MAN AT WAR:
John Gell in his troubled time

RON SLACK

**26, Glenthorne Close, Brampton.
Chesterfield. 1997**

ISBN 0 9509746 3 3

By the same author

Brassington Forebears: 1700-1900. 1984
Paupers Venture/Childrens Fortune: the lead mines and miners of Brassington, Derbyshire. 1986
Near to this place ... Brassington church memorials 1674-. 1988
Lands and lead miners: a history of Brassington, in Derbyshire. 1991

Printed by Mastaprint Limited, Sandiacre, Nottingham NG10 5HU

Contents

Foreword

This account of John Gell's life is derived mainly from material in the Derbyshire Record Office. The Chandos-Pole-Gell collection (D258) is the main source, plus, for the Civil War, the Sanders (D1232) and Gresley (D803/Z9) collections. For the chronological sequence of marches, battles and seiges in which Gell's troops were involved I am indebted to the book, "Derbyshire in the Civil War", by B. Stone (Scarthin Books, 1992). Dr T.D. Brighton's work on the Civil War and on Gell's role in it, published by the Bakewell & District Historical Society, was particularly helpful for biographical details of the participants. The portraits of Sir John Gell and his brother Thomas in the text of the book are from the unique illustrated edition of "Magna Britannia" in the Derby Local Studies Library. They and the cover portrait are included by courtesy of Derby City Library. I was helped by the comments and advice of Tom Hawley and George Power, who read a late draft of the book, though of course its shortcomings remain my responsibility. I am grateful too for the help of the staffs of the Derbyshire Record Office, the Local Studies Library, Derby, the Local Studies Library, Matlock, and Chesterfield Library.

The places in Derbyshire and neighbouring counties which were of most significance in Gell's life are mapped on page 80. Civil War strongholds are printed **bold.** The drawing of Hopton Hall before the large-scale alterations carried out in the early 1800s is from the Chandos-Pole-Gell collection and was first printed in the Derbyshire Countryside, October-December 1954.

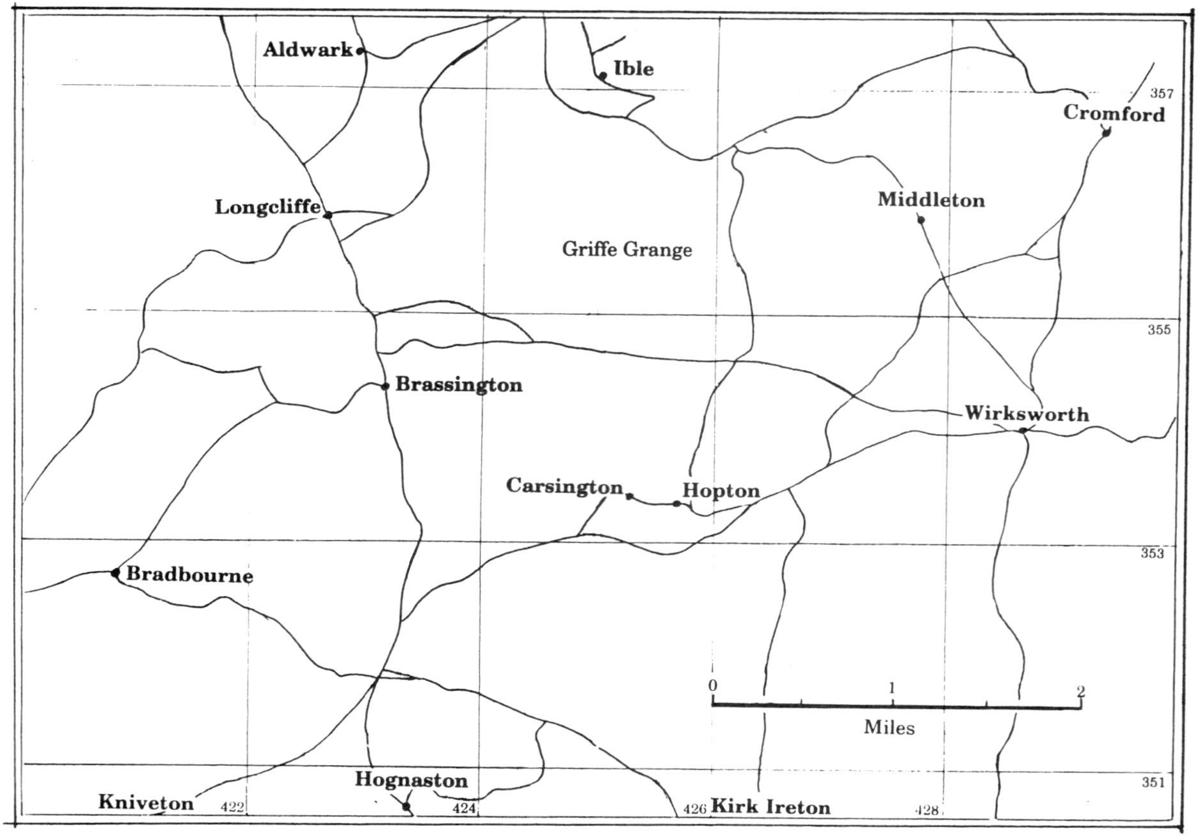

Aldwark
Ible
357
Cromford
Longcliffe
Middleton
Griffe Grange
355
Brassington
Wirksworth
Carsington
Hopton
353
Bradbourne
0
1
2
Miles
351
Hognaston
Kniveton
422
424
426
Kirk Ireton
428

CHAPTER 1

The Gells and Hopton

In September 1642 John Gell rode off from Hopton Hall to the Earl of Essex's headquarters at Northampton. There Essex, commander of the army which Parliament had raised to defend its rights against King Charles I, commissioned him, in the rank of Colonel, to raise a regiment of 1,200 men. With his commission in his pocket he came home to find his house ransacked and plundered and a royalist force causing mayhem in Derbyshire. Over the next four years, however, Gell was to drive out these and other invaders and hold Derbyshire for Parliament until the King was beaten. The regiment which he raised, maintained and led, remained an effective fighting force for the whole of the war and, in the face of severe disruption inside his own camp, Gell resisted every assault from the enemy and prevented the royal forces from gaining control of central England. When Charles surrendered at Newark in May 1646, part of Gell's regiment was serving with the army besieging him, while another was helping in the fall of the royalist garrison at Chester.

These Civil War years, 1642 to 1646, were Gell's finest hour. This singular man had many enemies, however, and his successes did not prevent a storm of bitter condemnation descending on him at the end of the war. He had accumulated enemies throughout a career which had begun with legal battles to fight off neighbours' attempts to seize parts of his inheritance, and had seen him advance steadily in the affairs of the county between 1620 and 1642, the years of his prime. As the war between King and Parliament approached, Gell had been ready for it. He was not a republican and certainly not a democrat, but absolute rule by a divinely-appointed King did not appeal to him either, and he did not hesitate to choose Parliament. His choice made a difference. Most of the Derbyshire nobility and gentry were for the King but were paralysed by indecision and dread of the approaching upheaval. Gell acted. Once he had made his mind up, he proved self-confident, energetic and experienced enough to burn his bridges and impose himself on the developing conflict.

Gell's enemies had much to complain about. This pugnacious, difficult man was no saint, confessing that he "used not to meddle with women, unless they were handsome". The moral flexibility implied by this remark seemed present in his politics, when he attracted accusations of opportunism and treachery by declaring himself for Parliament in the year when the King had transformed him from plain John Gell to Sir John Gell, Baronet. He was notoriously vindictive. When he married the widow of one of his enemies he was accused of doing so only to continue his vendetta against her dead husband by treating her badly. He pursued poor lead miners for the tithes, or tenths of their ore, to which he had a legal right, claiming that they would have no difficulty in paying the tithes were they not "given over to unthriftines and to be lavish and idle in expence". He was tried for treason and convicted of concealing it. He was angrily intolerant of dissent and was hated by some of his fellow officers and by many other people who worked with him. Even his faithful younger brother, Thomas, was provoked into an outburst in which he complained that in spite of twenty years of supporting him in all his ventures, he had received not a penny from him. And yet the most determined of his enemies conceded that this dictatorial commander did in fact confer with his officers before every military undertaking, and Gell was able to declare that he did so because "it concerneth theyre lives and the treuth is I am very tender of those brave and valiant frends that have been so faithfull in our servis".

The war touched everyone of his rank, but the contradictions in Gell's personality would in any case have prevented him from enjoying the tranquil life which both his ancestors and his descendants led as squires of Hopton. While quarrels with tenants and miners could be expected in the life of anyone whose income came from rents and lead, Gell's were conducted with an intensity which transcended legal formalities and earned him hatred. This complex man also read and perhaps wrote love poetry, and was a conscientious and loving father. Living in London after the war he wrote cordial letters to his son John at Hopton, advising him on the management of the Gell estates and always returning to his great love of falconry, putting John right on the proper rearing and training of his hawks. The restless, aggressive, ruthless side of him found fulfilment at the moment when he faced a life or death conflict. He fought his war in the same single-minded, thorough-going fashion as he had fought all his earlier battles.

Forebears

The wealth in land and lead which Gell later exploited so successfully had been accumulated over several centuries, mainly by his grandfather, Ralph, though there had been earlier entrepreneurs in the family. According to Burke's Landed Gentry, John Gell was descended from a Ralph Gell who held Hopton from Edward III (1327-1377). Such an early possession of Hopton was unknown to John, who fought a lawsuit to establish his ownership and claimed only that the family had held it from the time of Edward IV, a century later[1]. A fourteenth century Robert Gyle and a Ralph Gell who was at Hopton in the early fifteenth century[2] were probably also his ancestors. However, he was certainly descended from a John who died in 1471 and who was succeeded by his son, another John[3]. This second John held Hopton until his death in 1526 and it was his son, Ralph, who made the upward move socially from yeoman to gentleman - he is given both descriptions in two documents in 1537 and was a gentleman thereafter[4].

The township of Hopton was part of the Duchy of Lancaster's manor of Wirksworth, a royal possession since the Duke of Lancaster had become King Henry IV in 1399. It consisted of about 300 acres of cultivated land and about 400 acres of pasture and woodland[5]. The Gells had been increasing their estate in and around Hopton since at least as early as the days of Robert Gyle, who was living around 1400[6], but the family member who seems to have been the main entrepreneur before the Reformation was the John Gell who died in 1471. During his long life, this sixteenth century John Gell bought and sold property in Hopton and the neighbouring parishes and his son, another John, inherited a substantial estate in 1471[7]. This John Gell was also long-lived and an indication of his standing in the area by the beginning of the 16th century is seen in a bond of 1510 in which, still styled "yeoman", he was sufficiently prominent to join a local tradesman called John Fearne in presenting Wirksworth church with a third bell for its belfry, one "of good tone"[8].

By the Tudor period, then, the Gells were established as the owners of the small township of Hopton and by virtue of this as a family of weight in the Wirksworth area. They were still, however, big fish in a small pond. It was Ralph who gave them real financial muscle, and he did it partly at the expense of the religious houses who owned large tracts of land and leased lucrative mineral rights in Derbyshire. Henry VIII gave him his chance when he dissolved the monasteries and sold off their property. Like many others among the gentry, Ralph took this unique opportunity to enrich himself. He had already, in 1517, nine years before he inherited his father's estate, taken a thirty-one year lease from Dale Abbey of Griffe Grange, which adjoined Hopton[9]. Griffe provided pasture for the Abbey's sheep, which remained there under the terms of the lease. It was also, however, a rich lead-producing area, and the Abbey leased the mineral rights from the Crown. It was a valuable addition to the family's existing interests in mining and smelting and Griffe remained one of their main assets for 250 years. The lease was renewed for sixty-one years in 1537, together with other Abbey land in Brassington and Wirksworth. In 1546, after Dale Abbey's dissolution, Ralph paid the king £107-13-4d for Griffe Grange and its mineral rights, plus Dale Abbey property in Wirksworth and some land at Hognaston which had been the property of Rocester Abbey. There survives a receipt to Ralph for his £107-13-4d from Sir John Willins, treasurer of the Court of Augmentations, the agency set up to sell off the church properties. It records what was surely one of the best among many good bargains struck at the time.

Ralph invested heavily in one controversial class of property which was destined to cause trouble for his grandson. This was the tithe, or tenth of produce, due to ecclesiastical authorities. He leased tithes in his own part of the county and in the the parishes of the Peak District. As part of one agreement with Lichfield Cathedral he built a parsonage house at Bakewell which was later to be his son Thomas's residence before he inherited Hopton. Tithes which Ralph leased in the parishes of Hope, Tideswell, Holmesfield, Ashford, Birchills, Monyash, Over Haddon and Chapel-en-le-Frith included lead and were to be the issue over which Ralph's grandson John was to fight some of his longest battles, trying to collect his tithe ore from miners who denied his right to it. In 1553 Ralph made his biggest purchase when he paid the Duchy of Lancaster £289-6-8d for the manor of Wirksworth. Ralph's and his successors' position as lords of the manors of Hopton and Wirksworth entitled them to hold courts there and to demand ancient manorial dues from the tenants. Ralph continued to buy land in his own area and in other parts of Derbyshire and in 1562 leased the manor of Willersley from the Earl of Shrewsbury.

Ralph's will details his stake in the lead mining industry. In addition to the property, rents and tithes in the Wirksworth, Bakewell and High Peak areas, he left his "bole" or lead smelter at

Barrel Edge and "all my groves (mines) and all my woods for burning (smelting) withall", a vital part of the inheritance. The inventory taken of his goods when he died in 1564 included his bole, lead and blackwork (slag), valued at £318-8-0d, and coins and silver plate to the value of £360. Ralph was not the first Gell to smelt lead. His father John was operating a bole in 1516[10]. However he had by 1541 become the largest purchaser of ore and the largest producer of smelted lead in the Wirksworth Wapentake[11], selling his lead on the London market[12]. Ralph's income from the duties on lead ore which were included in the lease and later purchase of the Griffe, and from the tithes of Hope and the other Peak District parishes, is not known. However the Griffe duties at least must have been lucrative since the Wirksworth area was the largest producer of lead in the county at the time[13]. It was the wealth from lead which financed Ralph's land buying. There are records of the Gells' lead trade during the time of Ralph's sons and the industry was a mainstay of his grandson's position.

Ralph married twice, each time into a family prominent in the lead trade. Both marriages helped to cement the Gells into the county gentry. His first wife, Godythe Ashby, was the grand-daughter of Roger Foljambe, a member of the knightly Chesterfield family who had held the mineral rights in the Low Peak from the Crown[14]. Ralph and Godyth had three sons and five daughters, of whom only two sons were alive at Ralph's death. His second wife was Emma Beresford. The Beresfords, like Ralph himself, owed their gentlemanly status to their success in the lead smelting business, and four of Ralph and Emma's five daughters married into similar families - the Hurts, Lowes and Wigleys. These marriages ensured that his sons and grandsons had many blood ties among the lead-rich gentry in Derbyshire. At Ralph Gell's death in 1564 his two surviving sons by Godythe, Anthony and Thomas, and John, his son by Emma, were left estates at, respectively, Hopton, Bakewell and Kniveton. John died in the same year as his father leaving the Kniveton estate to his wife and young family. Ralph Gell has a monument, an alabaster chest tomb in Wirksworth church. He lies between his two wives, dressed in what looks like legal costume, with small sculpted figures on each side of the tomb representing the children of Godyth and Emma. Though there are no records of Ralph's being a lawyer, the fact that a John Gell, possibly Ralph's brother, was called to the Bar at Gray's Inn in 1521[15], and that his eldest son and members of later generations were lawyers, makes it possible that he was. His monument may be the evidence. Ralph's is the first family monument, another indication that by his time the Gells had become prominent in the area.

Anthony and Thomas Gell, esquires

Ralph's sons consolidated the family's position. Anthony, born about 1520[16], became an Inner Temple barrister in 1547 and prospered sufficiently there to reach the rank of Master of the Bench in 1569. He spent enough time away from his London duties to be appointed a JP on the Derbyshire magistracy. It was during his time that the present Hopton Hall was built, presumably replacing an earlier family home, and Anthony is likely to have been the man responsible[17]. By the time that he and Thomas, born in 1532, were granted a coat of arms in 1576[18], their rank had risen from "gent" to "esquire" in the Elizabethan social scale. The brothers continued the lucrative trade in lead, sold both in London and at Hull. A letter dated 20th September 1588 from Thomas Sacheverell, buyer for the lead merchant William Walthall[19], informed Thomas that he, Sacheverell, had weighed the lead which Gell had in Hull. It came to more than fifty-two fothers (approximately 52 tons), over a fother more than Sacheverell had paid Gell for. On the 26th Gell heard that he was to receive £12-10-8d for the extra lead, meaning that the price of the whole consignment was over £651 or at least £65,000 at today's value.

The family's success in the lead industry had made them wealthy enough by Anthony and Thomas's time to be on easy terms with the upper social ranks in Derbyshire. This is apparent from surviving letters. In 1575 John Manners wrote from Haddon Hall to thank Anthony for some legal work and to order three fothers of lead. He specified "boll" (bole) lead, produced by the old method of smelting, which used wind-power on hill-top furnaces. Although this was a less efficient method than the recently-introduced ore-hearth mills, where the draught was produced by water-power, it produced purer metal. Anthony was at the time smelting by both methods. Manners demonstrated a familiarity with Gell by telling him what the lead was needed for - the earl of Rutland "has a building in hand"[20]. Manners himself was in the smelting trade[21] but the Gells had by the late sixteenth century become pre-eminent in it. The gentry swapped favours. Manners asked Anthony for a loan of £20 in June 1583 and thanked him for it[22]. Two years earlier one of his letters contained thanks to Gell for a gelding[23]. In 1582 Manners asked Gell to dine with him at Haddon to discuss business[24] Henry Foljambe at Dethick asked Gell to favour "their poor township" by reducing the constable's tax asssessment[25]. Henry Berrisford at Peak Forest asked for Gell's help in getting the parsonage of Sheen for a friend - Gell's brother-in-law Wigley had the gift of the appointment[26]. Godfrey Wolstoncrofte wrote to Thomas Gell at Bakewell that he had "written sundry remembrances of commendations" to Gell, but "never received any answer" and, presumably to encourage a "remembrance" sent Gell a crimson velvet collar with a double row of studs for Gell's hunting dog, as he knew that Gell loved hunting[27].

Thomas at Hopton

Until Anthony's death in 1583 his brother Thomas had lived at Bakewell, presumably in the house which his father had built as part of his 1534 agreement with the Dean and Chapter of Lichfield. Ralph had agreed to "build and make on the said parsonage a competent dwelling house for that ground". This house, known as the Parsonage House, has survived and is now the Old House Museum[28]. On Anthony's death Thomas inherited his estate and moved into the family home at Hopton, where for the rest of his life he lived the life of a country gentleman. This no doubt included hunting. We have Godfrey Wolstonecrofte's word that he loved this sport. Thomas confirmed it by placing a hunting dog on the crest of the coat of arms which he and his brother had been granted in 1576. It wears a collar which looks remarkably like the description of the one sent to him by Wolstonecrofte. Thomas, aged fifty[29], took steps to provide himself with an heir and married Margaret Needham, daughter of William Needham of Thornsett. Margaret, however, died childless a few years later, and Thomas married again. This second wedding, in 1588, was to Millicent Sacheverel, daughter of Ralph Sacheverel of Stanton-by-Bridge, whose family had long been prominent lead smelters and merchants.

This second marriage proved more fruitful than his first, though it was five years before he and Millicent produced an heir, and Thomas did not live to bring him up. The couple's first child, the future Sir John, was born on the 22nd June 1593 and Thomas died on the 11th of November in the same year[30]. His widow, pregnant at the time of his death, gave birth to a second son, Thomas, who was christened at Carsington on the 20th September 1594. Millicent Gell, left alone at Hopton with two babies, did not remain a widow for long. Soon after Thomas's birth she married John Curzon of Kedleston and left Hopton which, during her sons' minorities, was occupied by Thomas, the son of her late husband's half-brother John[31]. At Kedleston, the two Gell boys acquired a half-brother in 1598 when Millicent gave birth to a third son, John Curzon. Their childhood and adolescence were spent as members of the Curzon family and their tie with John Curzon remained strong after John Gell's return to Hopton.

Royal ward

John Gell, as the fatherless heir to the Gell estates, was made a royal ward and Gilbert, Earl of Shrewsbury, was appointed his guardian. Two thirds of the estate was leased by the Queen in February 1595 to Shrewsbury for the duration of Gell's minority, at an annual rent of £23-7-2d[32]. The indenture recording this arrangement refers to John Gell as the Queen's ward and an endorsement on the cover reads "The queenes grant to the earl of Shrewsbury of the wardship of Jo: Gell 10 Feb: 1594 [1595 by modern dating]". However a later note comments "She grants the Earl two thirds of the estate & leaves the children to take care of themselves". Left without a father's protection almost from birth, John Gell was vulnerable to exploitation and this vulnerability must have been a factor in the development of his combative personality. He was defending himself when he was barely in his teens. In August 1595, when Shrewsbury had done nothing about the children, Millicent Gell's father, Ralph Sacheverel, wrote to him to ask what plans he had for his ward's future and for the letting of the property[33]. In the event, the estates were sublet and the widow's problems in bringing up her two baby sons were solved by her marriage to John Curzon. The care both of Shrewsbury's ward and of his brother were in the hands of their step-father[34].

The Curzons of Kedleston

In marrying John Curzon, Millicent Gell had bettered herself. The Curzons had been Lords of Kedleston since the twelfth century and the Hall in which the Gell brothers grew up was an altogether grander place than Hopton Hall. There was to be a new building at the end of the century and another, the present Hall, in the middle of the eighteenth century, but the one to which Millicent moved when she married John Curzon was a mediaeval mansion, much altered, no doubt, since it was built about 1200 but still containing a great hall with a Norman doorway and a buttery whose windows boasted painted armorial glass[35]. The Curzons were richer than the Gells, with land in many parts of the county and lead mining interests in the Peak. They had been influential for several centuries and by birth alone John Curzon's son could assume a position in the public life of the county which his Gell half-brothers would have to fight for. By this marriage Millicent had ensured that her children by Thomas Gell would be protected.

Precocious marriage

Curzon's stepson and ward rapidly outgrew his juvenile status. In January 1609, still only fifteen, John Gell married Elizabeth, daughter of Sir Percival Willoughby of Wollaton, in Nottinghamshire[36]. The bride's age is not known, but this marriage was early even for the time and Gell must already have possessed the capacity for defying and over-riding opposition, in this case from his mother and step-father. He must also, at fifteen, already have had the way with women which his enemies were later to include in a long list of complaints against him. Probably because Curzon insisted on carrying out his responsibilities to his stepson, Gell was separated from his bride and sent to Oxford in the following year, when he was seventeen[37]. He spent a year at Magdalen College which, from the rough sentence structure and haphazard spelling of his letters, does not seem to have taken his education much further than whatever he had received at home. He left the university without taking a degree and returned to his wife at Kedleston, where his first child, Millicent, was born in 1611[38].

Early fights

Gell's inheritance, or parts of it, seems to have been under threat almost from the death of his father. His mother's migration to Kedleston may have been one reason. The land at Hognaston which Ralph Gell had bought from Rocester Abbey in the previous century consisted partly of strips in different parts of the ancient open field system and partly of the enclosed fields which were then being formed from them. One of Gell's tenants, John Fearn, the first in a long line of adversaries, claimed that he "or some of his ancestors or kindred" had bought this ground from the Gells. His family had been neighbours of the Gells, and collaborators with them, since the fifteenth century, and his actions during John Gell's youth suggest that he was finding it difficult to acknowledge their recent rise up the social ladder. He was instructed by the Court of Wards to hand over the Hognaston ground and to "continue" to pay rent for it. Fearn refused and brought an action against Gell in 1606[39]. Gell's lawyer alleged that, "about a yeare or two since", Fearn had surrendered the land in the Wirksworth manor court and that Gell had then claimed the freehold. At a further hearing of the case in 1608 Gell himself gave evidence, at fifteen years old. The outcome of this dispute was that the court named each field and awarded two thirds of the Hognaston land to Gell. There were also two houses in dispute - Gell was awarded the "mansion house". The estate was let to John Fearn at £40 per annum, an arrangement which led to further legal battles, since Fearn turned out to be a poor payer. He was prosecuted late in 1614 for breach of a decree of the Court of Wards concerning Gell, "his majesty's ward" and in 1616 Gell himself, described as John Curzon's "late Ward" sued him for payment of his rent and £120 arrears.

Lord Of The Manor

Gell, or his guardians, had successfully fought off the attempts to take his Hognaston property. At the same time he also had to face down a determined effort to deny his claim to the manor of Hopton. His chief antagonist was again John Fearn[40]. The Court of Wards ruled in 1607 that Gell was the holder of the manor, citing documents from 1471, the year in which his ancestor had died. Fearn and other local landowners refused to accept Gell's claim and challenged it in the court of the Duchy of Lancaster in 1615. Another Gell tenant, Lawrance Allsopp, had been refusing to pay his rent into the Court of Wards during Gell's minority. Allsopp was supported by Fearn, who argued that although Anthony Gell had claimed that the manor had been granted to his grandfather, John Gell, and had descended to him through his father, Ralph, the reality was that the Gells were merely "Reeves and rent gatherers", holding office under the Crown, whereby they "intruded uppon his Maiesties possession intitulinge them selves to the sayde pretended manor of Hopton". The Attorney-General noted that Allsopp had in fact sold his land to the Committee of Wardship and ordered him to pay his arrears of rent. The Court ruled that "the sayde Gell was seised of the sayde Mannor of Hopton aforesayde". The grant of the manor was made by royal decree on the 11th July, 1615.

Gell's ownership of Hopton manor meant that his neighbours had a duty to attend meetings of the manor court and would be fined for not attending. In addition, much of their buying, selling and inheriting of land would have to be validated by the court, with a payment to the lord, Gell, in each case. Gell's court also had a role in the judicial process, being able to inflict fines of not more than 39/11d for various offences relating to debt, farming practices and public order. The manor court was still a significant part of administration and justice in the early seventeenth century and Gell immediately began holding sessions at Hopton, taking steps to compel Fearn and the others to attend his court and preventing them from using the one at Wirksworth. Fearn and his allies were clearly outraged at their neighbour's pretentions and returned to the attack, unsuccessfully, in 1617. One item of Gell's evidence reveals how seriously this dispute was taken. He alleged that on the death of Martin Marshall, "servant or clarke to Thomas Gell Esqr deceased", Fearn had entered Marshall's study, "rifled" it, and stolen documents which would have been useful to Gell's case. Marshall lived in Wirksworth[48], and Fearn's burglary, if it did in fact take place, could only have been possible because of the family's absence in Kedleston, as Marshall's study, and his papers, would have been in Hopton Hall if the family had been in residence. Fearn and every other land holder in Hopton had good reason to prefer the Wirksworth court to the one on their doorstep, run by their neighbour and rival, as was to be shown a few years later.

Family life

Gell and his wife soon had a large family. Elizabeth's mother Bridgett Willoughby wrote to her young daughter at Kedleston on May 2nd, 1611[41]. She had heard that Elizabeth was "breedinge childe" and assured her that she would send her anything she needed. Bridgett had already had the gown and other things made for the event and would send them by the next carrier. She hoped "to be shortly in the countree". Bridgett Willoughby's letters all sound a note of concern for Elizabeth's well-being which may have originated in the first place because of her youthful marriage but which later is clearly to do with ill-health. In this early letter Bridgett hopes that her "sister Curson ... may have joye and comforte" in the young Elizabeth. By the time of her mother's next surviving letter, written in January 1615, Elizabeth had had two more children, Bridgett (1612) and John (1613), and was expecting her fourth. Bridgett proposed that "if you fynde yorselfe well and able and dare adventure soe farr" she would be glad of Elizabeth's company for three or four days. She would send for her on the following Saturday. As in all her letters she asked to be remembered to her "brother and sister" Curzon, and invoked God's blessing on the Gells. Elizabeth drafted her reply at the bottom of this letter, making it clear that she was not well - "Havinge all other my deuty most humbly remembered, craving your blessing, I ... are readie both now and allwaies to doe my duty. At this time I shall not bee so well able to travell as I weare". The visit was not made and in March Bridgett wrote that she had not sent for Elizabeth because, in view of bad weather, she understood that Elizabeth "durst not adventure soe far consideringe in what case you ar". She sent a pair of old sheets to make "cloutes" and asked God to make Elizabeth "a gladd mother". She was clearly still worried about her daughter when she wrote in October, after the birth of the baby, William. "Daughter I have sent this bearer purposely to knowe howe you doe, and what rest you have taken this night, and shoulde be glad to heare that you weare well". She sent a chair "which I ordenarily used and liked myselfe", three pairs of rabbits and some peaches, and repeated her prayer that God should make Elizabeth a glad mother. A fifth child, Elizabeth, was born at Kedleston in 1617. The impression that Elizabeth was chronically unwell is strengthened by a further letter from her mother written in 1625. Bridget had written to invite her to a christening, but "if you shoulde not be well in health I woulde be lothe you shoulde com to hurt you".

Brother Thomas

While John Gell was at Kedleston, struggling with covetous and hostile neighbours to secure the family inheritance, his younger brother Thomas was carrying on the Gell tradition of having a lawyer in the family. Thomas Gell was in London, still at his studies, when he wrote to John at Kedleston in July 1619, declining his offer of horses to bring him home for the summer[42]. He could not "come this sumer into the cuntry without great hindrance to my studdy, especially because I am nowe neere the barre". In the same letter Thomas thanked his brother for two payments of £5, but reminded him that he had been promised £15 a quarter, "and the rest I shall expect from you at your better leasure". Thomas was playing his part in his brother's legal battles, as he was to do on many occasions afterwards. John had been in London on legal business and had entrusted an important document to be taken to Kedleston by a lawyer acquaintance of Thomas's. The document had not arrived and the lawyer had gone on holiday. Thomas and the missing lawyer's "chamber fellow" had searched his study, without success, and Thomas thought that "it was very ill done to trust an attorney with it and not to take it downe yourselfe, or have left your man to have seen it finished". He suggested that if the document did not turn up John should ask his cousin Lowe's advice. At this time their cousin Lowe, possibly Nicholas Lowe, was the family member who was usually called upon for legal help. He was descended from their father's half-sister Lucy, who had married Edward Lowe of Alderwasley.

Family disputes

Life at Kedleston became uncomfortable for the Gells and the Curzons. There are a number of indications. In 1619 two of John Gell's servants were included in a list of men with whom his mother had incurred heavy debts[43]. Debts cause friction and John Gell was careful with his money. A few years later he is seen justifying his non payment of £4 to one of his Curzon relatives . "It is soe small a some, and ... there hath beene a greater forbearance of a bigger some unto some of her freinds"[44]. There was trouble too between Gell and his step-father over land, stock and goods at a place called "Champians"[45], involving complicated arbitration by Nicholas Lowe. There were many other, later, quarrels with the Curzons. A draft letter to John Curzon itemises some of them and demonstrates Gell's ability to provoke hostility by the bluntness with which he approached people and problems[46]. The offended people included the younger John Curzon. Gell's uncle George Curzon, younger brother of his step-father[47], had warned him that he needed to make peace with the Kedleston family. The main charge against Gell was that he had acted against his half-brother and prevented him from obtaining a partnership in a mine in Wales. This, said Curzon, he had been told by Thomas Parker. Parker was the Wirksworth "barmaster", the administrator of the local lead industry. Gell denied telling him anything - "I did never open my mouth to any Parker in the world". He admitted failing to support Curzon but claimed that nothing he could have said would have helped him, and that it would have turned out to have been to both their disadvantages. He was aware that Curzon thought his conduct unworthy "and badd shite in my pottage", a typically earthy and extravagant expression. Clearly the quarrel was serious but he denied saying that he wanted to have nothing more to do with Curzon, though he was keeping quiet because "I would keepe his freindshipp if possible I could".

A second major quarrel was also over lead. Gell's cousin Lowe, like Gell himself a mine owner, had again been arbitrating, this time in a dispute between Curzon and two miners, Higget and Tompson. Lowe, however, had recently died, with his arbitration incomplete, and the elder Curzon had wanted to replace him but had been thwarted by Gell, who "desired respite of tyme but to speake wth them." The younger Curzon had become impatient and threatened that his father would take them to court - "proceede against them wth all extremity". Gell was in favour of quiet diplomacy, perhaps because he was not himself involved. He advised his step-father "to have the busines arbitrated, that pryvate busines needeth not to be publikly spoken of". Arbitration would be as effective as "ryger of lawe" in getting Curzon what belonged to him.

There were three other causes of displeasure at Kedleston. One was that he had failed to call on them when he was passing through, a simple complaint but one which probably implies a more general feeling of neglect. Gell was busy and may have had less time for his mother and step-father than they thought he should have. His plea was that he had only once failed to call when he was in the neighbourhood, on a day when he had heard "before I came into town, that you were all gone towardes Mackworth of hunting". Uncle George also let him know that John Curzon was annoyed at Gell's response to his request for a loan of £100. For whatever reason Gell had clearly not lent the money - "I protest I did answeare you with truth and if it had bene otherwaies I would have done otherwaies". Finally Gell professed remorse at an unspecified "accident" which had clearly hurt Curzon. He did not know what to do about it "more than desire at godes hands that it had never happened and could wish that my going to London on foote might have excused it or a greater penalty rather than such a thinge to hapen agayne". Gell ended his attempt at reconciliation by hoping that his step-father would be "pleased to afford me your fatherly countenance untill I shewe neglect of duty towardes you which assuredly shall never happen".

It seems unlikely that Curzon was particularly fatherly. A note written on a page of Hopton accounts of 1627 reads "Curzon and the foolish bitch his wife's acctt in their own hands of Mr Gell's estate, of which they cheated him of the greatest part"[48]. In fact Gell retained his inheritance, but the terms of this note, authorship unknown, suggest that his move to Hopton in 1620 was overdue

Return to Hopton

John Gell and his family moved from Kedleston at a time between August 1619, when letters were still being sent there, and April 1620, when they were addressed to Hopton. While there is plenty of evidence of Gell's legal struggles over Hopton manor and the Hognaston land, there is none to explain why he remained at Kedleston until he was twenty-seven years old. There must have been a good reason for his continuing to live with his mother and step-father for so long. It was not in character for this violently independent man to have remained under their roof any longer than was unavoidable and he must therefore have been prevented from reoccupying his father's house. The legal objections to his ownership of the manor may have been a factor, but the main obstacle is likely to have been his cousin Thomas, much older than himself, who had been in residence at Hopton since the family's move to Kedleston. However, while there is nothing to explain John Gell's continuing at Kedleston beyond the age of twenty-one, his cousin did not die until 1627[49], and the fact that John and his family did move back while his cousin was still alive, may indicate that a private family battle had taken place.

Back at last in his father's house, lord of the manor of Hopton, Gell was by 1620 his own man. His children, the sixth of whom, Elizabeth, was born in the year after the move, included two sons, making dynastic problems unlikely, and Gell was rich enough to live well and make his mark. While Hopton Hall, still a modern house in 1620, lacked the ancient grandeur of Kedleston, it had the advantages of comfort and convenience. It was typical of the small manor houses built during the Elizabethan period by families which had done well from the dissolution of the monasteries and the confiscation of their land. At the time it was built, probably on the site of an earlier house, it was one of the signs that the Gells were coming up in the world. It was substantially extended in the Georgian manner during the eighteenth century but its original projecting gable-ended wings can still be seen at either end of the facade. The house stands on a slight slope looking towards the wooded rise below Kirk Ireton, across what is now the Carsington Reservoir but was then the open country of the valley of the Scow Brook. At its back is the old road to Wirksworth. The few neighbouring houses of the very small hamlet of Hopton were at a respectful distance. The larger settlement of Carsington, with pubs and a church, adjoined Hopton, and was where the Gell children were christened and their daughters married, both ceremonies no doubt attended by the villagers. Most of the people of Hopton and Carsington were Gell tenants and John Gell and Elizabeth could now make close acquaintance with them. The family, still growing, could now settle down in their own house.

A fine figure of a man

His estate and manorial lordships confirmed, Gell began to make his way. There is no full-length portrait but half-portraits survive which suggest that he was below average height. They show him to have been sharp-featured, with a small moustache, and he gazed confidently out as he sat for the painter in armour and a full-bottomed wig. His expression in the picture is composed, alert and imperious. In 1621 he spent £7-8-0d on a wardrobe of new clothes[50] - a doublet, a jerkin, a cassock, or long military coat, hose, which were more breeches than stockings, a cloak and another coat. The lace and silk adorning these otherwise practical garments were the outward marks with which men of Gell's rank distinguished themselves from the yeomen, merchants, clergymen and lesser gentry with whom they dealt. They were also there in sufficient amounts to suggest that Gell was something of a dandy. A list of noblemen which Gell drew up at about this time, giving each man's family motto and a description of his coat of arms, reinforces the suggestion that, at least in his youth, Gell was concerned about the outward signs of his rank[51].

Literary tastes

The picture of the dashing young squire suggested by his decorative wardrobe is strengthened by the remarkable amount of manuscript love poetry among Gell's papers. Whether this was copied from published poets or was Gell's own work, it is in the extravagant contemporary style - "Why to a longing soule doe you denie/ the favor of your hand your cheeke your eye/ Can I commit adultry with your glove/ That with such killing frownes you oft remove/ Your pretty fingers from your dearest love"[52]. There are sonnets full of regret for lost love - "Peace my hearts blabb, be ever dumbe/ Sorrowes speake loude without a tongue/ And my perplexd thoughts forbeare/ to breathe yourselves in any eare/ Tis scarce a true or manly griefe/ Which gadds abroade to find reliefe". There are poems to his mistress, his rich mistress, his poor mistress and to his frowning mistress and there are reflections on "An indiferant affection" and "Upon the picture of a faire lady drawne unsuccessfully". The poems express fashionable attitudes and, while there is no evidence that Gell was ever so poetic in his relations with women, the fact that he read them indicates a sensibility which was obscured by the combative face he always presented in his public activities. There are long passages in Gell's best handwriting from Beaumont and Fletcher and from John Donne - "Yet love and hate mee too/ Soe these extremes shall neithers office doe/ Love mee that I may dye the gentler way/ Hate mee by cause thy loves too great for mee"[153].

Gell's literary taste extended to prose. Along with Donne's poems he copied out some of his prose work, including some from the collection of "Paradoxes and Problemes", like "Why doth the Poxe soe much affect to undermine the Nose?". Three commonplace books have long passages from many authors, including Latin ones such as Horace and Cicero[54]. Latin was the main component of a gentlemanly education in Gell's time and either he, just back from his year at Oxford, or other members of the Curzon household, practiced it to record the birth of his daughter Millicent in one of the commonplace books - "Millesant Gell nata fuit 3tio die Octob 1611 die Jovis (Thursday) sub planeta Mercurii". A second attempt by someone else, in addition to placing Millicent's birth between the hours of five and six pm, gave her planet as Jupiter.

Religious loyalties

John Gell was also concerned with religion and morals even though in these, as in his evident love of literature, his private reading and speculation were often belied by his actions. Gell was a Presbyterian. The family had been firmly protestant since the previous century, a stance which perhaps had its origins in the great gains which Ralph Gell had made from the Tudor monarchs' attacks on the Catholic church. Gell's eldest son John was to be described as "the most rigid Presbyterian in the county"[55] and, while he himself could never have earned that epithet, his papers make it clear that he shared the Presbyterians' belief in personal religion, their opposition to the episcopal structure of the Anglican church and their criticisms of the laxity of many Anglican clergy. In one paper, consisting of three and a half sides of very small handwriting, New Testament texts are used to draw lessons on salvation from sin, the achievement of grace and similar Puritan sentiments[56]. There are two small handwritten books of sermons[57] and, in Gell's handwriting, and in a forthright style which suggests that he may have been the author, there are discourses on three currently controversial church matters[58].

CHAPTER 2

The miners

The mining industry

The limestone upland pastures of the Peak District, including those to the south of the river Derwent around Hopton and the neighbouring villages, are honeycombed by the shafts and galleries of abandoned lead mines. The villages are set in a landscape dominated by thousands of grassy hillocks formed of the spoil from the mines, and by the remains of the miners' limestone buildings. In the seventeenth century twenty thousand people were employed either in the mines or the trades associated with them[1]. Derbyshire was the chief lead producer in England and lead was second to cloth in the value of national exports to the Continent[2]. The way in which the industry was organised enabled men such as John Gell and his ancestors to grow rich and, paradoxically, encouraged a spirit of robust independence in the mining villages.

Gell derived income from every stage of the lead industry, from the extraction of the ore to its sale as ingots ("pigs") of smelted lead. He owned shares in many of the mines of the Wirksworth area, and was the owner of two smelting mills in Wirksworth. From about 1638 he leased the mineral rights in the Low Peak, which entitled him to 1/13th of all ore mined, plus 6d for every load of about five hundredweight sold at the mines to merchants. The miners, while often trying to evade these duties, recognised their legitimacy. However, in certain High Peak parishes Gell claimed a further tax which the miners resented and strongly resisted. This was the tithe, or tenth of their ore and, since Gell showed the same energy and persistence in collecting tithe as in everything else, he became a hated man in the mining villages.

Tithe wars

The tithe had been paid to the pre-Reformation church and the miners had seen it then as a reasonable return for spiritual services rendered. Many of the tithes were held by religious houses and, at the dissolution of the monasteries by Henry VIII, were sold by the Crown to laymen, along with church land and property. Many others had already been sold or leased by the church authorities. The transfer of tithes from religious to lay hands was never accepted by the miners and by the seventeenth century this rejection had been extended to include tithes still held by the church. John Gell's grandfather, Ralph, had leased a third of the tithes of lead ore mined in the parishes of Bakewell, Tideswell and Hope from the Dean and Chapter of Lichfield Cathedral in 1549[3]. Ralph and his sons had successfully collected this ore but in 1613, when John Gell was still under twenty-one, the miners got their hands on "all the orders, charters, evidence and writings which doe plainlie manifest and sett forth" his title to the tithes and denied that either Gell or his guardian, the Earl of Shrewsbury, had any right to them. How the papers had come into the miners' hands is unknown, but the family's absence from Hopton and the consequent break in continuity, may have been at the root of their rebellion.

There was a fundamental difference between tithes and the traditional dues owed to the lessee of the mineral rights. The mining dues were ultimately Crown property and the structure of the industry was designed to collect the king's taxes. By Gell's time the lease-holder also held the ancient office of "Barmaster", which made him responsible for administering the system, supported by deputies and by miners' juries. They awarded title to mines to anyone able to demonstrate that there was lead to be mined, adjudicated the frequent disputes, and ensured that the miners and merchants paid their dues. Tithe holders, however, were on their own. Gell paid the rent for his lease to the Dean of Lichfield Cathedral, but for his return on this outlay he relied not on the Dean, who might have been expected to keep his side of the bargain, but on the miners, who refused to recognise it. He was confronted by a community of independent minded, tough and well organised workers, whose livelihoods depended on making the most of the lead they won so painfully from the rock underground. Gell also claimed tithes on hay and corn in a number of places and had to fight for some of those too, but the miners were more formidable opponents than the farmers. As far as he was concerned he was simply demanding what was rightfully his, but from the miners' viewpoint he was an outsider, with no rights. At the same time as he was repelling his neighbours' attempts on his land and authority Gell was also embroiled in a struggle with the miners of Bakewell and adjoining High Peak parishes. Though underage, he had been married four years and was a father. He was mature enough to demonstrate the pugnacious tenacity in defending what he regarded as rightfully his which was his lifelong characteristic, and when the miners at Bakewell refused to pay he immediately brought an action against four of them in the Court of Wards[4].

Giving evidence on 23rd November, 1613, Ralph James, one of the four miners, denied all the charges but made several submissions to be considered if the case should go forward. He played for time and pointed out that a similar case brought by Sir Francis Leake of Sutton Scarsdale, who claimed the other two thirds of the tithes, was being heard in the ecclesiastical court and suggested that Gell's case should be moved there. While denying that any tithes were payable he gave the game away by claiming that if nevertheless they had to be paid they were personal tithes, based on the miners' work, rather than "prediall" or those based on property. Although this was an irrelevant point if, as James was claiming, tithes were illegal, it would be an important one in the more likely event of the court's deciding against him and his fellow defendants.

Personal tithes were paid before the ore was dressed, leaving the expense of dressing to be borne by the tithe owner. Dressing ore was preparing it for sale, and was an onerous task. The lumps of ore-bearing rock were smashed into pieces about the size of peas and the resultant gravelly material was then "washed". Washing took several forms but in essence was the use of water to allow the heavier, ore-rich material to sink to the bottom, making it possible to skim off the waste from the top. The miners always accepted that they themselves had to dress the duty ore paid to the owner of the mineral rights.

In a submission which made it clear that the miners would continue to refuse payment of tithe, and that they were simply stalling, James made the impossible claim that the tithe holders should recompense the miners for the hard work, danger and costs spent in mining. He reminded the court of how he got his living, though he cannot have expected it to take him seriously in demanding bonus money for it - "leade oare is gotten by and with the labor and industrie of this defendante and others ... and gotten at their great charges and costs ... and with greate danger of theire lives insomuch that the same is many tymes digged for and gotten above fortie fathome depe in the earth".

There could never have been any doubt about the court's verdict since, whatever the morality of taking wholly unearned lead from the miners, Gell had an unassailable legal right to it. The court dismissed the miners' case and ruled that they were entitled only to a penny for dressing each dish (about sixty pounds) of tithe ore. In June 1614 the court noted that the miners had admitted that they had paid tithe to John Gell's father Thomas and instructed James and his co-defendants to show cause why an injunction should not be issued granting Gell possession of the tithes. In the following month the court granted the injunction "for payment thereof in such manner as yt was yealded and paied unto the wards father".

Gell had won his case. What followed was typical of all his later attempts to get hold of his tithes, the miners proving obdurate and resourceful in thwarting him. Sir Francis Leake wrote to Gell on the 6th August, 1614, reporting that the miners "neither care for your injunction nor mine"[5]. Leake recommended using Common Law and asked Gell to send his agent Francis Burton to Lichfield to collect documents which were essential for their cases. Gell, never one to stand back from a fight, went himself to Bakewell in September with Burton and summoned two of the four defendants, Thomas Wilson and Edward White, to meet him there. What Gell said to them was not reported but it is unlikely to have been conciliatory. The point of his being there in person was clearly to intimidate them. In his presence, and with two other Gell agents to add weight, Wilson and White were shown the injunction instructing them to pay the tithe and Burton asked them whether they intended to do so.

In his account of this meeting and of subsequent events, given in a statement which he made to the court in February 1615[6], Wilson held to the strategy followed by Ralph James and pleaded ignorance. He admitted that "one John Woodhouse shewed him ... a wrytinge, but what the effect of the same wrytinge was hee ... knoweth not for that hee did neither reade or heare the same, neither did hee ...observe whether the same wrytinge were in parchment or in paper nor whether there were anye seale fixed to the same". He claimed that, apart from the demand made at the meeting with Gell, no one had demanded tithe ore from him. He was unable to remember how much ore he and his fellows had mined since the previous September because he had not been asked for any at the mines where tithe had sometimes been been paid in the past. He agreed that tithe had been paid to Thomas Gell, whom he had known. Edward White was similarly obstructive. At the meeting in Bakewell he had told John Gell that he would pay the tithe if it were a legal requirement and he agreed that the injunction had been read to him. However, he was "unlearned" and had no idea what an injunction was. Like Wilson, he agreed that he had mined lead ore, though he did not remember how much. He had paid no tithe because no one had come to the mine to demand it and "hee doth not thinke that hee is bounde to carry ... tythes to anye other place".

Gell met with a more direct rebuff when, in June 1615, he sent his agent, a Kedleston yeoman called Richard Warde, to Bakewell, to collect tithe from Wilson's and White's mine. Warde testified to the court[7] that when he arrived at the mine there was ore "gotten and lying upon the banke". However, he was told by one of Wilson's workmen "that he would pay no tythe at all to the said John Gell", and that his master had said the same. Also present at this encounter was a partner of Wilson's called Hugh Whittaker. Whittaker put the miners' attitude beyond doubt - "hee would never pay any tithe of the said lead oare although hee was cast in the lawe to paye yt". On the 23rd June the court insisted that its injunction should be obeyed - "the defendants shall take at theire perill that the tythe oare shalbee payd upon demand made unto theire servants or workemen at the place where the said oare is gotten". By the autumn of 1616 Gell had had no success. The miners had combined to build a fund expressly to fight tithe cases and their lawyers were using delaying tactics. Gell, by now fighting in his own name, brought his case back to the Court of Wards and in 1617 submitted a long paper to this new hearing[8]. In the form of questions to the defendants, which was the usual procedure, it amounted to a comprehensive description of what was involved in the struggle.

Gell repeated the earlier assertion that the miners had always been paid a penny for dressing the ore, and asked what more had ever been paid and by whom. He also pointed out that the dressing process had recently been made much simpler and more efficient by the use of sieves, which had been introduced near the end of the sixteenth century. The pulverised ore-bearing rock was placed in a sieve and then plunged into water. The top layer of lighter waste material was readily removed from the lead-rich bottom layer of the resultant slurry. Gell maintained that in the days when the process was much more difficult the miners had dressed the tithe ore before paying it.

One of Gell's questions is worth quoting in full. In addition to expressing the enduring contempt of the gentleman for the lower orders, it perfectly embodies the exasperated, impatient response characteristic of him when confronted by what he regarded as unreasonable opposition - "Are not the laborers & mynrs for the most pte given over to unthriftines and to be lavish and idle in expence, doe they not often bargaine and sell awai the proffitt of their labors before they have gotten yt, to maintaine their idle expences to their greate losse, and might not otherwise manie of them growe riche, and most of them live well, and maintaine themselves honestlie". In the next question Gell asked what weekly profit the miners did in fact make, clearly hoping to demonstrate that they could afford his tithe.

One of the difficulties in collecting tithe ore from the miners was that many of the mines were remote and scattered. If a tithe gatherer was to be in the right place at the right time, when the barmaster measured the miners' ore in order to collect the dues, he needed the barmasters' cooperation This cooperation was not always given. Gell attempted to establish where the ore was measured and at what times and accused the barmasters of losing him money "by absence and negligence" when they should have been measuring and collecting the duty. Years later, when Gell himself, as holder of the mineral rights in Wirksworth, was chief barmaster there, it is apparent from his papers that his deputy barmasters were kept strictly to their tasks and carefully accounted for.

Gell argued that the miners' resistance to the tithe gatherers was a conspiracy. He alleged that they "combined or agreed togeather to with hould denie or refuse the payment of the tithe". Furthermore they "made or gathered a purse, or a great some [sum] or anie some or somes of money for the mainteyning of suites against the sd John Gell". It is clear that the miners imagined that their fund was big enough to pay any likely legal expenses. Certainly Gell faced prolonged litigation and one of his questions includes a claim that the miners were currently prosperous. He pointed out that mining profits rose and fell according to the price of lead and to the richness or otherwise of the veins in which the miners were working. At the present time, he said, there were "manie hundreds more" miners and workmen than at any time in the previous sixty years and profits were increasing daily. Such a boom is ample explanation for Gell's determination to get his hands on the duty his ancestors had enjoyed and for the miners' reluctance to pay it.

Gell repeated his earlier success in winning legal right to the tithe but still found himself unable to collect it and took further action at law. There are letters from Sir Francis Leake which show the two men helping each other in their common struggle. In July 1619 Leake wrote that he was proposing to petition the king and asked Gell to send him a copy of a petition that the miners themselves had presented[9]. Leake wrote again, referring to a injunction which he was seeking in the Court of Chancery and asking Gell to produce the records showing the origins of the tithes[10]. A list of these[11] shows that they included the original twelfth century grant of the tithes to Lenton Priory by William Peverel, the sale of one third of them to Lichfield Cathedral in the fourteenth century, the lease of Lichfield's third by Ralph Gell in 1549 and the lease of the two thirds to Sir Francis Leake after the dissolution of Lenton Priory. Among other documents were accounts of tithe ore collected at different periods, four of which, from the 1520s, included the "allowance given of 1d the dish for washing", though marginal notes to the list contain no mention of the great decline in the value of a penny which occured during the sixteenth century.

Rough play

Some of the miners did not restrict their opposition to the courts. In 1620 Gell collected his tithe ore at Bakewell only to have it hijacked "with force and armes"[12]. These were violent times, when it was normal for men to carry weapons, and these miners were clearly prepared to use them. Gell took them to court and they were found guilty of the charge, but his lawyer had once more to prove his right to tithe ore by exhibiting the ancient leases by Lichfield Cathedral, starting with one from 1314 and ending with the lease to Millicent Gell for her baby son. One miner at least agreed to abide by the courts' verdicts[13]. This was Ralph Staley, who agreed in 1624 to pay a third of the value of the tithe to Gell in return for a penny per dish for dressing the ore. This document mentions the fact that Gell had brought a lawsuit against miners who refused to pay tithe and had won it. Significantly, however, Staley promised not to pass his mines to anyone who intended to deny Gell his rights. Clearly legal entitlement was still not the same as possession, as far as tithe ore was concerned.

In Chancery

A reference in the agreement with Staley to the "due course of law" probably refers to a decree which Gell had obtained in the Court of Chancery in 1624[14]. This, like his authority from the Court of Wards, was doggedly opposed and in 1626 he brought an action in Chancery against miners who were refusing to obey it[15], naming Ralph James, Robert Jepson and James Walklate. Walklate entered a bond of £40 with the Derbyshire high sheriff, Henry Harpur, in May to appear in Chancery to answer a charge of contempt of court[16], yet by December the warden of the Fleet prison in London was issuing a warrant from the Court of Chancery for his and Jepson's arrest for contempt[17]. Two of the officers executing the warrant were Ralph Poyser, a servant of Gell's and later one of his deputy barmasters, and William Gell, presumably a relative. The collection for the miners' anti-Gell fund went on and the tithe gatherers continued to be obstructed.

In the Court of Chancery in 1627 Gell aimed for the organisers of the resistance to him. He brought an action for contempt of court against six men, accusing them of frustrating the 1624 decree by collecting money from the miners in Bakewell, Tideswell and Hope and threatening to remove their ore and bring legal action against them if they refused to pay[18]. The leaders were local gentry, Robert Allsop, Esquire, the miners' solicitor, and William Wright, gent, who held the mineral rights in Ashford and was presumably responsible for a decision to levy a 3d contribution in Ashford to contribute to the anti-tithe campaign. Allsop was accused of going "from one place to another amonst the myners", promising them that if they paid their contributions they would never have to pay tithe again. Gell maintained that the miners would rather pay tithe than the money demanded by Allsop and said that some of the miners had paid their tithe secretly, to avoid the wrath of William Wright and others. Allsop was further accused of threatening legal action against the tithe gatherers and Wright of seizing tithe ore after it had been paid.

Gell also accused the barmasters of taking part in the campaign. "Letters notes directions orders or prtended orders or coppies of orders" had been circulated, one of the chief letter writers being Henry Coupe, one of the miners' solicitors. These documents had been shown or read to miners, and the barmasters were accused of taking part in this persuading - "have you read or caused the same to be read in any church or chappell ... in publique manner in or after divine service upon the Sabath day or some holiday". Evidence was given by Gell's agent, John Woodhouse, that once, when he had bought twenty loads of ore, Henry Platts, deputy barmaster at Ashford, had demanded the 3d "towards the maynteyning of the suite fr the tyth oare against Mr Gell & the lord Dencourte [formerly Sir Francis Leake, created Baron Deincourt in 1624]".

Evidence was given by one Tideswell miner of the treatment received by Gell's agent Ralph Poyser in March 1627, when he attempted to claim tithe ore from John Wrigget and Thomas Ashton. Poyser produced a copy of the Chancery decree, sealed with the royal "great seal", as his authority. Wriggett thereupon knocked him to the ground while Ashton threatened him and "called the kings brode seale a bobi [trick] that hi brought to scare men with all". A warrant for the arrest of John Mitchell, one of the six named in the contempt proceedings, has an instruction to the constables to "command him to bringe the order of the Chancery which hee vyolently tooke from the forsaid Raphe Pyser" on July 3rd.

There was evidence from two Tideswell yeomen, one of whom was eighty-six years old "or there abouts", who had been tithe gatherers, that the tithe had been paid "till now alate [of late] that this sute begun". A third yeoman testified that at a meeting in his (the witness's) house Allsop had contended that only the four miners named in the Court of Wards proceedings were obliged to pay tithes. In June the Court of Chancery noted that Allsop, Wright and their four co-defendants had failed to answer the charges against them and instructed them to appear within a month, bringing with them the letters circulated by Coupe. The court continued to take evidence throughout 1627 and its commissioners called witnesses to a meeting at Brassington as late as 12th November "by nyne of the cloke in the morning". Brassington was chosen for the hearing because it was then on the main road between Derby and Manchester, and had half a dozen inns. The Court met at one of them, the New Hall, still standing at the side of the main north-south road through the village and now called the Tudor House. Among the witness summoned there were Jepson, Walklate, Woodhouse and Poyser.

The court's verdict, given in January 1628, must have infuriated John Gell[19]. It noted that an order issued in May 1627 had ruled invalid Allsop's contention that only the four miners named in the order of the Court of Wards were obliged to pay tithes, and that the order "should stand against all the miners". It ruled that Allsop "had comitted a contemp in stirring upp the myners against the performance of the said decree". However, in spite of this, Gell's case was dismissed because the decree referred to miners and since "the saide Alsoppe was noe myner the same did not extend unto him and the plt [plaintiff] failed to prove the rest to be myners". Allsop and the others were "discharged of their said supposed contemp" and were free to continue to thwart Gell's attempts to collect his tithe.

The contest was inconclusive. Gell certainly collected some tithe ore. A letter of 1632 from Henry Harpur[20] refered to a stock of tithe ore collected on behalf of both Gell and Deincourt and asked Gell whether he wished it to be sold or smelted. Presumably referring to the tithe gatherers' past problems, Harpur promised to "keepe the oar in safetie" and to "husband yt better then yt hath bene formerley". On the other hand Gell's servant Thomas Stopard confessed in 1643 that "wee are at your great charges to looke for yr tith oare and get verie litle"[21]. There are lists of recalcitrant miners in the liberties of Tideswell, Hope, Ashford and Barlow and a request from a Gell tenant who owed six months rent to be allowed to earn it by collecting tithes in Bradwell. "Some menn doe soe abuse yr servants & denie the payinge of the tythe oare that hath paid none this year or tow". Ominously, Gell is asked to "send mee a muskett by these bearers".

Assault and battery

When Gell intervened personally in the tithe dispute by going to Bakewell to bring pressure on the miners he demonstrated that he was prepared to go beyond litigation and take physical action when his interests were threatened. We can guess that the Bakewell confrontation was not a diplomatic one, and the assaults on his servants are a reminder that violence was common at the time. He showed his own tendency to use force during a meeting of his manor court at Hopton a few years later. A Wirksworth man called Richard Wigley had arrested Gell's servant Booth and brought him to the court to answer charges brought by Thomas Stone, a kinsman of John Fearn. A note on the cover of an unrelated document among Gell's papers refers to this incident - "one letter in which mention is made of his having beaten a Bailiff for arresting a man at his court"[22] - and what happened on this occasion seems to justify Fearn's apprehension at the prospect of Gell's being lord of the manor. On arrival at the court Wigley was assaulted by Gell and others and "verie violently dealt withall, both by word and deed" . Worse, when he returned to Wirksworth he was confronted in the market place by six men who "drewe upon him, and if he had not over run them home, they had slayne him". The six, who were presumably Gell's men, hacked at the door with their swords and threatened to kill him. Wigley made the allegations of these outrages to Anthony Fearn, brother of John. Fearn wrote to Stone in 1622 asking for the truth about them and also wanted to know what Gell had been saying about him, as Wigley "sayth Mr Gell did me wrong in his speeches, without any cause given him by me"[23].

The obnoxious barmaster

Gell's extreme animosity toward Richard Wigley had its roots in lead mining quarrels. Gell was a mine owner in the Wirksworth area and Wigley was a deputy barmaster and associate of one of the best hated men in the Wirksworth area, Richard Carrier. Carrier was the Vicar of Wirksworth and, along with his wife Jennet, was carrying out the duties of barmaster first on behalf of Jennet's grandfather, Robert Parker, and later for her father, Thomas, who lived in Yorkshire. In both roles he was Gell's natural enemy. As Vicar, he claimed, and had been awarded the tithes of lead ore, and in Wirksworth Gell found himself playing the opposite role to the one he was playing in Bakewell. He was no doubt as unwilling to pay tithes to Carrier as the Bakewell miners were unwilling to pay them to him. As barmaster Carrier conducted the business of the industry in a way which provoked determined opposition from the miners. In addition to the usual dues, Carrier and Jennet demanded an extra tax called "gifter ore", and were ready to use violence to enforce their authority.

By 1627 a commission of the Star Chamber was investigating complaints made against them, and evidence given by Wigley and others revealed the conflicts in the industry. Jennet was accused of producing a knife on one occasion, saying "shee would take a short course with them, & being desired to put up her knife shee said it was but a hanging matter if she killed one of them". She denied saying this and claimed that the knife was for nicking a tally stick to record ore measurements, but the picture is clear enough. Carrier himself was accused of saying that "hee was Barmaster, Judge, Justice & Lord of the Mine, & whosoever resisted hee would set them in the stocks by the Neck, Middle, or Legg"[24]. Wigley was not the only associate of Carrier's with whom Gell's quarrel became physical at this time. Gell attacked William Hopkinson, a member of a prominent Wirksworth lead mining family[25] and also close to Carrier. Gell was "presented" to a meeting of the Wirksworth manor court on 2nd May 1622 and fined the standard 3/4d for "making an affray" on Hopkinson[26].

Until he was finally deposed Carrier was allowed to continue to collect the dues, while John Fearn was appointed to administer the industry. Fearn wrote to Thomas Gell in 1631 reciting Carrier's continuing offences and asking Gell to acquaint the "great ones" with the situation[27]. According to Fearn Carrier was conducting a reign of terror among the miners and there was no one brave enough to stand up to him. Among the associates whom Fearn named as helping Carrier were Richard Wigley, William Hopkinson and Hopkinson's brothers. Carrier's terrorising was " chiefly through the speeches & doings of the Hopkinsons". A further letter to Thomas Gell from Fearn in April 1632 referred to material which Gell was collecting as evidence against Carrier, whom Fearn described as "the arch enemy of our parish"[28]. Gell's list of Carrier's offences, with the names of witnesses prepared to swear to them, describes attacks on miners, confiscation of ore, perjury, "vexatious" law suits, and threats to jurymen and witnesses at miners' courts[29].

Thomas Gell, ever his older brother's faithful ally, had influence in government and used it against Carrier. Fearn's letter was prompted by his seeing a letter to Gell from Sir Kenelme Digby' solicitor. Digby was a member of the king's inner circle of advisors, and certainly one of the "greate ones". In his listing of the court records and other material with which Gell was to proceed against Carrier, Fearn named many of Carrier's associates, including three Hopkinson brothers who were "all dependants of Carrier and always opposite to your brother". Years later Thomas reminded his brother of the help he had given him at this time - "it was by my meanes that Carriers malice against you took noe effect to your prejudice, but to his owne great losse, which was donne by my friends, at my instance without anie charge of yours"[30]. However, John Gell paid a lawyer's bill of £2 for "drawinge and ingrossinge additional articles against Carrier and his wife" in 1632, and clearly took a leading part in the anti-Carrier campaign[31].

It was probably Gell's opposition to the Reverend Carrier that led him, along with his servant Ralph Poyser and Poyser's wife, to be summoned to appear before the Commissioners Ecclesiastical at Lambeth Palace on the 22nd November 1632 "to answere unto such matters as shall be objected against you and to receave such further direction therein as to justice shall appeare lawe"[32]. Assessing the truth of the allegations against Carrier is complicated by the fact that he was an obstacle to a takeover of the mines of the Dovegang area of Wirksworth currently being engineered by Sir Robert Heath, the Attorney General, and his partner Sir Cornelius Vermuyden, who was driving a sough to drain the mines of the Dovegang[33], but there is no doubt about the strife and John Gell's violent treatment of Richard Wigley and his fight with William Hopkinson were two among many confrontations between the Carrier faction and the miners and mine owners.

The Dovegang plot

Gell's different role in the Wirksworth mines, where he was a tithe payer rather a gatherer, did not in fact make him a friend of the working miners or of his fellow mine owners, and in the Dovegang episode he took the part of the powerful outsiders who dispossessed the locals. The background to the Dovegang takeover was the King's chronic shortage of money during the period when he was governing without a Parliament. In addition to the revenue from leasing the mining dues he collected a tax of 48/- per "fother" (about 1 ton) of smelted lead[34]. He was assured by Heath that he could greatly increase this income by making arrangements with the miners to preempt their ore at an agreed price. This was in fact impossible as the mining rules stipulated that the miners could sell their ore to whomever they chose. Ore prices furthermore fluctuated according to the price of smelted lead, to the quality of the ore, and to the difficulty of mining it. Heath nevertheless made an arrangment with a Derbyshire ore-buyer, William Rowland, in 1629, asking him to be prepared to buy the preempted ore. There was never any ore delivered to Rowland but Heath used this illusory promise to persuade the King to grant him title to the mines of the Dovegang, and persuaded Rowland to help in removing the owners in return for a promise that as soon as they were evicted, he would be made Royal Commissioner entrusted with buying the preempted ore. The Dovegang mines were known to be rich but had been inaccessible for many years because of flooding. The existing owners, whose titles the King ignored in granting them to Heath, had been attempting to dewater their mines since about 1618 and strongly resisted their eviction, bringing a succession of lawsuits against Heath and his agents. Richard Carrier was one of Heath's biggest obstacles. As defacto barmaster he controlled the local industry and he and his wife owned some of the Dovegang mines. It cannot be a coincidence that procedings against him began in 1627, the same year in which Heath began his move to preempt the miners' ore.

Gell's half-brother John Curzon was the only member of the local gentry, apart from Carrier, who opposed Heath. Gell found himself collaborating with old enemies like John Fearn in shared hostility to Carrier and it was this hostility which prompted them, at least while Carrier was still barmaster, to give their support to Heath. Ferne's letter of 1632 to Thomas Gell had noted that, in addition to opposing Gell, Carrier was "likewise against the king in the preemption". Gell's motivation probably included also the fact that Heath was influential with the King. By the end of the decade, when Heath was out of royal favour and Carrier ejected from the barmaster's position, and when Gell himself had taken the lease of the mineral rights, he joined Heath's accusers[35].

While Fearn's main role was to curb Carrier's activities, Gell played an active role in dispossessing the Dovegang miners. Heath's contention was that the mines were too far below the water table ever to be successfully drained by the methods then being used. The Dovegang owners had employed a succession of engineers and had at one stage pumped the mines dry enough to be worked. This success was temporary and by the time that Heath began his operations the miners' current engineer, John Bartholomewe, or "John the divisor", had begun the construction of a sough, or drain. This was the method used by Heath's engineer, the considerably more accomplished Dutch expert Sir Cornelius Vermuyden, who had recently drained the East Anglian fens and was in favour at the royal court. Bartholomewe claimed that he would soon have drained the mines, an unlikely claim since Vermuyden was to take twenty years to complete his sough. Heath took Vermuyden as his partner in the enterprise. Gell's role was to lead a commission which surveyed the area in 1632. It was set up by the Dutchy of Lancaster to determine the extent of the Dovegang, the number and location of the mines and the names of those who "pretend to have title" to them.

Gell and his fellow commissioners, Edward Revell and William Hampes, who was later to be barmaster for the Dovegang, met five deputy barmasters and twenty-four jurymen at the Dovegang in

June 1632. These jurymen seem to have been confused men, judging by the evidence they gave in various lawsuits later brought against Heath. Although they were described by Heath's opponents as "divers ignorant and inexperienced men" they were in fact local miners who must have been knowledgeable about the industry and several of them gave evidence against him later. In 1632 they were probably unaware of the full implications of Heath's proceedings and, as was alleged, were probably under pressure by Gell when they approved his commission's findings. These included a very generous definition of the boundary of the Dovegang and a statement that all the mines were flooded to the extent that they had made no profit for at least six years. Gell counted thirty-three mines, of which Heath owned thirteen. Jennett Carrier had shares in four mines and five others had shares in two while the rest were unclaimed.

All these findings were later strenuously denied in court but in 1632 the King confirmed Heath's and Vermuyden's rights to the mines "accordinge to the boundaries and limitts distinguished and sett forth by a mapp lately made by vertue of a comission out of our said courte of duchie", and all former owners were threatened with a fine of £500 if they did not allow Heath and Vermuyden full possession. The miners who refused to go quietly were driven out either by threats or by direct violence. Among the men who used these strong-arm methods was Johannes Molanus, a Dutchman who had served Vermuyden during the fen-draining exploits which had earned him his knighthood. Molanus was later to be one of Gell's closest allies. In helping to dispossess the mine owners of the Dovegang, many of whom were his neighbours, Gell had demonstrated his willingness and ability to execute the King's plans, however unpopular.

CHAPTER 3

Royal favour

Loyalties

The court of the Duchy of Lancaster was a royal court and its appointment of Gell to provide the official document on which Heath could base his seizure of the Dovegang mines indicated that at that time the King trusted him. And yet Gell could never have seemed a natural supporter of Charles I. The Presbyterian beliefs expressed in his papers would themselves have made him an opponent of the King. Presbyterians advocated the replacement of the rule of bishops by the rule of presbyteries composed of elders and laymen. Their ideas were anathema to the High Church royal establishment at a time when religion was a vital part of politics. In politics, as a member of a rising class of new gentry, Gell could have had no sympathy for Charles's insistence on the divine right of kings to rule unfettered by their subjects. He owned a book explicitly challenging the King's pretensions - "The question is whether the king without assent of parliament may sett Imposicions upon the wares and goods of Merchants exported and imported out and into this Realme"[1]. When a choice had to be made he can have had no difficulty in choosing sides, but he was loyal to the crown until the King made his decisive break with Parliament. He was rewarded for his loyalty and by 1632 he had already moved forward.

Militia man

John Gell's first official appointment, made in 1624, was as a captain of foot in the trained bands, or county militia, with responsibility for the administrative areas, called hundreds, of Scarsdale and High Peak. In spite of the fact that in 1630 he refused to pay the levy which raised money to support the militia[2], he retained the post for at least ten years, as on the 20th of May 1634 he was informed by John Manners that there was to be a muster at Chesterfield on June 16 and was asked to be there, with his officers[3]. On the 17th, at a muster of the High Peak militia at Bakewell, "Capt Gell" was paid £15 for his services[4]. On appointment in 1624 Gell wrote to Sir Peter Frescheville of Staveley, one of the Deputy Lords Lieutenant to whom he was subordinate, asking for his advice on appointing officers and NCOs and exercising the soldiers[5]. Gell had a copy of a training manual, "The pathwaie to martiall discipline" by Thomas Styward, published in 1582[6], and he lent this to Frescheville for his opinion on its usefulness. Frescheville returned the book on the 21st August, suggesting that it be brought to the musters - it has a section "of mustering and training". Gell seems to have taken him at his word, since the book is badly worn. It is also heavily bloodstained, suggesting that it was taken into battle as well as to training parades. Frescheville also suggested that Gell should seek advice from the High Constable of Morleston "who hath beene for a long tyme very well acquainted with that service".

In the event Gell did not need the help of the High Constable as in October he received official instructions on how he was to carry out his duties[7]. These came from the Lords Lieutenant of the county, the Earl of Devonshire and his eldest son, William Lord Cavendish, and instructed that once the men were trained they were to be mustered for inspection at a time and place appointed by the senior Deputy Lord Lieutenant, Sir Francis Coke. Gell was to instruct the Petty Constables of each parish to recruit a file of ten soldiers, choosing for convenience men who lived near each other. The Constable was to choose "leaders Bringers up and Midlemen" from the most expert of the militiamen and these NCOs should exercise their men "upon holidaies and Sondaies after evening prayer". Gell himself was to choose the training grounds. In order to avoid "putting countrie to charge of powder" the training was to be restricted to drill except that, once they had mastered the drill they were to be allowed to fire blanks - "false fyer, and a litle powder in the pan". Gell was instructed to submit reports each quarter and notify their Lordships of any defaulters. Frescheville wrote in 1626 giving more exact instructions as to how the militia exercises were to be ordered - Gell's lieutenant and sergeants should each exercise ten men on each of five holidays so that the whole of the training requirement of his two hundred men could be completed in five days[8]. During his decade or more as a militia captain he learned how the military force of the county was organised and how it could be raised. He became familiar with the rank and file and their officers and he became experienced in the minutiae of training and controlling a militia force. This was the knowledge and expertise which he was to need when it fell to him to raise a regiment and fight a war in Derbyshire.

Gell may have had other practical experience. At least one writer has claimed that he fought on the Continent during the Thirty Years War, which began in 1618 and ended in 1648[9]. There is an item among the family archives which suggests that, however unlikely it may seem that he should have left his family and his responsibilities to go away in the wars, he did in fact undertake a brief adventure in 1627, when he was thirty-five years old [10]. This is a draft or copy , unsigned, unaddressed and undated, of a letter, in one of the commonplace books. The writer states "I have no great skill in warrfare yet I served about two yeares in the borders of France under the late Duke of Buckingham". Buckingham was the court favourite and chief minister to both James I and Charles I. His campaign in France started and finished in 1627, though there were preparations in 1626 and attempts to renew it in 1628. It was designed to relieve the protestant Huguenots of La Rochelle, under siege by the French royal army, and was the last in a series of grandiose failures engineered by Buckingham. 3,000 English, from an original strength of 7,000, made a precarious dash back home after six months campaigning, leaving the Huguenots to their fate. The story is made more plausible by the probability that Gell knew Buckingham, who was married to Lady Katherine Manners, daughter of the Earl of Rutland and a neighbour at Haddon.

Receivers for the Duchy

That he kept the Militia post in spite of his reluctance to pay his dues argues that he carried out his duties satisfactorily, and there was a further indication of royal favour to Gell and his family in 1632. On 30th June the King granted the office of Receiver and Supervisor of the Honour of Tutbury successively, for life, to Thomas Gell, John Gell and John Gell the younger[11]. This was a Duchy of Lancaster appointment - the Honour of Tutbury was the name given to the Duchy's Derbyshire and Staffordshire estates - and the Receiver was responsible for collecting Duchy money. At a time when the King was anxious to exploit every possible source of revenue it was an important job and Thomas was being instructed in 1637 to ensure that all fees due to the King on the deaths of Duchy of Lancaster copyholders were paid[12]. By a custom which survived until the form of tenure known as copyhold was abolished in 1925, a fee was due whenever copyhold property was transferred either by sale or inheritance. Thomas was sent a schedule of property on which inheritance fees were outstanding. In the same year Thomas ordered that defaulters' property should be seized in lieu of unpaid Duchy rents[13]. The brothers carried out their duties well enough to prompt John's appointment as High Sheriff for the year 1635.

High Sheriff and Ship Money

The office of Sheriff had lost some of its functions with the creation of Lords Lieutenant in the sixteenth century, when it had become an annual appointment. It was still important, however, in the administration of justice and in carrying out special duties for the King. Gell's year as High Sheriff was politically important because it was the first year in which the King's "ship money" was imposed on inland towns. This tax had been levied on coastal towns in the previous year and was one of the devices by which Charles I raised revenue during the period between 1629 and 1640 when he governed without Parliament. The Petition of Right, a catalogue of Parliament's grievances against the King which Charles had reluctantly signed in 1628, had forbidden taxation without the consent of Parliament. Ship money was therefore of doubtful legality, notwithstanding the fact that when the famous Parliamentarian John Hampden was tried in 1637 for refusing to pay, the Court of Exchequer declared that the King was entitled to levy it. Ship money was one of the grievances which were to bring King and Parliament to war, and the enthusiasm with which John Gell set about raising it in Derbyshire made him personal enemies. The Privy Council assessed Derbyshire at the cost of providing a ship of 350 tons, with a crew of 140 men. In the list of counties Derbyshire's liability was put at £3,500 but in an accompanying calculation of the cost of buying the ship and manning it for six months the figure became £3,780[14]. According to one of Gell's own records he raised a total of £3,684-15-6d, made up of £120 from the nobility, £108-10-6d from the clergy, £175 from Derby, and the rest of the sum, £3,281-5-0d, from the six administrative units called hundreds[15]. This last figure included an assessment of £40 for Chesterfield, listed under the hundred of Scarsdale.

The Privy Council instructed Gell to levy the tax by assessing hundreds and parishes in a similar manner to the one used in levying other common taxes and to instruct High Constables of hundreds to decide parish assessments[16]. In September the Petty Constables sent their "presentments" of the number of people in their parishes whom they judged capable of paying the tax[17] and in the following month Gell sent them instructions detailing the amounts of money to be collected, sometimes the names and assessment of large tax payers, and the person to whom the money was to be handed over[18]. In the two largest towns in the county this was the Mayor and the acknowledgement which Chesterfield's Mayor, Reignalde Bretlande, sent back to Gell that he had received the ship money writ has survived[19]. In Derby the burgesses, or town councillors, questioned their assessment. Gell wrote for advice to the Privy Council in September and was warned by the Secretary, Sir John Coke, that "you will hardly avoid censure if you suffer either Derby or any other of what qualitie soever to free themselves from your power"[20]. Coke, in the words of a covering letter from his son John, used his influence "to procure there for your full satisfaction"[21]. The Privy Council's decision gave Gell what he wanted. They pronounced that although Derby's tax had been set at £120 it was permissible for him to alter it, and the best rate would be the one which the town usually paid[22]. They had written to the officers of the town to this effect to ensure that there would be no further dispute. From Derby's final assessment of £175 it seems that the corporation had made a mistake in crossing swords with Sheriff Gell, though the town was one of a number of late payers who were reported to the Council later[23].

The details of the parish assessments show that Gell observed the principle of ability to pay. £16-16-0d was demanded of Stanton and Newhall, "whereof the Ladie Darcy is to pay £12-0-0d". At Walton upon Trent Lady Ferrers paid £12, the parson £3 and the rest of the villagers £4-4-0d. The squire of Tissington, Sir John Fitzherbert, was assessed at £12 and his tenants at £7-12-0d. At Hope the ship money total of £58-4-0d was raised from Rowland Moorewood (£7) and twenty-five others who paid £1, £2, or £3 each. Eyam's £40 was paid by nine people. Gell assessed himself at £12 and the rest of the people of Hopton and Carsington at £6, though a separate, perhaps preliminary, list of the Hopton and Carsington ship money payers[24] includes a "Mr Gell", assessed at £1-3-10, who was presumably either John Gell's brother Thomas or his son John, and sixty-two others paying a total of £6-8-10. There was one villager with an assessment of 12/8d and no one else with as much as 10/-. Thirty-two people in Hopton and Carsington were to pay less than 1/-. Clearly most people in the county paid very little and many paid nothing.

Some Constables sent nil returns and at least one explained why. This was Nicholas Woodcocke, Constable of Weston Underwood, who declared that "All the men within this constablery are poore tennants & doe sitt upon the racke". Weston Underwood was assessed at £5-12-0d and, though in this case no one is named, the money was presumably to be raised from the parson or other Weston gentry. The tax fell most heavily on such members of Gell's own class, and they deeply resented it. However, Gell kept in mind the Secretary's warning and pursued his task with zeal, raising more money for the king than any subsequent sheriff, more, his critics alleged, than had been assessed. The order to Gell and the other High Sheriffs had anticipated this possibility, forbidding them to levy "more of the saide men then shall suffice for the necessary expences of the premisses, or that any one shall detayne by him the money or any part of it" [25]. If more was collected than had been assessed the excess was to be returned to the tax payers "by ratable portions".

The most bitter of the conflicts caused by Gell's determined tax-collecting was with Sir John Stanhope of Elvaston. Elvaston had been assessed at £32[26] and, as in every other parish, its richest inhabitant was asked to pay the lion's share, in this case £24. Gell failed to collect the whole of Stanhope's £24 - there was still £7-13-0d owing on his list of defaulters. He had in fact failed to collect any money at all as Stanhope had claimed to be unable to pay. The shortfall was in the money raised by "distraining" [seizing] and selling Stanhope's cattle. Stanhope was very ill, too ill to plead his own case before the Privy Council. After the Earl of Chesterfield, Stanhope's brother, had spoken for him, the Privy Council ordered that the money should be paid. Stanhope died in 1638 and and in 1640, by which time Parliament was sitting and ship money had been declared illegal, Dame Mary, his widow, obviously smarting from a sense of injustice, petitioned for the return of the £24 and payment of damages for Gell's treatment of her husband[27].

If her account of what happened is true Gell had indeed behaved with deliberate malice designed to hurt Stanhope. By Dame Mary's account Gell's collector, Richard Ward, had seized six milk cows worth at least £24. Instead of selling them on the spot however, Ward had driven them three miles to Derby, penned them for eight days without food, driven them a further ten miles and only sold them when they had so deteriorated as to fetch only £16. He returned a fortnight later and was about to drive off two draught oxen to cover the remaining £8 when Stanhope's ox-driver, who had told his master what was going on, "expostulated" with him. Dame Mary's account has the two men exchanging words and Ward then telling the driver, William Wood, that if he stood in front of the oxen and turned their heads he, Ward, would be satisfied and would not take them. Ward appears to have been as unsuccessfull in collecting ship money as he had been with tithes twenty years earlier.

After hearing Ward's report Gell included Stanhope among the defaulters on the list presented to the Council. This is the story used by Gell's critics to illustrate his boundless and cunning malice[28]. However, the story of William Wood and Richard Ward is clearly unbelieveable and it is entirely believeable that Stanhope's original six cows might be worth only £16. A much more likely explanation of Gell's behaviour, consistent with his behaviour at other times, is that he was exasperated by what he would see as Stanhope's arrogant intransigence, particularly after Ward's failure to distrain the oxen. Gell ascribed this failure to "riotous" opposition, much more plausible than the "gentle manner" with which William Wood behaved in Dame Mary's version. Gell won his case and the continuation of the affair by Dame Mary's accusations against him, of malice and dishonesty, were probably behind the malice which he certainly did show against the Stanhopes during the Civil War, in which they were royalists. Dame Mary alleged that Gell had "raised £200 more at least than he had the direction to do, which he hath ever since kept to his own use", a damaging accusation which must have infuriated Gell.

The frequency of the use of distraining is suggested by a report to Gell from the High Constable of the Scarsdale Hundred in November 1635 that parish clergymen and Constables were being negligent in collecting the money and that "there is noe wayes to come by your moneyes yet unpaide but to send prsentlie to distrayne them"[29]. The Constable, James Foljambe, warned Gell that "you must be certen in this resolucon, wthout alteracon otherwyse you will occasion you selfe endles trouble". The arrival of the bailiffs was painful and Sir John Stanhope was not the only one to resist. Sir Arthur Ingram of Walton was distrained for his assessment of £12 and a letter of December 5th from Gell's collector Richard Taylor reported first that he had received £10 from Ingram's servant Paul Flecher and then, in a postscript "since I writt this letter I understand that willfull Paul

Flecher will not pay the £X for Sr Arthur Ingram"[30]. The £10 was presumably an error as the following day, no doubt after the application of some pressure on Flecher, Foljambe wrote to Gell that he had received a bill of exchange from Taylor for "£12 received by him from the handes of Paule Flecher for the money imposed upon Sr Arthure Ingram, knight"[31].

Gell's brother-in-law, Percival Willoughby, seems to have helped him in tax gathering. In 1636 Percival, who had been living in Derby since his marriage in 1631, wrote to Gell about his efforts to enforce the recovery of £31-10s from one of Gell's debtors[32]. Percival did not identify either the debt or the defaulter, but the date makes it likely that it was unpaid ship money. His efforts included issuing a writ to be executed by the Under-Sheriff of either Staffordshire or Derbyshire, provision for the debtor to be held in Stafford jail if he were arrested there, payments to be made to the Under-Sheriff and the engagement and payment of an agent to help in the debtor's capture. Percival, Elizabeth Gell's younger brother, was a highly regarded doctor[33]. He was a friend of William Harvey, famous for discovering the circulation of the blood. Percival seems to have been on good terms with his brother-in-law. This letter has a warm and friendly tone.

There were anxious letters from the hard-pressed. In October the widow Pheallycea Agarde complained "I have been charged with £12 for Ship Money, a sum that will prove heavy to me as, of all my husband's estate, I have only my jointure, not amounting to £300 by year. All the other estates descend to his heir and for the most part lie in other counties. His personal estate went towards payment of his debts and legacies"[34]. A much more humble complainant found it difficult to pay his assessed ship money tax of 16/-. He had no money and "a very smale stock, & they make there cessant [assessment] by land which is verie hard for poor tenants"[35]. This problem had been anticipated in the order issued to Gell by the Board, who instructed that while the assessments should generally be on the same basis as other taxes, namely on land, that nevertheless rich men without land should be taxed and poor men with land should be spared[36]. If the above complaint were true, Gell was in this respect failing to carry out his orders.

Eckington's parson, Doctor Lowe, who was also the Master of Corpus Christi college, Cambridge, enlisted the help of the Earl of Manchester to appeal against his assessment[37]. Manchester was

Lord President of the Council, Lord Privy Seal, a zealous member of the Star Chamber Court and "one of Charles's most trusted and loyal adherents"[38]. He wrote to Gell in November 1635 pointing out that Lowe's assessment of £17 was disproportionate in a parish assessment of £50 and hoping that "it might bee speedily rectified, & his majesties service carried with that justice & equality that your diligence may finde commendations, & noe just greivances bee given to any". This intervention could hardly be ignored and Gell acted promptly. While Eckington's assessment remained at £50 the parson's own became £7 and James Foljambe, relieved at one dispute settled, could write "Doctor Lowe hath satisfied Mr Sheriffe and so I am discharged thereof"[39]. How the missing £10 was raised is not revealed by Gell's accounts. Manchester's references to justice, equality and grievances must have reflected the reputation which Gell's tax-gathering had earned him. In a letter from the Privy Council in January 1636, signed by Manchester, the bishop of Coventry and seven others[40] Gell was reminded that his orders had included a recommendation that the clergy should "receive all due respect both to their persons & calling" and he was instructed to let the Council have the assessments for the Derbyshire clergy "with convenient expedition".

As well as Gell himself, the local collectors were accused of being over zealous. In November 1637 Sir Francis Coke wrote to his father, the Secretary of State Sir John Coke, at Melbourne, asking him to intercede on behalf of Francis Eyre, former Constable of Bowden Middlecale[41]. As the village Constable Eyre had had the responsibility of collecting the £47-4-0d at which Gell had assessed Bowden Middlecale and was currently being persecuted by members of the local gentry who accused him of collecting more than the assessed sum. Coke pointed out that his accusers were rich while Eyre was poor. An attempt by Coke to persuade Gell to clear the matter up was unsuccessful and it was referred to the Privy Council. In December the Council wrote to Gell, Coke and the current High Sheriff, Sir John Fitzherbert of Norbury informing them that Eyre was accused of collecting £6-14-0d too much, enclosing Eyre's petition denying the charge and instructing them to examine him and his accusers[42]. They were to settle the differences if possible. If they decided that either Eyre or his accusers were at fault they were to punish the guilty parties. If they could follow neither of these courses they were to report back and await further orders. Eyre was distrained for £20 and Francis Coke wrote to Gell later, regretting that they had not managed to settle the matter without bringing in the High Sheriff and doubting that the Privy Council would agree on such a high level of distraint[43]. Coke asked Gell to "persuade Francis Eyre to give this £7-14s [sic] to them and make a clean end of the matter".

Gell made many enemies during his year as High Sherrif and it was alleged that he had "soe highly misdemean'd himselfe that he lookt for punishment, from the parliament" and that he took up the Parliamentary cause in 1642 only to avoid this punishment[44]. Any tax-collector, particularly one responsible for a tax of disputed legality levied by an unpopular King, was bound to have made enemies and Gell conducted himself as tax gatherer in the way that he conducted all his affairs - to the utmost of his ability. Apart from the evidence that he stuck too rigidly to land holding as the basis of assessment in the case of men with small incomes, and that he was late in sending in his accounts[45] he seems, in his rough and ready way, to have collected the king's money as he had been instructed, in such a way "that no inequalitie or other miscariage may either retard or disgrace the service"[46]. He responded to the Earl of Manchester's rebuke over his assessment of Doctor Love and to much less high and mighty interventions. Helen Wolseley of Ravenston wrote to him on September 27th to say that the £6 at which she had been assessed was beyond her ability to pay - "this is the playne truth, and noe fayned excuse"[47]. He seems to have fore warning of Mrs Wolsely's problem as relief came for her before she had posted her letter. On the edge she wrote "Sr I humbly thanke you for your abatement and if you had knowne my weake estate you would have cut off more from the first demaunde".

Gell's assessment methods were questioned. There was a letter from the Secretary of State, Edward Nicholas, in Westminster in February 1636 noting that he had not sent an explanation "of how the money required for setting forth a ship by Derbyshire was assessed"[48]. Gell replied to this letter on the 14th March[49]. He explained he had been instructed to raise £3,500. The tax had been split among six hundreds, which he named, two corporate towns, Derby (£175) and Chesterfield (£40), the nobility (£120) and the clergy (£90). After naming the hundreds he went on "in all which hundredes there is not anie poore men that doth paye soe farre forth as I doe Knowe of". There was money outstanding and when it was received he expected a surplus, which would be returned, as he had been instructed. Gell had, in fact, made up a shortfall in his receipts from his own money, and his successor as High Sheriff, John Milward, was instructed to repay him when the outstanding sums had been collected[50]. There is no evidence that he was corrupt and the claim that he was afraid of Parliamentary punishment has nothing to support it. He was as whole-hearted in his service to Parliament after 1642 as he had been to the King, for much less reward.

JP and Deputy Lord Lieutenant

As far as the royal service was concerned it was presumably because he had performed well as Sheriff that Gell was given a further promotion in 1636. This was to the Magistrates' Bench as a Justice of the Peace[51](Cox, 1890). It is difficult to imagine him showing the measured gravity ideally required of a magistrate, and he lacked the legal knowledge which his uncle Anthony had brought to the Bench. However, he carried out his duties and his papers include a record of the cases he dealt with in 1641 and 1642, including fines imposed for bastardy and public disorder - "Jo: Nun de Hopton £5 to keepe the peace towards Richard Radford of Duffield, nailer"[52]. Being a member of the county magistracy was a valuable position for a man with political ambitions. It brought him more power and influence, both of which were further increased two years later when he was appointed one of the Deputy Lords Lieutenant, with responsibility, under the Lord Lieutenant, for the county militia and for public order[53]. Gell was one of fourteen, the others consisting of one viscount, four baronets, five knights and three esquires. Gell's half-brother, John Curzon, who had by then been granted the first of two baronetcies, was one of his colleagues in this important layer of authority in the county.

Sir John Gell Baronet

Gell was now in the thick of Derbyshire politics and it is likely that the hope of further service from him weighed as heavily with the King as gratitude for services already rendered when he granted Gell his next honour. This was the baronetcy, granted in January 1642 when war between King and Parliament was beginning to seem inevitable and when Charles needed allies. The King had granted a baronetcy to John Curzon in the previous year, probably with the same motive, to go with a so-called "Nova Scotia" baronetcy given in 1636[54]. This variety of baronetcy had been created, like the original one, to raise money, in this case supposedly to colonise Nova Scotia. Gell's title, and all others granted after January 1641, were abolished by Parliament in 1651, on the assumption that the King "to promote his designs against the parliament, did use meanes to draw unto himselfe a party to assist him, and did give titles of honor, dignities, and precedences by patents, unto sutch persons as he thought were or might be servicable to him"[55]. Whether the honour genuinely signified the king's favour or was merely the bribe Parliament later thought it to be, it was an expensive one for John Gell. Payment for honours was an important source of royal income. Gell sent £450 to Thomas in London to make the necessary payments[56]. £300 went "to a courtier for a warrant for a Baronett", presumably the basic fee. The King received further payments for £7 each "for the kings hand" and "for the privie signet" and £64 was paid "for the fees at the great seal". Apart from these payments to the King there was an attorney's fee of £25 and numerous small sums for messengers, porters and "for expedition", which sounds like a euphemism for greasing the path. Gell's drive and ambition had brought him a long way and he no doubt thought that this expenditure was money well spent.

The Chaworth inheritance

While Gell was enjoying royal favour he was, at the end of the 1630s, engaged in a lawsuit whose bitterness may have tempered his loyalty to the King. This concerned his claim to a six-year lease to property at Merton and Tytheby, in Nottinghamshire. The property had been leased to Gell in 1637 by his kinsman Henry Sacheverell, who was the executor of the will of its former owner, Sir George Chaworth[57]. The price was £800 and after the death of Sir George's widow in August 1637, Gell "entered into the said premisses ... clayming the said terme of six yeares". However, the ownership of the property had had an involved history and in order to validate his claim Gell cited a number of indentures and agreements, dating back to an indenture entered into by Sir George's grandfather, also Sir George, in 1583, and this Sir George's will, made in 1589. He found himself baulked by the senior branch of the Chaworth family in the person of George, Lord Chaworth and, after his death, his son and heir John, who had taken possession of the evidence and refused to allow Gell the rents of the property. Gell presented a Bill of Complaint in the Court of Requests and petitions to the Court of Wards, the House of Lords and, after Lord John had obtained an Inquisition verdict in Gell's absence, to the King[58]. As usual the legal battle in London was being fought on Gell's behalf by his brother Thomas. Gell was sure of the justice of his case and Thomas reassured him - "The Lord Chaworth hath not yet answered, he is loath to come to his triall and hath used all the delayes that possiblie he can. I doubt not but to bring the business to a good end, and thinke that I have soe proceeded as I shall ere longe put him into a chase"[59]. This was in May 1638 and as the six years slipped away and proved Thomas to be over-optimistic, Gell saw himself getting no return on his £800. The King was his last hope. Gell pointed out that Lord Chaworth had obtained an injunction preventing him from continuing his legal challenge but that since Chaworth's mother was the holder of the freehold he was not entitled to it. Three years of the lease had already gone and his case was unlikely to be decided quickly, even should it come to court. The lease was likely to be expired before any verdict was reached. Meanwhile, if Lord Chaworth or his mother should die, Gell would be in danger of losing his arrears of rent. He asked to be allowed to continue his case.This petition was as unsuccessful as the previous ones and Gell was left feeling cheated and bitter.

CHAPTER 4

Family matters

Godyth Ashby=**Ralph Gell**=Emma Beresford
d 1564

Anthony Gell **Thomas Gell**=Millicent Sacheveral=JohnCurzon
d 1583 d 1594

Sir John Gell 1593-1671 = Elizabeth Willoughby d 1644
Thomas Gell 1594-1656
Sir John Curzon 1598-1686

- Millicent b 1611 = Richard Radcliffe
- Bridgett b 1612 = John Wigley
- **Sir John Gell II** 1613-1689 = Catherine Packer
- William 1615-1642
- Elizabeth b 1617 = Henry Wigfall
- Eleanor b 1620 =Anthony Allsop

A faithful brother

With one important and disastrous exception John Gell derived vital help and support from his family. His brother Thomas, based in London, was his industrious and usually uncomplaining ally in times of trouble. A lawyer in the family was bound to be of exceptional value to such a litigious man as Gell and Thomas seems to have taken part in almost all his legal struggles. A set of accounts, "Money laid out for my brother Gell in Michaelmas terme 1641"[1] demonstrates that John kept his brother busy. There are payments to the Assize Clerk, including one of £20, and to the Attorney General. Robin Woodcutter is paid for his affidavit and travelling expences. 17/6d is paid for a dinner for counsel and 8/8d for a supper. Several of John Gell's agents receive payments via Thomas. A calculation in a different hand reckons that Thomas has paid out £132-9-2d and that, after £100 has been received, £32-9-2d "remaynes due to my master". Thomas's ability to mobilise "the great ones", in John Fearn's phrase, in support of the miners and specifically to defend his brother from attacks by Richard Carrier was only one of a number of occasions on which Gell depended on his younger brother. Thomas pulled strings to get John made Justice of the Peace and drew up his patent of baronetcy[2].

Marriage alliances

John Gell's daughters and his eldest son married into families who enhanced his social status. The marriages also united families who took the same side as Gell when the war broke out. Not all the Derbyshire gentry families were united in this way. For instance, the Secretary of State, Sir John Coke, whose mother, like Gell's, was a Sacheverell, was compulsorily retired in 1642 after a lifetime of totally faithful royal service[3]. In spite of this royal career, however, he was sympathetic to Parliament during the war and his elder son, Sir John, was a firm Parliamentarian. His younger son Thomas, however, took the king's side and was ruined by it. Three of the Gell daughters married into Derbyshire families. Elizabeth married Henry Wigfall of Renishaw in 1636, Eleanor married Anthony Alsopp of Allsop-in-le-dale in 1637 and Bridgett married John Wigley of Wigwell Grange in 1638[4].

The oldest daughter, Millicent had earlier made what sounds like a modern romantic match. Her husband was Richard Radcliffe of Manchester and while it is not known what previous connection the two families had, the meeting between the two is described in a letter which Richard's father William wrote to Gell in December 1635[5]. Addressed to "his noble frende" Radcliffe's letter mentioned "kind and bountifull entertaynement" his son had had at Hopton, and "it seemes my sonne hath taken such lykinge of one of your daughters as he hath importuned mee soe far as that I would give way to him to solicit his sute". Radcliffe was of the opinion that if Gell approved he would like to see the match made quickly since he had heard "of your noble desertes" from many people. In reply Gell wrote a negotiating letter about financial settlements, characteristically trying to drive a hard bargain, warning Radcliffe that his son could not expect Millicent to come with a large dowry[6]. Radcliffe was accomodating. He would not "presse you with any unreasonable demands" in respect of either the amount or the time when the dowry would be paid, and promised to match whatever Gell put up. In any case his son and his wife would have his estate eventually but for the present he was thinking of a grant of £800 and an estate of £250 a year. He hoped that there would not "bee a breache betwixt us". The wedding took place and in the war which broke out a few years later Millicent's husband helped to hold Manchester for Parliament[7].

Son and heir

In the important matter of finding a suitable partner for Gell's heir the family did not wait for romance to strike again. Thomas Gell, in London, played a part in the search and produced a draft letter for his brother to send during any negotiations[8]. Expectations seem to have been high as the draft is addressed to "My Lord". He received a letter in March 1638 from a John Byrche of Cannock describing Byrche's efforts on behalf of Thomas's nephew[9]. Byrche had spoken to a Sir William Whitmore "in the business concerninge your nephew", and Whitmore had told him that his daughter lived with his brother, Sir George, who was in charge of her affairs. His, Sir William's, only responsibility was to provide a pension for her which, Bryche thought, would be £3000, plus "a fathers blessing at his death". Byrche proposed that if it seemed a suitable match he would take John Gell along to Sir George Whitmore's house for the two to get acquainted, "and if upon private confessenne with them it were conceived they could like eche other" further negotiations could take place. Miss Whitmore and John Gell seem not to have liked each other however as by May 1638 Thomas was writing to his brother describing further efforts[10].

Whether as a result of this determined search or by John's own choosing, he did find a bride. She was Catherine Packer, daughter of John Packer of Shellingford, Berkshire[11]. By design or not, Gell's heir had made a suitable match, suitable, that is, from a social point of view and, as it turned out, from a political point of view also. Packer had been a faithful royal servant, his posts including that of clerk of the Privy Seal to Elizabeth and to James I. He had bought the manor of Groombridge in Speldhurst, Kent and Charles I had given him Shellingford manor in gratitude for his loyalty. He also owned Donnington Castle in Shaw, Berkshire. Packer was elected MP for Looe in Cornwall just before the beginning of Charles I's personal rule and by the time that Parliament was recalled in 1639 his attitude to the King had changed. He may have been converted by the constitutional arguments of Sir John Elliot, a friend and fellow Parliamentarian, but he was generally regarded as a greedy and treacherous man and his new loyalty was condemned as ingratitude when, in 1640, he refused a royal request for a loan. Shellingford was seized by the royalists and Donnington Castle garrisoned for the King - it withstood three sieges during the Civil War[12]. The young John Gell had married into a family of national eminence - of his four Packer brothers-in-law Robert was an MP, George a fellow of All Souls, Philip one of the original fellows of the Royal Society and John a fellow of the Royal College of Physicians.

John Gell the younger was a convinced Presbyterian, was old enough to fight and, it can be assumed, willing to do so. The fact that he did not take part in the war and lived until 1646 with his wife's parents, was probably because his father had decided that, with Hopton plundered and the estate in enemy hands for part of the war period, this was the most likely way for the family to survive. He did in fact assist the Parliamentary forces. An account presented to his wife in 1645 reveals a list of debts incurred in 1644 for transporting money and supplies to the armies of the Parliamentary generals Waller, Browne and the Earl of Essex, manouevring in Oxfordshire and Berkshire during that year[13]. Waller was supplied with bread and cheese, wood, hay, bedding, labour and "imprest horses". There are general entries concerning provisions and money sent to Essex and Browne, and one which reveals that sixteenth century soldiers were not fussy about their meat - "for horse meat to Collo: Vandrose". There was transport "for carting money to the armys". The agent presenting this bill added a letter which makes it clear that these services to the Parliamentarians involved real sacrifice. It is clear also that at times when the King was in control of their neighbourhood the family had to help him too - "... I verily beleeve that you will scarce have any profitt for this yeare that is to come, unlesse it please god to mend the times, for it is worse now with us then it hath been, because paying to both sides".

Gell had turned most of the estate over to his son in 1636, by an indenture which included a provision that John pay his father and mother an annuity of £10 and keep them in board and lodging[14]. The list of possessions transferred to John included the manor of Wirksworth, Hopton Hall, possessions in Hopton and other parishes in the Wirksworth area, those in the High Peak parishes of Hope, Bakewell, Bubnell, Chapel-en-le-Frith and the tithes of hay and corn. This transfer was inspired not by any wish to be rid of the burden of the estate, nor by benevolence, but by a fear that it might be forfeited. Gell had made disloyal noises against the King at the time and was making sure that if the King moved against him he would have nothing to lose. This is revealed by a letter written fifteen years later, when he was in fact in danger of losing everything, though not to the King but to his executioners. Parliamentary commissioners, charged with seizing the estate after Gell had fallen foul of the winners of the Civil War reported that it had been transferred to his son "upon occasion of some words given out concerning the late king, for which he feared to be questioned" [15]. They noted that the indenture of 1636 had had no practical effect at the time, but that the situation had changed in 1644, when the son married.

On this occasion Gell settled the whole estate on John[16] and that this transfer was a serious one is indicated by the fact that the settlement included an annuity for Sir John not of £10 but of £1100. The shrewdness of these moves was proved in 1651, when John was able to show that the estate in fact belonged to him. Gell's heir proved a loyal son and a capable manager of the family fortunes. Lists of tenants, their holdings and their assessments for rent, rates and tax during the 1630s have later annotations in his hand[17]. According to a letter written in 1638 to his brother Thomas, the property which Gell handed over to his son in 1644 was worth an annual £1500 in rents[18].

This income would be considerably boosted by the family interests in lead. In 1644, in addition to his uncertain hold over the tithes of the High Peak mines, Sir John held the joint lease of the barmastership of the Wirksworth Wapentake, owned shares in mines there and elsewhere and owned two smelting mills at Wirksworth. The value of the barmastership varied according to the economic state of the industry but an indication of its worth was given in 1651, during proceedings to seize the estate of Thomas Coke, who had chosen the royal side in the Civil War. John Gell junior and his partner, John Milward successfully pleaded that they had paid Coke £1000 for a six-year lease in 1648[19]. Sir John, however had held the lease, sub-let by Coke, for at least nine years by then, as the deputy barmasters were presenting him with their accounts as early as 1639. These were the accounts in which they recorded the amounts of ore mined in each liberty and calculated what was due to Gell in tax. The most complete accounts which survive are from the 1650s. In one year, 1655, after the younger Gell had renewed his lease for a further six years, the income from the four liberties in the Wirksworth area was £1022[20]. The industry had become more productive with the completion of the Dovegang Sough in 1650, but the incomplete accounts from the 1640s include tax ore worth about £145 from the liberty then producing the most ore, Wirksworth, in 1642. Two years later £111 was received for 117 loads of tax ore in Elton[21]. Sir John's lease probably cost him less than his son's £1000 and, with an income from mining dues of £145 in one year from one liberty, would have been very profitable for him.

The figures for sales from the Gell mines are even more fragmentary than the tax figures, but those which contain the Elton tax ore sales also include sums of £60 and £29 received from two ore buyers in 1644 and £340 from another in 1645. John Gell had been smelting earlier than 1633, when he was sued by a former employee[22]. Nether Mill, which had been built in the late sixteenth century[23], was bought by Gell in 1640[24] and Upper Mill was in use before 1647[25]. Detailed accounts for the two mills' operations start in 1648. In that year Nether Mill made a profit for John Gell junior of £18 for the first quarter[26] and £23 for the second [27]. At Upper Mill, where the tenant was Johannes Molanus, the profit was £40 for the five months January to May[28]. The lead industry was unreliable but it was prospering during Gell's time and a further annual income of £1000 to add to the £1500 from rents does not seem an unreasonable estimate.

The black sheep

John Gell's younger son William, born at Kedleston in 1615, grew up to be the archetypal black sheep of his family. Like his uncle Thomas he was fated to see his brother inherit his father's estate, though in 1631 his father had made arrangements for some of his rents to be devoted for six years to raise money for William and his sisters[29]. In the 1636 indenture the younger John Gell agreed to provide board and lodging for his brother "if the said William Gell ... shall need & will come to the said John Gell his brother". William, however, was expected to make his own way in the world. To that end, after a short period at home, he was sent off to London in 1631, when he was sixteen, to live under the eye of his uncle Thomas[30]. Thomas, with the help of William Rowland, an agent of John Gell's, found him lodgings and paid his bills for food and clothes. Rowland negotiated an annual bill of twelve marks (£8) for William's "diette lodginge and washinge" and Thomas footed bills for a "cloth sute, cloake and stockins", a hat and other clothes. There are also frequent unexplained sums paid to William, all noted in the accounts which Thomas presented to his brother. He engaged a teacher, Mr Conradis, "to teach Mr William Gell to write a good secretarie and Italian hand, as also to teach him to cyfer and to keepe a merchants booke". If Wiliam proved unable to learn book keeping, Conradis was to be paid £1 less. However, he seems to have been a good teacher. By the time that William was writing home a few years later his handwriting is far more neat and legible than either his uncle's or his father's and his letters better organised.

In the matter of book keeping William was sufficiently capable to be apprenticed, in or about 1633, to a London merchant, Thomas Northey[31]. This arrangement was an expensive one. Northey was paid an immediate £200 and Gell also entered into a "bond" of £1000 with him as surety for William's "good and true behavour". William borrowed his father's alarm clock, and Gell wrote a fatherly letter to him, concerned that he should not lose sleep - "I am not against it, that you make use of the allarum delivered to you out of my study, whereby you may be wakened at what houer you please: so it do not call you from sleep unseasonally, for I would have you to have a speciall care of your health" [32]. He went on to recommend William to imitate the ancient Roman Cicero's style in his letters home. All went well for three years. William behaved himself and Northey was sufficiently confident of his honesty to trust him with money, including on occasion some large amounts. All changed when William struck up an acquaintance with a neighbouring youngster, Thomas Birkett.

The relationship between the two was later to be described by John Gell as the story of how a guileless young man was corrupted by rogues. In Gell's version Birkett, while described as a merchant, spent most of his time in taverns and gaming houses and was a notorious conman. He boasted that he could win money from anyone at a game called "even and odd" , except "such as knowe the tricke of it", and had in fact won over £500 from William Gell "and other young gentlemen". He was equally successful with dice and cards, boasting that he had won £200 in that way from William "and if his father would have settled his estate on him hee would have fooled him and have gott it on him every penny". Birkett had a wide acquaintance with the underworld and was able to show William a much more exciting side of London life than he was likely to find in the house of Mr Northey. Sadly for him Birkett's amusements turned out to be not only expensive but, possibly, unhealthy. It was alleged by one of Birkett's friends that William "had a foule disease and that hee went to doctor Butler for him".

This may have been a lie but one of the first of Birkett's circle whom William met was Anne Harbine, alias Anne Kelley, "a woman of an infamos life". Birkett knew that William often carried Northey's money and Anne was the instrument for parting him from some of it. William was young, country bred and, according to his father, of an "easie nature". He was assured by Birkett that Anne was "a woman of a great fortune and a cleane reputation", of "good worth and qualitye" and he must have found her exotic and exciting. Birkett "taught her how to spoile him" and saw to it that one of their amusements was dicing. Once William had been hooked Anne was supplied with "false dice"and their victim was soon losing Northey's money. In a succession of visits to Anne William lost £40, most of which went to Birkett.

Birkett led young William on a round of taverns and gambling dens, introducing him to a rogues' gallery of characters whom he persuaded Gell to believe were honest merchants, like himself, "that desired to play at dice privately". The sessions were staged at the Three Tuns, near Guildhall, and a tavern in Lumber Street called the White Horse, "where there is a tennis court of the backside, and a gameinge house". William played even and odd, dice and cards with his new companions, spending more and more of Northey's money until they had taken £200 from him. As with Anne Harbine's winnings, Birkett kept most of this "as the principall man that had power with [William]", and "tooke delight to bragge of his owne witt and cunninge and the folly of the said William Gell".

William's trusting master at length noticed that his money was disappearing and in 1635 and 1636 Gell had to take time from his duties as High Sherrif and ship money collector, as well as the arrangements for the marriage of William's sister Millicent, to conduct what must have been painful meetings with his son and with Thomas Northey. Northey was persuaded not to call in Gell's

£1000 bond and Gell paid Northey £150 to cover most of William's embezzlement. There is a note on the back of one of the legal papers to the effect that in 1636 Gell, having paid £150 the previous year, now owed Northey £70. In the draft of a petition to the king about the affair, Gell claimed to have paid a total of £400 to Northey. He was also obliged to pay another £70 in 1637 to cover William's debts with a mercer. This man clearly knew all about William's escapades as when his money was returned to him he acknowledged that "Mr Birkett did much hurt" to the young man. It says a deal for John Gell's powers of persuasion and, perhaps, for William's charm that after this catastrophe Northey was prepared to reinstate him as his apprentice after William had promised to mend his ways. His father warned Birkett to "forbeare the companie" of William, which Birkett "faithfullie promised that he would doe".

Birkett, however, was unable to resist the chance of easy money and William seems to have learned nothing. Northey too seems to have been remarkably gullible as William soon re-established himself as a trustworthy apprentice. Birkett proposed that William should get whatever money he could lay his hands on and that the pair of them should go to France, where he promised that William would quickly win back all the money he had lost. William fell in with this idea, took £70 from Northey, and fled to France with Birkett. Inevitably the £70 was soon transferred from William to Birkett, and William was reduced to selling his clothes to pay his debts while Birkett left him "to shifte for himselfe" in France and crossed back to England.

John Gell now owed Northey another £70 if he was to avoid having to redeem his £1000 bond. He decided that, though Birkett and his accomplices had committed no crime, and that in fact he did not know who the others were, he must make some attempt to recover his losses from them. Any loss would have been painful for a man like Gell, seriously interested in money, and these losses were great enough to be painful even for a wealthy man. £500 in 1636 was the equivalent of about £50,000 at the end of the twentieth century. He consulted his lawyer brother and Thomas drew up a summary of the case as he saw it, beginning "A man binds his son prentice with a London marchant..." He ended his paper with the question "whether the father may have an action in the case against B: for either of these sumes or what other remedy he may have". Gell decided that he did "have an action". He petitioned the king, and Birkett and others were arrested.

Gell's case was given a hearing in the Court of Requests, where "in regard ye plt hath his sonne uttly ruined & undone by ye defendt & hath bin forced to pay all ye money of wch his sonne was cozend hee prays relief". Gell's "bill" to the court told the sad story. William Rowland frightened Anne Harbine into a confession of her part in William's downfall and at a hearing at Brassington in September 1638 Gell produced four witnesses who declared that they had seen Birkett and his friends gambling with William and had heard them boast of their success in cheating him of his money. The four were all Derbyshire neighbours - John Buxton, gent, of Brassington, Robert Cowper, yeoman, of Atlow, Thomas Adams, tailor, of Chaddesden and Rowland Woodhouse, husbandman, of Hulland. That these four Derbyshire men, of widely differing social standing and with ages ranging from twenty-four to fifty, should all have spent time in London in the company of a gang of shady rogues, some of whom they knew well enough to name, seems a remarkable combination of circumstances.

Birkett's opening shot was to enter a "demurrer" to Gell's bill of complaint in November 1639. In it he made a complete denial of all charges and submitted that the bill was unfit to be considered. It was "altogether unfitt for a courte of equitty, and contayneth very scandalous rayleings and approbrious language, and alsoe such criminous and felionous matters as is properly examinable and punishable in the Star Chamber". Birkett maintained that it was unfair to ask him to accuse himself by answering Gell's questions. The court, however, rejected Birket's demurrer and instructed him to answer the bill. In his answer, submitted in March 1640, he admitted winning £20 from William "by fair play", and to have accompanied him to France, though only because "ye apprentice pswaded him unto it". He denied cheating and said that the men whom he had said were men of honour were in fact honourable. He denied ever meeting Anne Harbine or saying that she was a respectable woman. He pointed out that he was only nineteen years old at the time he met William Gell and claimed that it was William who had persuaded him to go gambling. Although innocent he was anxious to get rid of John Gell as he intended to set up in business and needed to avoid scandal. He therefore offered to pay Gell some of the money . He also claimed that one James Warren of Lincolnshire had a letter of attorney from Gell, dated 7 December 1638, authorising Warren to clear up the business, and that Gell had signed a deed on 5April 1639 releasing him from all further demands. Gell denied both of these assertions.

In November 1640 Birkett submitted statements from two witnesses for the defence, one of whom was among the men named by Gell's witnesses as Birkett's accomplices. The other was a barber surgeon who further blackened William Gell's name by accusing him of contracting a "foule disease" four or five years previously. Gell had come to him for help, saying that he had caught the disease from one woman. The witness, Thomas Hall, said that he had treated him for about three or four months, using remedies obtained from a Dr Butler, and had not seen him since. The other witness admitted winning "sixe or seven pounds" from William at the Three Tuns, said he had heard that William and Birkett had been to France and accused Rowland, acting for Gell, of forcing him to pay £5 for the sake of a quiet life. He had heard of Birkett's and others' arrests but did not know what any of them had paid and "beleaves thatt if the defendt had payd 20L to the sd Rowland hee might have bin quiett".

In addition to his difficulties in getting what he could from Birkett, Gell also seems to have had problems with Northey. Evidence was given that Rowland had had to threaten Northey with court action when, in spite of Gell's having repaid the money embezzled by his son, the merchant refused to surrender his £1,000 bond. Rowland and Northey had exchanged "ill tearmes and language" in the course of their argument. Northey is unlikely to have returned Gell's £1000, deposited for William's good behaviour, since, whatever the degree of influence exerted by Birkett, William had been a spectacularly bad apprentice. Gell must have had to swallow his anger and disappointment.

While his father was struggling to save something from the disaster, the young man himself, left high and dry in France, had gone off to the wars[33]. William travelled across Europe to Germany with a protestant army, suffering hunger and frost-bite, before borowing money from a comrade for a passage back to England. He told his mother of his adventures in a letter written in June 1638, swearing that after the suffering he had endured as a soldier he would never displease her and his father again.

With his troublesome son back in England, penniless, Gell considered what to do and discussed it with his brother[34]. He approved of Thomas's conduct of the legal action and confided that he could meet his losses over William since the family land was worth an annual rent of £1500, and though he was not actually drawing that much rent at the moment as "I doe not streane the teanants to that", he would "heareafter". As early as the 1630s black sheep were being sent off to the "Colonies" or as far away as their fathers could send them. In John Gell's time the colonial options were fewer than they subsequently became and he proposed two possibilities, which he put to his brother. He asked Thomas to send William to the Low Countries if he could, but if not, to Virginia. He was to tell Rowland that "I entreat him to see William on shipboard". In the event the choice was the Low Countries, and William was instructed to join a Lieutenant Coke, presumably a member of the Derbyshire family to whom the Gells were related. Gell tried to make the best of things, writing William the jaunty letter in which he claimed to have seen service on the Continent himself[35]. He was encouraging - "You undertake that which becometh you, whom I have ever thought a stoute man". He went on to stress that the prime military virtue and necessity was discipline.

Thomas had entrusted Coke with William's supervision. Inevitably there was a hitch. In the same letter in which William told his mother about his German adventures he revealed that, though he should have gone with Coke, the 30/- Thomas had sent him by Rowland was not enough because there had been no ship ready to sail and he had had to find lodging while he waited for one, "my unckle not considering this & what a deere place Gravesend is where I did lye". There was a ship leaving within two days but he had not got the 5/- for the passage across to Holland. He asked Elizabeth to help as he did not wish to cause any further grief to her or disgrace to his friends. He was particularly troubled because Rowland had implied that he was not interested in whether his mother was alive or dead. Elizabeth had obviously been ill for some time and William protested his concern - "I would intreate you not to thinke soe hardly of mee that I should speake soe slightly of my owne Mother & the best freind I have in the world. Indeade I did aske whether you had your health any better then you used to".

This was in June 1638 and Elizabeth must have sent him the money as by the following year he was safely under the strict supervision of Lieutenant Coke in Utrecht. A letter to his father dated 6 November 1639[36] reveals that Coke had been given money for William and was doling it out to him at 3/- a week. Coke had allowed him a further £5 for clothes. William was abject in confessing his sins and thanking his father for "such favor at your hands". He had further annoyed Gell by not writing to him and promised "the best obedience that I can". In a second letter on 23 November[37], William repeated that he was living on the 3/- a week prescribed by Thomas - "as my unckle write" - and that he needs more "for it is very small not suffissient to keepe good gentlemen company". He also needed more for clothes "for we have had a hard march wch hath woare my cloths very much". William was still finding it expedient to protest his remorse "I rest your sorrowfull sonne in that I have soe much displeased you".

The last of William's letters to survive is one which he wrote to his father from Utrecht on 28 November 1639[38]. He thanked Gell for arranging extra payments from "my Captaine" - "praise god that I have soe good a Father for I have deserved the contrary". He would "not only promise but performe the best duty & obedience that I am able". There is no hint of deviousness in these letters, nor of devilry. They chime with John Gell's description of William as being good-natured and with Birkett's opinion that he lacked judgment. William sounds like a little boy lost, knowing the hole he has dug for himself and praying for the time when he can get himself out of it. Laid up with frost-bite in Hamburg or eaking out his 3/- a week in garrison at Utrecht, he must have thought of Hopton as the Promised Land. William survived his soldiering and returned to England, though when he did so he seems to have remained in London, under his uncle's supervision. He was in there in the autumn of 1641, when £4-2-6d was "laid out for William Gell" by uncle Thomas[39]. The hardships he suffered on the Continent may have permanently damaged his health as he survived his return only until November 1642. William was buried at Wirksworth on the 14th[40], aged twenty-seven.

CHAPTER 5

The coming of war

The King and his Commons

It was during the war between Charles I and Parliament that Gell's qualities of energy and determination, as well as their dark obverse, his domineering intolerance, were employed to their best effect. For the first four years after his accession in 1625 Charles was at constant loggerheads with Parliament. It was inevitable that he should be, since he believed that he was appointed by God, and that he had a duty to God to rule. Being a man of principle he found it intolerable that he should have to compromise with Parliament or any other institution. The main quarrels concerned his attempts to impose uniformity in religion, his arbitrary imprisonment of dissidents and his refusal to accept that Parliament alone had the authority to raise taxes. There was also a suspicion that the king might not be as anti-Catholic as Parliament thought proper, especially as his queen, Henrietta Maria, was a Catholic. Catholics had been persecuted during the reign of Elizabeth and any hope of an improvement in their situation which might have been introduced by James I after his accession in 1603 was dashed by the Gunpowder Plot of 1605. Their worship was forbidden and could only be carried out in secrecy. Those Catholics who refused to accept Anglican worship were known as "recusants". The collective term used by the Parliamentarians during the Civil War for their enemies was "malignants" or "delinquents" and, among these, special venom was reserved for "papists". While most English Catholics hoped only for a quiet life, they sided with the king when a choice had to be made, in Derbyshire as elsewhere.

Charles's efforts to raise money by extra-Parliamentary levies were unpopular and largely unsuccessful. In Derbyshire a royal "benevolence" of 1626 raised the insignificant sum of £20-4-0d from the hundreds of Wirksworth and Appletree and nothing from the other four[1]. In 1628 the Commons won a crucial victory in its constitutional argument with the King when it forced him to sign the Petition of Right. This was principally concerned with the liberty of his subjects, especially in regard to taxation, and by 1629 Charles had come to the conclusion that his vision of English government could not be reconciled with the claims of Parliament and dissolved it. This attempt to return to absolute royal rule, however, came far too late and the king's attempts to raise money, in particular by the ship money taxes and, of special interest to Derbyshire, by exploiting the Duchy of Lancaster's ownership of mineral rights, caused increasing resentment. The king's personal rule came to an end in 1640 when he needed money to fight the Scots, who had rebelled against an attempt to impose a new church government on them. Charles was forced to call a Parliament to get it. The elections produced a hostile House of Commons, of which the Derbyshire members were typical. Sir John Curzon, whose election campaign was actively supported by Gell, and John Manners, later Earl of Rutland, were the county members and Derby returned the Recorder William Allestree and Alderman Nathaniel Hallowes. Of these only Allestree subsequently supported the King. Charles found this Parliament, aptly remembered as the Short Parliament, so uncongenial that he dissolved it in May 1640. His problem persisted, however. The army levied to fight the Scots, four hundred of whom came from Derbyshire[2], was defeated at the battle of Newburn Ford in August 1640, and the Scots demanded money as the price for leaving England. Charles called another election in the autumn and a new Parliament met on 3rd November, subsequently to be known as the Long Parliament. Again Gell took part in the election campaign for his half-brother, who was again returned. Manners lost his seat to Sir John Coke the younger while Allestree and Hallowes kept theirs.

The Long Parliament proved to be the nemesis of revived monarchical rule. All the resentments of the previous eleven years found full expression. Arbitrary courts, the main instruments of royal rule, were abolished, ship money was declared illegal and the King's faithful servants, William Laud, Archbishop of Canterbury, and Thomas Wentworth, earl of Strafford were removed. Laud, who had persecuted nonconformists, was impeached for high treason, sent to the Tower in 1641, tried in 1644 and executed in 1645, insisting to the end that both he and the King were true protestants. Strafford's policy had been to establish the King as the holder of executive power, with Parliament having only an advisory role. He had underestimated the determination of Parliament to establish its sovereignty. Having tried and failed to impeach him it used the ancient method of "attainder". A Bill of Attainder was passed, removing all Strafford's rights, and the King, in an attempt to appease his enemies, signed his death warrant. Strafford was executed in 1641. In a move which made any further personal rule by the King impossible Parliament passed the Triennial Act, providing for elections every three years and making it illegal for Parliament to be dissolved except by its own consent.

A further ingredient was thrown into the already explosive political mix when the Roman Catholic Irish rose in revolt in October, claiming to support the King against the rising power of Parliament, "such factious and seditious Puritans", whom they feared, with reason, would be far more oppressive to their religion than would the King[3]. Parliament now had the fear that the King would use the Irish rebel army as a weapon against them. The power of raising an army to put down the rebellion was constitutionally reserved to the King and Parliament moved quickly to deprive him of it by passing the Grand Remonstrance, a comprehensive list of his misdeeds, designed to demonstrate his unfitness to to rule. Curzon and Hallowes both voted for it. The conflict between the two arms of government became physical when the King attempted to arrest and impeach five of his tormentors, an act which Parliament described in a printed broadsheet published on the 17th January 1642 as "seditious"[4]. It had become obvious that the King's choice was between submission to the will of Parliament or armed resistance. His action against the five MPs aroused great hostility in London and Charles made what proved to be a fatal decision and left the capital for York, much more friendly territory for him.

Petitions

Gell kept himself informed of these developments, to the extent of having summaries made of Parliamentary proceedings[5]. The King's move to York was deeply disturbing to moderates, including Presbyterians like Gell, who would much prefer Charles to have stayed in London and made his peace with Parliament. Curzon did what gentry in Nottinghamshire and other counties had already done and, with Gell's help, organised a petition to Parliament, presented on the 14th March 1642 with over seven thousand signatures[6]. This expressed support for Parliament, urged it to continue to negotiate with the King and ended with a an obviously heart-felt plea for peace, so that "in the blessed peace of the gospell, we may sit every man under his own vine and figtree, and enjoy a happy peace to us and our posterity to the world's end" . There were also petitions to the King from many counties, including Nottinghamshire, and Gell received a letter from an old friend, Emmanuel Bourne, the puritan vicar of Ashover, anxious that Derbyshire should follow suite[7]. Bourne had been told by "Chesterfield men" of a letter written by Sir Francis Rhodes and other local gentry to those in the south of the county, suggesting a meeting to draft a petition from Derbyshire. The gentry in his part of the county had asked him to pass this information on to Gell, and he hoped that if a meeting was arranged Gell would be informed of it. He hoped that any petition that was agreed would ask the King to return to Parliament and "take their approved counsells". In a postscript Bourne left it to Gell to engage whomever he thought best in the enterprise. Bourne's letter was dated March 23rd and the following day Luke Whittington, the Mayor of Derby, wrote to Gell reporting the Chesterfield initiative[8]. He had already written to the High Sheriff and "to the most of the gentlemen in these parts, and they have appoynted to meete at Derby upon Munday next at the White Hart where I shall bee glad to see you to afford them your best assisstance"". He asked for Gell's help in publicising the meeting. The petition drawn up at the White Hart[9] was signed by seventy-six men, who were probably all present at the meeting, and presented on the 6th April to the King, who had arrived in York on the 19th March. It expressed fear that the King's departure from London would hinder "the reformation of those greate grievances which had crept, both into the Church and Comon Wealth, and likewise an obstruction to the relieffe of those pressures, under which wee yet groane". It asked "With bleeding hearts we humbly beseech your Majestie You will be graciously pleased to return unto & reside near your Parliament, Your highest Court and Councill, whereby we conceive your Royall Crown is made most glorious to your self & your Posterity". The petitioners ended by assuring the King that they would "defend youre Majesties Royall person, honour and Crowne, The power and priviledges of Parliament, The right and liberties of the subjects and the power and puritie of the Protestant religion".

Gell had again helped to draft the document, and had circulated copies to village Constables, asking them to obtain signatures and return the copies to him. Emmanuel Bourne received his copy on March 30th and wrote to Gell to tell him that people trusted him "to be a meanes that the hands of gentlemen and others about you be procured and to stirr them up to goe in person" to present the petition at York[10]. He commented "I know you took great care and paines besides costs in the last petition" and revealed a great misunderstanding of Gell's commitment by suggesting that, because of these efforts, he might be excused from attending the king and send his brother and son instead. Bourne noted that the petition had only one request, that the King should live near Parliament - "I could have wished, it had been added, that he would accept of the advise of his parliament (as best approved) and put away from him evil counsellors". Many of the gentry who signed this petition, as in the case of the one to Parliament, were royal sympathisers who would later declare for the King. It was moderate, more moderate than the one presented by Nottinghamshire gentry, which did have a hostile reference to the King's "evil counsellors". It was possibly more moderate than Gell would have wished.

There can have been very few gentry in Derbyshire who did not view the approaching conflict with dismay, but Gell may have thought that their petition to the King was lukewarm in its support for Parliament. According to Bourne, he had left the White Hart meeting early, and he may have been dissatisfied with the outcome. He had a draft copy of a petition from Nottinghamshire to Parliament expressing strong support for the Commons[11]. This was a far-reaching set of demands, demonstrating that there could be no reconciliation between the King and his more extreme opponents. It asked Parliament to define the King's rights according to Magna Carta and the Petition of Rights, and to punish "grand delinquents, remove evill councellors, malignant persons, unjust magistrates, unworthy ministers and place good in their stead, disarm papists, secure and confine their persons". Parliament should punish anyone abusing "good Christians", establish free elections and, in an early bid to save the environment, close unnecessary ironworks and coal mines to preserve wood. Local courts should be established to make it easier to use the judicial system, which should be cleared of obstruction. Finally, emphasising the religious side of the conflict, the petitioners demanded that "idolatry and superstition" should be eliminated from the royal court and from the country.This petition was never sent, but Gell may have been contemplating a similar one from Derbyshire to counteract any doubt arising from the one to the King.

Mobilisation

However, the King had made his mind up, and had already sent his Queen, Henrietta Maria, to France and Holland to sell the Crown jewels to raise money to pay and equip an army. On the 15th February Parliament had passed the Militia ordinance, placing the army under the control of Lords Lieutenant appointed by them and on the 12th June the king appointed "Commissioners of Array" to raise troops in each county. Responsibility for raising troops for Parliament in Derbyshire lay with the Lord Lieutenant, the Earl of Rutland. His appointments of

Deputy Lords Lieutenant in March 1642 demonstrated that the gentry were reluctant to make any move that might be thought to favour Parliament over the King. Of the men who had served from 1638 only Gell, Curzon and Sir Thomas Burdett accepted office[12]. Rutland called a meeting at Derby on the 5th July to "consider of the safe keeping of the magazin" and of what other measures were needed[13], but was himself reluctant to take the irrevocable step of mustering the county's forces. In August a committee was appointed to raise the militia[14]. This was headed by three of the county's MPs, Curzon, the younger Sir John Coke and Nathaniel Hallowes, and included Gell, his brother, and Henry Wigfall of Renishaw, his son-in-law.

The new committee seems to have been no more active than Rutland had been. In August the King marched south and raised his standard at Nottingham where, among other recruiting efforts, he tempted the Derbyshire miners by offering 5/- each for their expense in joining him, weekly pay of 6/- and, after the war, relief from all lead duties[15]. He had already by then appointed Henry Hastings, son of the Earl of Huntingdon, as Sheriff of Leicestershire and instructed him to enforce the Commission of Array, which he did with some success. Less effective was a move by the Earl of Devonshire from York to execute the Commission of Array in Derbyshire. The choice between King and Parliament became impossible for the gentry to avoid. The King was in Nottingham for two weeks. He had little success in recruiting townsmen there but, through the efforts of Sir Thomas Bushell, chief barmaster of the High Peak liberties, he had some success with his offer to the miners. Bushell had the King's declaration posted in village churches and offered the local barmasters 12/- for every miner they persuaded to join the King and, while most of those whom he recruited soon changed their minds, 1,000 eventually took the King at his word and joined his army. The miners were not natural royalists. They made clear what the attraction was when they replied to the King's declaration with a petition[16]. In this they declared their willingness to continue paying the traditional dues, "being your Majesties ancient and undoubted right", but pleaded for the abolition of tithes - "the greatest grievance your petitioners have long undergone, is, the exacting and taking of Tythes, Tenths, and customary duties of lead-oare, which (your petitioners are informed, by learned Councell) is not due by Law". Ironically, Gell's long years of legal struggle over tithes were now recruiting men to fight him in earnest. The King's answer to this request was, of course, to agree to do away with tithes. He moved from Nottingham on 13th September. In

Derbyshire the following day he demonstrated that no effective action had been taken by Parliament's supporters by reviewing the trained bands, recruiting 500 men from them and dismissing the rest. On the 15th the King entered Derby, where he raised a forced loan of £500 from the Corporation and seized all available small arms, promising their return once the rebellion had been put down. From Derby he moved to Uttoxeter on his way to Shrewsbury, where he was joined by Bushell's 1,000 Derbyshire miners. These men were drafted into the royal life-guards[17].

Gell's move

It was left to Gell to take control for Parliament. While the King was in Derbyshire Gell was at Northampton, where on the 22nd September the Earl of Essex, Commander-in-Chief of the Parliamentary forces south of the Trent, granted him a Colonel's commision to raise a regiment of 1,200 men "to be raised out of the Trayned bands of the County of Derby, and of such voluntiers as shall be in that County"[18]. The first major battle of the war, the indecisive battle of Edgehill, was fought in October 1642. Early in the same month Gell and his brother Thomas, after an optimistic and unsuccessful attempt to enlist miners in Wirksworth, went on Essex's advice to Hull, which was garrisoned for Parliament and which they knew well through its role as the outlet for Derbyshire lead exported to London and the Continent. There Gell persuaded the Governor, Sir John Hotham, to provide him with 120 men as the nucleus of his regiment[19]. Returning via Sheffield, where his little force helped to suppress a royalist rising, Gell recruited a further 200 men in Chesterfield and marched to Wirksworth on the 26th October. During his absence a royalist force led by Sir Francis Wortley had established itself in the north of the county, and Hopton Hall had been plundered. Wortley fled without a fight when Gell arrived. Among the plunder taken from Hopton was Gell's patent of baronetcy, or so he alleged in 1652 when Parliament was investigating titles awarded by Charles I - "his mansion house at Hopton in Derbyshire was plundered by the special command of the said late king"[20]. The claim that the King was personally responsible for the attack on Hopton was probably made to impress the Parliamentary commissioners who were considering taking his title away. On another occasion Gell described what actually happened - "Major Gilb Kniveton for a privat grudge procured sum of his late Majesties forces to goe to my house and plundred it to a third, myself then being out of the cuntree wheather word was sent me that in case I did come home my skinne should bee pegged full of bulletts"[21]. On the 31st October, having raised another 200 men from his estates, he marched to Derby and occupied it for Parliament. For the next four years Gell and his household moved into four rooms at the White Hart inn[22] near Allhallowes church[23], where he and his family and friends dined and supped at a cost of 1/- a meal and their servants at 6d[24], washing their food down with a couple of bottles of claret, a bottle of sack or, occasionally, two bottles of white wine[25]

Sir John in his warlike pomp

Committee of war

While taking practical steps to remove royalist forces from the county Gell also moved to enlist some of the leading figures of the county in running the war. At his request Parliament restaffed the Deputy-Lieutenancy in November[26]. One of the accusations made against him later was that he tried to exclude all but his own small circle of relatives and allies from the conduct of the war and it is certainly true that in 1644 and 1645 he resisted the appointment of a number of his opponents to the Derby Committee. At the beginning of the war, however, he tried hard to recruit allies and the sixteen nominees to the new Deputy Lieutenancy included some of the leading county gentry whom Gell was anxious to bring into the war. Some of these were reluctant to commit themselves and refused to serve, among them Sir John Coke the younger, Sir Edward Vernon of Sudbury, Sir Samuel Sleigh of Ash and Sir Edward Leech of Shipley[27]. Two who did agree were Thomas Gell and Henry Wigfall and the absence of Coke and others meant that the body was dominated by Gell and his relatives. To finance the gathering war Parliament appointed commissioners to receive subscriptions of money and plate from supporters. Sir John Curzon was sent to the county with instructions to set to work gathering these "subscriptions", assisted by a body of commissioners, who included Curzon, Gell, Gresley, Hallowes and Sir John Coke. Coke wrote to his father on November the 14th 1642 to tell him of these developments[28]. Early in 1643 Parliament set up County Committees to finance local military operations and Gell was instructed to form one in Derbyshire "to meet at such times and places you shall think fit, for raising of men, arms, horse and ammunition and ordering all things necessary thereunto"[29]. This committee was dominated by Gell until late in 1644, enabling him to conduct the war in his own, vigorous, way.

Gell's chief target in his efforts to overcome the inertia among the gentry was Sir John Coke, Curzon's fellow MP for Derbyshire ,who refused to have anything to do with him. Coke was a neutral, deeply distressed at the turn of events, and Gell reported his reluctance in a letter to William Lenthall, Speaker of the House of Commons on the 13th December[30]. Gell and others had "desired Sir John Coke to join with us, but he absolutely refused, for what cause we know not but believe it is his dislike of the business ... other instances of his lukewarmness are given, and the whole is submitted to the judgement of the House". Gell pointed out in this letter that "we have many Malignants in this County and men of great power with whom he is more conversant than with us". These were the men who had made a firm commitment to the king and Gell's actions aroused them to action, albeit verbal only. While at Chesterfield he received a letter of protest from a group which had met at Tutbury and included the Earls of Chesterfield and Devonshire, Sir John Harpur of Calke and Sir John Fitzherbert of Norbury. Gell's answer was typically robust - "that it seemed strange that they should grow so quickly jealous of hym, theyre owne countrieman, well known to them, and that had no other end, than the clearing of his county from theeves and robbers, to mayntaine the laws of the land and the liberties of the subject, according to the ordynance of Parliament, and yet for a long tyme they could suffer Sir Francis Wortley and others to robb and spoyle without interruption"[31]

There are two unaddressed and undated copies of letters from Gell which may have been sent to the same group. They were certainly addressed to county gentry who were uneasy at his actions. In one, Gell said that he had heard that Wortley was back in the county and hoped that he "and the other gentlemen that were too forward to write to mee about the peace of the county" would now help at least by lending horses[32]. A second letter reported that the danger from Wortley had gone, but that he might come back and that, in any case, Gell intended to continue what he had started[33]. Gell denied that he was carrying on the war by "my owne conceit" and defended himself from what sounds like an accusation that he kept away from the action - "For my personall presence, I never knewe that any commander should be so desired". He ended this letter by telling his critics "to rest assured that no man doth more desire the peace of the county than John Gell". A delegation from the Gell party, consisting of Sir George Gresley, Lt-Col Thomas Gell, Captain Thomas Sanders and Nathaniel Hallowes, met the royalists who had written from Tutbury at Etwall, in a last attempt at compromise. Gell was called upon to disband his forces and refused to do so[34]. The royalists called in Hastings, by now commanding the royalist forces in Leicestershire with a commission as Colonel-General, to defend them from the Derby troops. The battle lines were now clear.

The nature of the war

Allegiance in this war was determined by a mixture of politics, religion, class and self interest. During the seventeenth century England began with the authoritarian monarchy which James I inherited from Queen Elizabeth and ended with the constitutional monarchy offered by

Parliament and accepted by William and Mary, after the expulsion of James II in 1688. The Civil War accelerated this revolution. The political choice was real for many of the gentry and nobility in 1642. Religion was a vital element in politics. The Long Parliament had a large Presbyterian majority, committed to reforming the church on Presbyterian lines, and fiercely anti-Catholic. Religion and politics proved stronger motivators than class, and the gentry and nobility split, though the minor gentry and the urban merchant classes were predominantly for Parliament, and in Derbyshire the nobility all chose the King's side. Only at the end of the war and in the period leading to the execution of the King in 1649 did strong democratic movements emerge. Ideology did not at first extend below the gentry. In this swirl of loyalties many considered their own class and self interest and in Derbyshire the overwhelming aim of the leading men of all persuasions was to avoid the threat to the established order which was posed by war. They avoided the choice as long as they could.

Civil war soldiering began as a confused and amateurish business. When the political conflict moved to war there was no national army for either side to woo and, while there were a few with Thirty-Years War experience, most of the commanders were new to military matters. All over England local nobles and gentry made up their minds and recruited their tenants and neighbours by personal loyalty or by promises or coercion. While the constitutional authority to raise the militia lay with the King, in practice the outcome in each county depended on the local balance of power - in Leicestershire Henry Hastings succeeded in mobilising the militia for the King, while in Derbyshire the Earl of Devonshire failed to do so, leaving Gell to outmanoeuvre the rest of the hesitant neutrals and royalists in the county. In Derbyshire, as elsewhere, the troops were raised by individual gentry, and there was always a tendency for Gell's heterogeneous force to fragment.

Most of the recruits to the armies of both sides, in all parts of the country, were in fact not the local militia who, if they had overcome their reluctance to fight for either side, would have been expected to respect and defend their own areas. The soldiers were volunteers, attracted not by religious or political loyalty, but by the promise of regular pay, free clothing and plunder. There were many men in seventeenth century England for whom the promise of a free pair of good boots was a powerful attraction. While it was clearly important to both King and Parliament that agriculture, trade and industry should be disturbed as little as possible, the commanders had difficulty in preventing the troops from treating the areas under their control as enemy teritory, to be plundered while they had the chance. As with their captains, who were always liable to switch allegiance to other commanders on the same side, the loyalty of the soldiers could not be taken for granted, and in their case the switch was sometimes to the other side of the conflict altogether. In this respect Parliament was at first at a disadvantage since it was much more difficult for it to express its ideals in an inspiring slogan than it was for the royalists to provide a loyal rallying cry for the King's troops.

There was local fighting all over the country, often characterised by inadequate attempts at coordination, and the two sides managed to concentrate their forces sufficiently for only three major battles, Edgehill in October 1642, which was a confused draw, and Marston Moor in July 1644 and Naseby in July 1645, both of which were decisive Parliamentary victories. Combined efforts in the counties were hampered by weak command structures and by local antagonisms, never fully suppressed by the army commanders. Naseby, for instance, was won without Gell's help, although he had been ordered to take command of a brigade drawn from several county forces and follow the king's army. He failed to get it organised in time, giving his enemies the chance to raise doubts about his loyalty. Fortunes in many areas shifted from month to month and it was a triumph for Gell that, though several parts of Derbyshire, north and south, were taken by royalist troops at different times, Parliament remained in the ascendancy throughout. Both sides were short of money to fight the war. While Parliament had the great advantage of help from sympathetic rich citizens of London, its armies were often badly paid or not paid at all and there were many mutinies. Derbyshire suffered as much as anywhere from this feature of the civil war.

The Derby regiment

The three men who accompanied Thomas Gell to Etwall were convinced Parliamentarians. While most of the gentry feared disorder above all else, and had agonised over a choice they dreaded making, Gresley, a deputy-lieutenant, had brought a troop of cavalry to join Gell at Derby and remained loyal to him for the whole of the war. He admitted that he was "the onely gentleman of qualety in this county that cordyally appeared to be on our side"[35]. Gell chose his first two officers from those closest to him. Thomas Gell was commissioned Lieutenant-Colonel in November[36] and raised a troop of about a hundred and thirty men. For his Major, Gell chose his tenant Johannes Molanus, the Dutch servant of Sir Cornelius Vermuyden who had distinguished himself in the ousting of the mine owners of the Dovegang in the 1630s. A Captain Vermuyden was probably the son of Sir Cornelius. A company of infantry was raised in Derby itself by Robert Mellor, whom Gell commissioned as Captain. Mellor was the son of Henry Mellor, who had been the first mayor of the town under a new corporation granted in 1637[37]. He was to become one of Gell's opponents. Other early appointments were Charles White of Nottingham and John Mundy of Markeaton, both made Captain after bringing troops with them.

Another who brought an armed unit to join the regiment, and who thereby obtained a commission, was Thomas Sanders of Little Ireton. His contribution was an infantry company of two hundred men and he was appointed Captain. While Gell could rely on the loyalty of his brother and Molanus, he and Sanders became irreconcilable enemies and when Sanders was later to declare that Gell was a greater enemy to him than any Cavalier, Gell was happy to agree. They were temperamentally unsuited. While Gell was intolerant of any opposition to his authority, Sanders, coming from the same social class, resented his pretensions. Sanders was also pious and straight-laced and hated Gell's more relaxed morals and earthy and violent language. They were divided also by their politics, which in the seventeenth century went with religion. Gell was a conservative Presbyterian and for most of the war was in tune with the dominant party in Parliament, believing in a national church run by elders rather than bishops and favouring the establishment of a constitutional monarchy. He was to find himself disillusioned by the outcome of the war. Sanders was more radical and was eventually to support the Independent faction, so-called because it advocated independently-governed local churches. The Independents were to become dominant in the army and to expel men of Gell's persuasion from Parliament, before trying the king for treason and executing him. The enmity between Gell and Sanders also arose naturally from Sanders's attitude to his military service. He regarded his two hundred foot soldiers as a private army, as he was later to regard the company of cavalry which he raised. Gell was noted for the thoroughgoing zeal, extending easily to violence, with which he defended what he regarded as his rights, and was the last man to have been happy with a semi-independent unit in his regiment.

Gell almost lost a vital part of his regiment at the very outset of the war. This was the company which he had brought from Hull, volunteers raised in London and commanded by a Welshman, Captain Humphrey Mathews. They had been sent with other troops to escort two artillery pieces from Coventry[38], when a Captain Aldridge from the Hull garrison arrived in Derby on November the 25th 1642 with a warrant from Sir John Hotham to arrest Captain Mathews and to send him, together with all his money and property, to answer charges brought against him in Hull. Aldridge had a letter from Hotham to the troops advising them to accept him as captain and, after Mathews had been sent back for his trial, Gell "commanded drummes to beate for the sayd Mathews Company to come togeather to their Colours in Allhallowes churchyard". With the troops assembled, Gell had Hotham's letter read to them. Personal allegiance mattered in this war and, for whatever reason, the volunteers refused to serve under Aldridge, declaring that if they were not to see Mathews again they would disband and return to London. Twenty of them signed a petition to Gell, declaring their attachment to Mathews, "for the love of whome next unto god and the Cause wee have ventured our lives", and asking him either to restore their captain or let them go[39]. At this moment of crisis Gell took charge of the situation by inviting them, if Mathews should not return, to take a third option and join his own company, accepting him as their "Coll and Captaine". Clearly impressed by Gell's dynamism the men accepted his proposal. They were to prove loyal to him for the whole of the regiment's existence. Mathews was cleared of the charges against him and was commissioned Lieutenant-Colonel with a regiment at Gloucester. He remained aggrieved at what had happened, however, and blamed Gell, though it is difficult to see why, and his version has not survived. The story was told fifteen years later by the clerk, and later Ensign and Lieutenant of the company, William Thomas[40]

By the end of 1642 Gell had gathered an effective fighting force for Parliament. He later claimed in fact that he had raised the whole of his regiment of 1,200 men by the 25th November, though that must have been an exaggeration, since, in the letter written in the following month in which he complained to the Speaker of Sir John Coke's foot-dragging, he, Gresley, Thomas Gell and Hallowes reported "We have at the present about 700 men under Sir John Gell, but not all armed and not one week's pay aforehand". The men whom Gell and his officers recruited to augment the Hull volunteers included Derbyshire miners and Derby townsmen whom Cromwell described as "a set of poor tapsters and town apprentices"[41]. Gell took recruits where he could find them. He was finding it particularly difficult to raise cavalry and in an effort to do so had written for help to the City of London[42]. Citizens were invited to raise cavalry troops to serve in Derbyshire "and afterwards wee shall pay them. We have already raised some companies of foote, which have donne good service both in this & our neighbour counties. Our cheife want is horse..." The contemporary terms for the three types of soldier were "horse", meaning cavalry, "foot" or infantry, and dragoons, which were mounted infantry. Typically the dragoons rode to the battlefield, dismounted and fought on foot. Gell welded the very disparate results of his recruiting efforts into a regiment which one of his most severe critics admitted was a force of "good, stout, fighting men"[43]. This critic went on to describe them as "the most licentious ungovernable wretches, that belonged to the Parliament", but in fact, however badly they behaved, Gell certainly governed them, and they earned a reputation as disciplined soldiers in an often undisciplined war. He had enough men and guns to garrison and fortify Derby but neither at that time nor later was he properly equipped or supplied to wage war elsewhere. The fact that he managed to do so would in any other war than a civil war have ensured his fame, rather than the notoriety and lack of reward which he in fact received for his achievement.

Money matters

By the early weeks of 1643 Gell had Parliament's instruction to form the Committee which was to run the war in Derbyshire. Among other calls on its funds the Committee had to find a weekly Parliamentary levy of £175, imposed under an ordinance passed on the 24th February 1643. A further Parliamentary ordinance of the 31st March 1643 created a Committee of Sequestrators for the county, to seize the estates of royalist sympathisers[44]. The members of the six-man committee included Curzon, Gell, the younger Coke and Hallowes.

The poverty of the Parliamentary cause had been apparent in the letter sent in December 1642 to Speaker Lenthall[45] and in a polite request for arms to Sir John Coke the elder on Christmas Eve[46]. This poverty dictated the robust interpretation of his authority from Parliament which Gell was to make for the whole of the war. Gell was soon sending out letters to the gentry informing them of his commission and asking what money, horses and arms they would contribute[47]. The stated war aim of Parliament was to return the King to constitutional ways and not to depose him. Gell's letters therefore described his commission as being "to raise 1200 men for service of the king and parliament" and pointed out in his usual blunt style that these troops could neither be raised nor maintained "without chardge". All contributions should be sent to Nathaniel Hallowes and would be accounted for and repaid. Constables were instructed to bring "8 or 10 of the alert horses and mares within your constablery with sadles & brydles"[48] and a declaration was published that although horses had been seized from the market, they were to be used to prevent certain troops from plundering and that "all men shall have liberty to trade and stay in Derby without molestation"[49]. Gell was clearly having to police his new regiment. He wrote to the High Sheriff acknowledging that there had been complaints that his men had terrorised people and stolen arms and other possessions[50]. He insisted that this was without his consent "& expressly against my mynd, for no man nor woman shall be wronged by them in the least degree by my consent". He asked the Ssheriff to instruct Constables to report such incidents to him at Derby "where he or they offending shall receive condyn punishment according to his or theire respective offences". This plundering was exploited by his enemies. Hastings issued his own declaration, forbidding looting and threatening punishment, including death, and promising that his own forces would not confiscate property[51]. This had its effect. Fourteen South Derbyshire villages combined to write to the Mayor and Corporation of Derby to complain about their treatment at the hands of Gell's troops, thanking the King for sending Hastings to protect them and urging Derby to disband Gell's regiment[52]

Derby was an open market town, with no defensible fortifications, and Gell and his Committee did their best to put this right. The monied citizens of the town were required "as you tender your owne & your neighbours safety" to send labourers, with tools, to help in the construction of earthworks[53]. In these early days the citizens, solid for Parliament, gave generously, as Nathaniel Hallowes's accounts show[54]. In November 1642 they raised over £1300 in gifts and loans. Hallowes, the first treasurer of the Committee, compiled a list of money, plate and other goods given or lent for the war's expenses during the period November 1642 to August 1643. In line with Parliament's professed loyalty to a constitutional monarch these donations and loans were made "for the defence of the king and both houses of Parliament and kingdome". Hallowes accounted for a salary for himself of £88-8-10d, earned for "receiving and paying £10613 at 2d per pound". Most of the 498 contributors seem to have been willing ones. There were 93 from Derby, and the 405 county contributors, while concentrated in the south of the county, did include people from as far north as Chesterfield,

Chapel-en-le-Frith and Flagg. The names were mostly the ones who might have been expected. At Brassington, for instance, the six richest farmers gave a total of £32 while at Bakewell £15-30-8d was collected from "divers well affected people" and £4-16-4d from "divers poor people". One apparently very generous contribution of £5 came from John Allen of Alderwasley, a labourer. There is a list of the contributions from the villages of Appleby Hundred. Many of the contributions from the comfortable burghers of Derby were large and freely given.

The cause was helped by some contributions which were either handed over unwillingly or extorted from royalists. Lady Stanhope of Elvaston is unlikely to have been happy to make her contribution of £31-7-9d, plus £60 worth of cattle and sheep, even if it was for "the defence of the king", and the enormous sum of £3000 was simply "brought from Mr Sacheverell of Morley". £77-11-4d was similarly "brought by Rich: Horne from Sr Edward Mousleys". The staunch royalist Sir John Fitzherbert of Tissington is listed as contributing £40 to the Parliamentary cause while another involuntarily gave £33-8-0d "found in a barne at Longenor of Sr John Harpur of Swarston". A separate list of payments made between March and August 1643 includes £80 from Lord Deincourt and £10 from Gilbert Kniveton, who might be thought to have got off lightly after plundering Hopton Hall but who was nevertheless unlikely to have been happy to help the Parliamentary cause[55].

Hallowes handed over most of the money he received to Gell's Commissary (quarter-master), who was Molanus until 7th January 1643 and Henry Buxton thereafter. Molanus received £2287 and the payments made to Buxton up to 11th September 1643 came to £8,261. In the following two years, according to a statement made at the end of the war, about £40,000 more was collected by Hallowes's successor, Gervase Bennet, and paid to Gell's agents[56]. Hallowes recorded payments amounting to £40 for about forty tons of timber for the fortifications at Derby and £10 "for one and twenty ould sheepe and six fatt lambs when the souldiers wanted pay", indicating that the difficulty in paying the troops started early in the war.

Soldiers' pay

There are no accounts of how Molanus and Buxton spent the money they received from Hallowes, though a surviving account by Thomas Gell indicates the scale of the expense of running the war. This account of expenditure on one company of the regiment presents a picture for the first half of 1643/44 of regular and uniform payment to the troops and of payment for goods and services[57]. Starting with 6th April, when the company apparently consisted of ten "comon soldiers", two sergeants and two corporals, the accounts have weekly payments of 5/4d to the soldiers, 10/6d to the sergeants and 7/- to the corporals. The company rapidly put on strength. In two months there were a hundred and twenty-eight soldiers, led by a lieutenant, an ensign, a "gent o' the armes", who may have been a quartermaster, and three each of sergeants, corporals and drummers. The lieutenant was paid £1-10s, the ensign 13/8d and the drummers and "gent o' the armes" 7/- each. The wages paid to most of these Derbyshire troops were less than those quoted in an official list[58]. Sergeants', corporals' and dragoons' wages were about half the official figure. In the cavalry the lower ranks were paid the stipulated wage while sergeants and officers made do with less. Gell was paying £700 for ten troops of cavalry instead of the official figure of £956.

There were payments for quartering of soldiers and officers, for arms and their repair and for shoeing the dragoons' horses. 2/- was paid "to a man for bringing bease [cattle] from Boulsover" and £2-10s "to ye Carrier for bringing match [for firing muskets] from London". The total expenditure on this one company was £217-12-10d in April and May and £466-14s during the next four months. In spite of Hallowes' purchase of sheep to feed unpaid soldiers, it seems that up till the middle of 1643 the Committee's income was adequate for Gell to run the war without the problem of unpaid troops which he was to face later. From October the lieutenant received varying amounts which were presumably to pay the men, suggesting that money supply was becoming more erratic, and the total expenditure for the next six months was £457-3-11d, £150 of which went on "severall jorneys about the states service".

CHAPTER 6

Into action

Command structure

For most of the war Gell's commander-in-chief was the Earl of Essex, who approved of his performance and supported him. In December he instructed the Derbyshire authorities to associate themselves for military purposes with the counties of Staffordshire, Leicestershire, Nottinghamshire, Lincolnshire and Yorkshire[1] and in January 1643 appointed Lord Grey of Groby as commander-in-chief of this Eastern Counties Association. There were local rivalries between the families of Grey and Hastings which made the two natural enemies quite apart from their opposite allegiances in the war[2]. Grey was given special responsibility to protect Nottingham and entered the town in June 1643 with a force of about six thousand men commanded by Sir John Meldrum. Grey's immediate subordinate was Thomas Ballard, appointed Major-General of the Lincolnshire, Nottinghamshire and Derbyshire forces by Essex in January 1643[3].

The local Parliamentarian with whom Gell had closest contact was Colonel John Hutchinson, his opposite number at Nottingham. He was the son of a Nottinghamshire knight, Sir Thomas Hutchinson, and began his Parliamentary service by seizing the county powder magazine at the beginning of the war[4]. He was commissioned as Lieutenant-Colonel in a local regiment and was a member of the Nottingham Parliamentary Committee. In June 1643 he was appointed by the Committee and Meldrum to command the garrison in Nottingham Castle, and in November was commissioned to raise a regiment of infantry. He was then appointed governor of town and castle by Parliament. Hutchinson was in the same situation as Gell, and suffered from the same internal feuding as was to go on at Derby. He was a more extreme Presbyterian than Gell and was to sign the death sentence against the King in 1649. He and Gell were mutually dependent as Nottingham would certainly have fallen if Hastings had managed to take Derby and Gell would have been unlikely to hold on if Nottingham were held by the enemy. In spite of this there was soon bad blood between the two and the biography of Hutchinson written by his wife Lucy contains some of the most extreme criticisms of Gell's character and of his behaviour during the war.

Grey proved ineffectual and the command of the Eastern Counties Association was taken from him in August 1643 and given to the Earl of Manchester, with the rank of Major-General. One of Manchester's senior officers, commanding the Lincolnshire force, was Oliver Cromwell, who was also an MP. Later in the war Gell found himself dealing with Lord Ferdinando Fairfax and his son Sir Thomas. Lord Fairfax had been appointed commander of the Yorkshire forces in December 1642 with his son as his second in command, leading the cavalry contingent. From February to December 1644, the county was required to raise £516 for the maintenance of Fairfax's army[5] and in late-1644 Derbyshire was transferred to a Northern Association, under Fairfax's command.

The enemy

Gell was threatened by a ring of garrisons, three of them held by royalist troops for the whole of the war. These were Newark, in Nottinghamshire, a royalist stronghold which was to witness the final surrender of the King in 1646, and two established by Hastings, Ashby in Leicestershire and Tutbury, to the south-west in Staffordshire. Also in Staffordshire, the towns of Lichfield and Burton were held at different times by royalists and by the Derby regiment. For part of 1643 and 1644 there were royalist garrisons in Gell's own back-yard, at Bolsover Castle, which was owned by the Earl of Newcastle, at Wingfield Manor and at Chatsworth. Gell's persistent local enemy was Hastings, whose hold on Tutbury and Ashby enabled him to mount a permanent threat to the Derby garrison. Hastings was a vigorous and persistent adversary who was to present a danger to Gell's forces for the whole of the war. After his appointment as Sheriff of Leicestershire in July, 1642, he raised a troop of cavalry and fought at the battle of Edgehill in October. He returned to Leicestershire with a commission as Colonel-General of the county and was created Lord Loughborough by the King in October 1643[6]. Hastings was personally popular and quickly raised a permanent force large enough to enable him not only to fortify and hold his father's house at Ashby, which resisted several sieges, but to attack Gell's and other Parliamentary forces. More remote but far more threatening whenever they approached Derbyshire were the two main royalist armies. By the end of November the King, his court and his army had established their headquarters in Oxford and

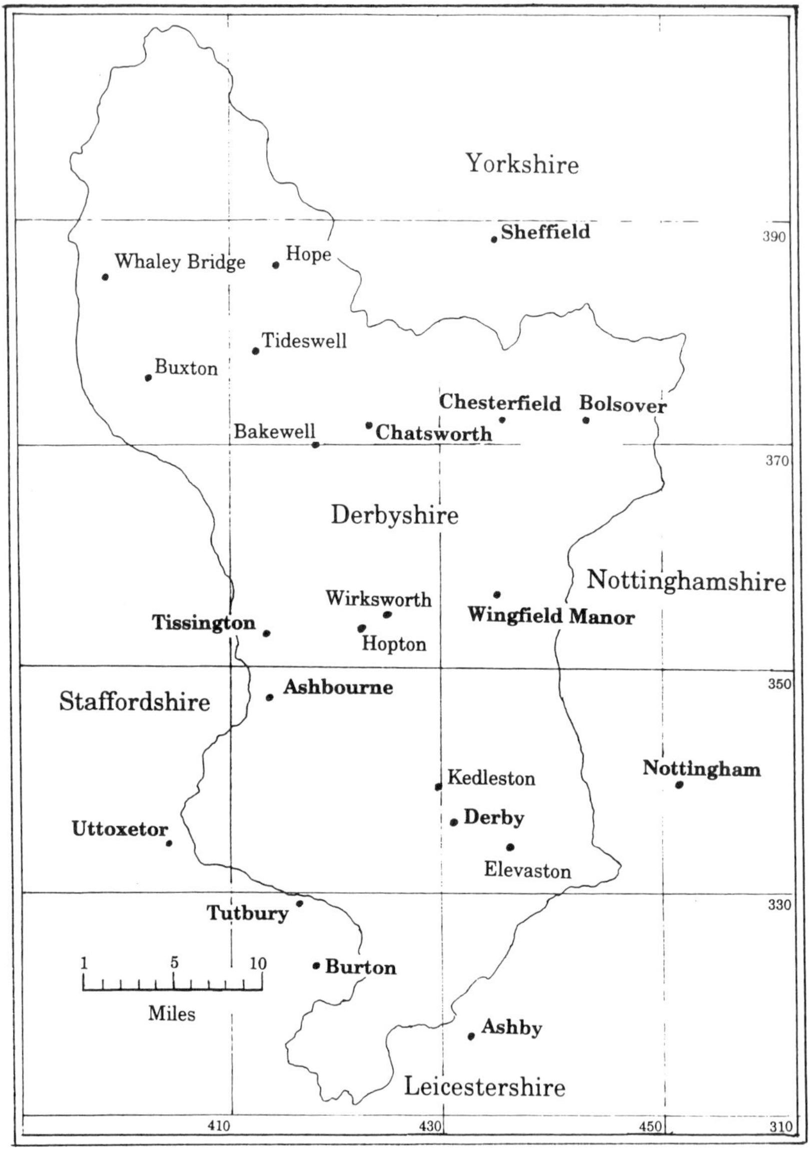
Yorkshire
Sheffield
390
Whaley Bridge
Hope
Tideswell
Buxton
Chesterfield
Bolsover
Bakewell
Chatsworth
370
Derbyshire
Nottinghamshire
Wirksworth
Wingfield Manor
Tissington
Hopton
350
Staffordshire
Ashbourne
Nottingham
Kedleston
Derby
Uttoxetor
Elevaston
330
Tutbury
1
5
10
Burton
Miles
Ashby
Leicestershire
410
430
450
310

a second royal army commanded by the Earl of Newcastle was operating in Yorkshire. It was vital for the King's success that he gain control of the midland counties which lay between the two armies, since with these counties in Parliamentary hands it would be difficult for them either to communicate or to join forces. Control of Derbyshire was also important because of the revenue raised from farming out the duties paid by its highly prosperous lead industry. Lead itself, of course, was a vital war material, used in the manufacture of gun metal and ammunition.

The fight at Bretby

The pattern of Gell's war, set in 1642, persisted until the end. It consisted of removing enemy troops from Derbyshire and sending contingents to help in neighbouring counties. So for the next four years the yeomen and husbandmen driving their cattle to market in Wirksworth, Ashbourne and Derby, and the strings of packhorses carrying cloth to and from Manchester or pigs of lead to the ships at Hull and Bawtry, shared the rough Derbyshire roads with Colonel Gell's soldiers. The villagers at home or in the fields saw the Colonel, his Majors and Captains, leading their armed and armoured cavalry, infantry and artillery pieces trotting, trudging and rattling across their countryside, away to fight battles in Staffordshire, beseige forts in Nottinghamshire and Cheshire, or bring relief to their comrades in Chesterfield or Sheffield. The newly appointed Major Molanus was soon in action[7]. Philip Stanhope, Earl of Chesterfield, brother of Sir John of Elvaston, had fortified his house at Bretby for the King and garrisoned it with forty musketeers, eighty cavalrymen and four guns. Early in December Gell sent Molanus and Sanders there with four hundred infantry, Captain White's troop of dragoons and two guns. The house withstood artillery and small arms fire and so Molanus sent his men in to storm it. The Earl and his son Ferdinando fled, leaving the Countess to face Molanus's thirsty soldiers. She showed herself to be made of sterner stuff than her husband and refused Molanus's demand for money to buy the men drink. They thereupon looted the house and took the earl's guns and ammunition back with them to Derby.

Crossing the borders

From the beginning Gell's regiment was called upon to serve outside the county. The letter to Speaker Lenthall in December explained - "We have been lately pressed by my Lord Fairfax to send him some forces, and by the Northamptonshire men to do the same by them. Also our neighbours in Nottinghamshire have desired help from us against the Malignants there". In the letter which Sir John Coke had written to his father in November he had noted that Gell had received instructions from the Earl of Essex, though he did not know what they were. When Gell himself wrote to the elder Coke at Melbourne on Christmas Eve he told him that Essex had asked the Derbyshire Committee to send some of the regiment to Sheffield, which they had done. However, they had also been asked to send troops to Nottingham. They were willing to do this but were very short of arms. They asked Coke if he could help by sending arms to them. They would be returned - "Let them be marked with your mark, and you shall have them, or others as good, safely returned to you"[8]. Gell pointed out to Lenthall that if it were not for him Derbyshire and "two or three neighbour counties" would have been lost to the royalists, a similar point to one made earlier by Sir John Hotham when he was reporting his transfer of 120 men to Gell[9]. Hotham saw that if Derbyshire could be held for Parliament, "as they have assured me with these men they quickly can", it would give "great security to Yorkshire, Derbyshire being the best pass into Yorkshire, should any forces be sent from the king's army".

The request made by Nottingham in December 1642 was met first by sending Captain White and his troop back to their home county to help in organising the town's defences and then, at White's request, reinforcing him by three hundred foot soldiers under Major Mollnus's command. Molanus was recalled after nine or ten days to help repel an incursion into Derbyshire mounted by Hastings immediately after he had fortified Tutbury Castle and Ashby. While Gell's force was divided by his Nottingham expedition, Hastings advanced and secured the Swarkestone Bridge, a vital crossing point over the river Trent, and fortified Sir John Harpur's house there. Gell marched the whole of his regiment and stormed the bridge on 5th January 1643, driving off Hastings's troops and capturing Harpur's house. Of the seven hundred men engaged on each side, Gell lost one and Hastings seven or eight. This victory was an important one since by retaining possession of Swarkestone Bridge Gell was able to hold up subsequent advances from Leicestershire.

No sooner was the southern flank of the county secured than Gell was called to help in the West, where Hastings had taken Stafford, and Molanus was sent with two hundred musketeers to Uttoxeter. On this occasion, however, because he received no support, Molanus was forced to retreat, and brought his troops back to Derby. He was immediately dispatched, with the rest of the regiment, to Ashby, where Gell had been ordered to join with forces under Lord Grey and Sir William Brereton, commander of the Staffordshire and Cheshire forces, in an attack on Hastings there. This was launched on the 17th January 1643 and was successful in driving the enemy into the fortified church and castle. The victory was lost when, just as the Parliamentary force was about to bombard the besieged royalists, Grey received a letter from the Parliamentary committee at Northampton telling him that Prince Rupert was on his way from Banbury to relieve Ashby. Grey ordered a retreat to Derby. His and Brereton's troops were Gell's unwelcome guests in Derby for about a week, causing him a problem in paying for their quarters and provisions. The allies were so at odds during this time that Grey and Gell both wrote to Parliament[10]. Gell claimed that he had paid £400 and refused to pay a further £300 because he was already in debt in Derbyshire and under military pressure from Hastings. Many of Parliament's supporters in the town had complained to him about the behaviour of Grey's troops and, because of the contributions the townsmen had made to the cause, they expected him to take action. Significantly, showing more political shrewness than he was later to be given credit for, he wrote that "we must be very tender for the present how we raise money".

Gell continued to be over-worked. In February he provided Captain Mundy's unit to help in fortifying Sheffield, garrisoned Burton-on-Trent with Molanus's company, and sent Captain Stafford from Thomas Gell's company to Whaley Bridge to guard the routes from Lancashire. The most onerous call came from the Earl of Essex who, on the 24th February, ordered Gell to send as many men as he could spare to join a force under the command of Major General Ballard in an attack on Newark. Molanus, whose own company was still at Burton, was put in command of five hundred men and sent off on this latest expedition, leaving Derby defended by infantry of Captain Mellor's company, and by Sir George Gresley's cavalry. The Newark episode proved to be Gell's first set-back. Ballard's attack captured the enemy trenches and the Parliamentarians occupied them, Ballard's own Lincolnshire troops taking the eastern side of the town while Molanus and a Nottingham contingent under Colonel Hutchinson lay on the west. Ballard then left the Derbyshire and Nottingham troops at the mercy of the Newark garrison by ordering the withdrawal of part of the Lincolnshire contingent and sending an inadequate number to reinforce Molanus and Hutchinson. These Lincolnshire men soon fled under attack by the garrison troops and Hutchinson and Molanus were forced to retreat, losing men in the process. Molanus blamed Ballard for the disaster and told Gell that if he and Hutchinson had not defied orders from Ballard they would have lost all their guns[11]. As it was, Gell lost one gun and men whom he could not afford.

The seige of Lichfield

Molanus had little time to rest in Derby. During his absence Gell had responded to a further call and had taken Gresley's troop to a potential Parliamentary disaster at Lichfield, leaving Derby defended only by Captain Mellor and his company of Derby townsmen. Molanus marched there to join him. Lichfield had been occupied by the Earl of Chesterfield, after his flight from Bretby, and a contingent of Essex's army under Robert, Lord Brooke, had moved there on the 1st March to remove him. Brooke, inspecting the progress of the siege, had been shot dead by a sniper, leaving the Parliamentary troops leaderless and demoralised, and it was a tribute to Gell's reputation that he was regarded as the man to restore order. Gell, no doubt eager to resume hostilities with Chesterfield, offered £100 for the Earl, dead or alive. However, the siege was ended by more conventional means. Gell used a mortar to bombard the defenders into submission. They surrendered and Chesterfield was imprisoned, first at Wingfield Manor and later in London. Gresley, Thomas Gell and Hallowes reported to Speaker Lenthall on 13th March "... our Colonel Sir John Gell upon the sad occasion of the unhappy death of that noble Lord Brooke was sent for post to Lichfield to settle those then almost distracted soldiers, where yet the necessity of that service continues him, and .. by his being there those soldiers were continued together, and that town and divers prisoners - some of great quality - taken"[12].

The battle of Hopton Heath

Characteristically for this war, Gell had spent only a short time with the Lichfield garrison when he received a letter from Sir William Brereton, suggesting that they should jointly attack Stafford[13]. Gell agreed and arranged to meet Brereton at Hopton Heath, about three miles from the town. He marched there with a force consisting of Molanus's five hundred Derby foot soldiers, Gresley's troop, about four hundred cavalry of Lord Brooke's regiment and five hundred

Staffordshire men, a total of about fifteen hundred men. Gell had some artillery, including the mortar from Lichfield and fourteen assorted cannon. He arrived at Hopton Heath early on Sunday the 19th March and awaited the arrival of Brereton from Newcastle-under-Lyne, deploying his men along a ridge overlooking the road from Stafford as well as Brereton's approach route. Gell set out his small force sensibly, perhaps drawing on tactical skill learned from his years with the militia, or from Continental experience, or perhaps from his study of Styward's textbook, which may have acquired its bloodstains during this battle. The foot soldiers were positioned with the holes of a rabbit warren in front of them, hampering any cavalry charge they might face, while the dragoons and some of the artillery pieces were placed behind a wall on their left. To their right Gell set his cavalry, with more artillery between them.

The Stafford garrison had been reinforced by royalists fleeing from Lichfield and by a force led by the Earl of Northampton, who took command. Northampton arrived to face Gell at about 3 o'clock with a force of about eleven hundred cavalry and a hundred foot. The royalists had some artillery, including a large piece called "Roaring Meg". Brereton had arrived by then, bringing two troops of cavalry and three of dragoons, while his foot soldiers were still making their way to the battle-field. The royalists first shelled the Parliamentarians, killing some of them. Their cavalry then charged both Gell's dragoons and his and Brereton's horse, putting them to flight and capturing some of their guns. At this point, with disaster apparently certain, Gell dismounted and moved among his infantry, making sure that the pikemen and musketeers were ready for the next charge[14]. When it came the first volley of musketry killed many of the royalist cavalry. Northampton himself had his horse killed under him and, refusing to surrender, fought on foot until he was killed. A second charge was also repelled by the musketeers, who had by then been reinforced by two hundred men of Brereton's infantry. Gell is said to have been wounded during the battle, possibly in the neck as there was evidence of it in his doublet, which survived in the family, and in a surgeon's bill for £10 for treating it[15]. The wound was not disabling, and Gell himself did not mention it in his own account.

Brereton wrote an account of this battle without mentioning Gell's part in it[16]. He ascribed the flight of his cavalry to "the wisdom and goodness of Divine Providence", because the royalists were thereby encouraged to charge the infantry, with disastrous results for themselves. A royalist pamphleteer, reporting that Gell had been injured but not killed, accused him of cowardice - "He is not too forward to come into danger"[17]. However, Gell always had his own apologists and one of them put his version in a pamphlet entitled "A case for the city spectacles", published in 1648[18]. This described how Brereton "wheeled about and left Sir John to hot service, which he performed with such valour as gained the day (no thanks to Sir William). There was slain the Earl of Northampton, and foure or five hundred more after which Sir William appears again and makes a fresh onset on the dead bodies, and plunders them of their cloathes, and Sir John of his honour; for the credit of the whole business was laid upon Sir William". Brereton admitted that the bodies of the royalist soldiers were stripped and plundered, and that the Earl of Northampton's was treated no better than any of the rest.

The royalists decided against another attack and encamped for the night, while Gell and Brereton, whose defeated troopers had returned, counted their losses and, with their men exhausted, withdrew from the field. While Brereton returned to Nantwich, Gell marched through Uttoxeter to Derby, taking the naked body of the Earl of Northampton with him. At Uttoxeter he was asked by the earl's son to return the body. Gell, however, hoped to use this trophy as barter for the return of the artillery pieces he had lost at Hopton Heath and refused to hand the body over until the artillery was in his hands. Artillery pieces were too valuable, however, and his offer was turned down. The Earl's body was carried with the returning troops to Derby and buried in the Cavendish family vaults at All Saints church. The king had granted an amnesty to Parliamentary supporters in Derbyshire but Gell's refusal to hand over his dead enemy was regarded by the royalists as barbarous, and a royal proclamation was issued, excluding him. While the battle had been a failure for the Parliamentarians, who had lost most of their artillery and baggage and had left their enemies still in occupation of Stafford, Gell himself had shown conspicuous courage and leadership in stiffening his infantry when the flight of Brereton's cavalry had left them to withstand Northampton's cavalry charges alone. His failure to observe the normal rules of the time and return his enemy's body was another manifestation of his single-mindedness - he badly needed his lost artillery and had no scruples in using the dead earl to try to retrieve it.

Thomas Gell at Sutton Scarsdale

Gell's next action was in Derbyshire, against Lord Deincourt, who twenty years earlier had been his collaborator in tithe battles with the miners. Deincourt had fortified his house at Sutton Scarsdale, near Chesterfield, and had been helping the garrison which the earl of Newcastle had established in February at Bolsover, the only royalist garrison in the county at the time. He had previously been reluctant to help either side and his jumping off the fence may have been prompted by his forced contribution of £80 to the Derby Committee's funds. Whatever the reason his position between Derby and Chesterfield made him a danger and on the 8th April Gell was asked by the Staffordshire commander, Colonel Lewis Chadwick, to send men to augment a force of three hundred cavalry which he had gathered to remove Deincourt. Gell immediately sent his brother and Molanus, with five hundred men and two guns. Besieged and bombarded in his house, Deincourt held out for some time but eventually surrendered, with very light casualties on the Parliamentary side. Deincourt was put on parole to appear at Derby, an arrangement which would not have been likely if Sir John had been in charge, and naturally went to Newark instead, to join the royalist garrison there. This move seems to have caused him further losses as, in the words of Sir George Gresley, who referred to Deincourt as "that lump of fleshe", "which perfidious dealing of his, our very adversaries have since, in some measure, revenged, for the garrison at Bolsover pillaged the house, and those of Newarke caused him to unburye his money and bestow it against God and the Kingdome; his lands the cavaliers have leased"[19].

There was no rest. On the 21st April Prince Rupert, moving north after capturing Birmingham, recaptured Lichfield after a siege of eleven days, and was expected to make Derby his next objective. However, after the town's defences had been strengthened in preparation for the coming assault, and extra men called in from neighbouring garrisons, Derby was spared because Rupert was needed by the king to fight Essex's army in the south. He did, however, take Burton, whose garrison had been withdrawn to take part in the defence of Derby, and left a detachment to hold the town. Gell moved quickly to retake it. He asked Lord Grey to join him and the two met on Egginton Heath and drove the royalists out. Gell then put in Captain Sanders with his two hundred men and later reinforced him with sixty dragoons.

Captain Sanders deserts

Having, by a combination of luck and his usual energy, survived this threat from the south, Gell was soon in danger from the north. The threat there was from the Earl of Newcastle. The garrison at Bolsover had been carrying out raids in the north of the county and in north-west Nottinghamshire. Nottingham was also threatened by the garrison at Newark, by one established by Newcastle at his house at Welbeck and by the Earl of Chesterfield's house at Shelford Manor, in the Vale of Belvoir, occupied by his son Philip. Thomas Gell was at Chesterfield with two hundred men and was ordered to move to Sheffield, under imminent threat from Newcastle's army, which had just captured Wakefield. On his way there Gell heard that Sheffield had fallen and retreated to Derby, which Sir John now assumed would be the next target. He called in the Burton garrison, as he had done when Prince Rupert was expected and discovered, to his fury, that Captain Sanders had deserted him - "In the meane tyme that wee left Captayne Sanders at Burton, one Mr Houghton, a Lancashire man, was made Colonell, and hee made the said Sanders his Leiftennant Colonell, soe that Colonell Gell lost that great company and above sixty dragoones horse and armes, which was a great losse to Derbyshire when the enemy were soe aboute us"[20]. Gresley's account of this desertion is more explicit than Gell's own - "Captaine Saunders, who had one hundred and eighty of our foote, well armed, and some horse, raised in our county, and intended principally for this countries service, under our regiment, he refused in this our extremity to come unto us, yet he sent us his coulours and commission, but kept our men, armes, and horses; all which he turned over to Colonell Houghton; and was for that good service made his liefetennant-colonell"[21]. This desertion probably indicates that the corrosive enmity between Gell and Sanders was already established. In Sanders's own version of this episode is heard a wounded, whining tone of self-justification which was characteristic of his explanations of his clashes with Gell. He had raised the troops himself, doubted the validity of Gell's commission, had been "thrust out of the county" by Gell in order to put him "in danger of ruine"[22] and had accepted Haughton's commission only to save himself and the Burton garrison[23]. The point about the troops being raised by him and, by implication, his to dispose of, illustrates an attitude which made it impossible for him to serve happily under Gell.

The Queen's march

Gell was saved again by the scattered and disorganised nature of the war at this time, when Newcastle was forced to turn back after the recapture of Wakefield by Sir Thomas Fairfax. There was only a brief respite. At the end of May he was ordered to join a force commanded by Lord Grey which was being essembled to stop the Queen, Henrietta Maria, from reinforcing the King's army. She had landed at Bridlington in February with arms and supplies for the King, and had been waiting at York since then for an opportunity to join her husband at Oxford. Grey's army of about five thousand included his own Leicestershire men, a Nottingham contingent under Lieutenant-Colonel Hutchinson, and a contingent from Lincolnshire led by Oliver Cromwell. Gell and his men were under the command of Lieutenant-General Hotham, who was already becoming a lukewarm Parliamentarian and was later to be executed for trying to betray the Hull garrison. Hotham objected to taking the obvious course of marching into Yorkshire and preventing the Queen from leaving York. Grey's army instead attacked a royalist garrison at Wiverton. On hearing that the Earl of Newcastle's army had marched out of Newark to attack them, Grey withdrew to Nottingham, ignoring pleas from Major (later General) Ireton that it "would be a deed of great dishonour to him to retreat, and that they were there to fight with them"[24]. According to Mrs Hutchinson, "and then was Nottingham more sadly distressed by their friends than their enemies: for Hotham's and Gell's men did not only lay upon free quarter, as all the rest did, but made such a havoc of friend and foe, that it was a sad thing for anyone that had a generous heart to behold it". As on every occasion before the formation of the New Model Army in 1645, the indiscipline of the men and the disunity of Grey's commanders made his force impotent. When the Queen marched to Newark between the 4th June and the 16th the Parliamentary army broke up. Hotham was arrested by Cromwell and Hutchinson, Cromwell moved off to Peterborough, and Gell returned to Derby.

Gell, in his own frustrated words, had "marched upp and downe in the Vale of Belvoir for the space of one moneth"[25] and, after the failure of the combined Parliamentary forces, the Queen's army now menaced his own position. She had failed in an attack on Nottingham and marched on to Newark, where she was joined by Hastings. Her next target on the way to Oxford was bound to be Burton, and Gell, calling for help from the Nottingham garrison and from Staffordshire, moved his troops to Egginton Heath to await their arrival before reinforcing the Burton garrison.. "But", said Gell, "nobody would come". Without help he had to retreat to Derby and on the 2nd July the Queen's troops stormed Burton, killing many of the defenders and capturing many more, including the newly-promoted Lieutenant-Colonel Sanders, his commander, Haughton and his Major, Nathaniel Barton. By the 13th July the Queen was in Oxford. This major blow was only slightly offset by a small success achieved by Thomas Gell. A royalist sympathiser, Sir Richard Fleetwood, had fortified his house at Wootton Lodge in Staffordshire and had been intercepting the weekly carriers plying between London and Manchester. Thomas took about four hundred men, stormed the house, and brought Fleetwood and others prisoners to Derby.

The return of Captain Sanders

An attempt to besiege Hastings in Tutbury Castle, helped by a contingent from Nottingham, was aborted when the Nottingham force was withdrawn after a report that Newcastle was on his way to break the seige. Gell had hoped to relieve the pressure on Derby by taking Tutbury. An additional motive for the effort was that Sanders, Haughton and the others taken prisoner at Burton were being held there. In the event Sanders was exchanged and returned to serve again as Major, under Gell, in a new regiment of cavalry which he had raised himself. This development, which was to make it impossible for Gell to exercise full control over the Derbyshire troops, was forced on him. On his release Sanders had gone to London and obtained Parliamentary permission to raise money in Derbyshire for the formation of a contingent of cavalry to operate in the county[26]. Such an addition to the Derbyshire force was needed and Essex granted him a commission. While Sanders and his friends regarded the appropriate rank to be that of Colonel, Essex restricted him to Major, presumably in an attempt to preserve a single unified force in Derbyshire. However, Sanders was given the power to appoint his own officers and to have command of all the cavalry in Gell's regiment except Gell's own troop, an arrangement guaranteed, in the words of one of Sanders's allies, to cause "inconveniences"[27]. Sanders's own interpretation of the arrangement was "I acted, he had the honour"[37], an interpretation which Gell was not likely to share. However, with the alternative prospect of a second regiment under a Colonel Sanders[29], Gell wrote to him on the 12th December 1643 accepting the arrangement - "I am contented you shall have full power and authority to constitute and appoint captains and all other inferior officers belonginge to a regiment of horse accordinge to an agreement formerly made betwixt us before the Comittee at Derby and accordinge to the effect and purport of a comission granted unto him the said Major Sanders by his Excellency the Earl of Essex. I onely desire to except my owne troope"[30].

Sanders appointed a number of captains who shared his religious and political views and were to prove allies in his quarrels with Gell. The most prominent were Nathaniel Barton, Joseph Swetnam, Robert Greenwood, and Robert Hope. Barton, Sanders's former Major at Burton, and Swetnam, were clergymen, Swetnam being the vicar of All Saints in Derby, while Greenwood's civilian role was running a leather manufacturing business in Ashbourne[31]. Robert Hope of Derby served as Lieutenant in Greenwood's troop until being appointed to command his own in June 1644. In the months ahead, contemplating his fractious regiment, Gell may have brought to mind the words of his military bible - "where many divisions are: there happens the sooner discord and disorder". To add to Gell's problems Sanders also joined the Committee, under an order of Parliament dated the 16th October 1643[32], together with an ally, Captain Robert Mellor, the Derby alderman with a commission in Gell's own company.

The defence of Nottingham

After Tutbury, the next episode in Gell's war was one which provoked the greatest slurs on his military performance. Part of the Nottingham garrison had been sent to help Cromwell face the army of the Earl of Newcastle, which was advancing into Lincolnshire. This left the town with only four hundred men and fourteen guns to man its defences. Colonel Hutchinson expected to be attacked by a detachment from Newcastle's army and once more called on Gell for help. Gell sent Molanus with three hundred dragoons to occupy the town while the citizens were evacuated into the castle. Hutchinson's retreat to the castle was opposed by many of the townsmen, who feared that they or their houses and property were being left undefended against enemy occupation. A number of these dissidents were arrested and taken back to prison in Derby by Molanus after the evacuation of the town had been successfully accomplished. Molanus and his men were soon back, recalled by Hutchinson to remove a royalist force from Newark which, as feared, had occupied the town on the 18th September and begun to bombard the castle.

According to Gell's own account[33] Molanus drove the enemy out of Nottingham, capturing a hundred and fifty prisoners and relieving the soldiers and townspeople in the castle, who were almost starving. Mrs Hutchinson's version[34], is that the royalists retreated without fighting and that Molanus's men allowed them to go, while they themselves plundered the empty houses. In her account of this, as of other events, Mrs Hutchinson seems to have allowed her detestation of Gell to cloud her vision. Gell had, after all, answered a desperate call for help from her husband, and it seems unlikely that a force of enthusiastic royalists, with the possibility of taking a crucially important Parliamentary stronghold, would have simply run away. Their commander was Sir Richard Byron, a notably resolute soldier.

Molanus, however, does seem to have let Gell down the following day, when he refused to join Hutchinson in an attack on the fortified bridge over the Trent and returned again to Derby. Mrs Hutchinson was scornful of Molanus' caution - "The major of Derby, an old dull-headed Dutchman, said ten thousand men could not do it", and Gell probably agreed with her since, ten days later, he sent Molanus back to do the job, nettled no doubt by a letter from Hutchinson saying that "if he be pleased to send any of his men, they might come and see the fort taken"[35]. Molanus this time had three or four hundred cavalry and dragoons, according to Gell and six score in Mrs Hutchinson's version. Whatever the number, Gell's and Hutchinson's men drove trenches toward the bridge and within a day or two were ready to attack. By then, however, the fort was empty. The royalists had fled to safety in Newark during the night. Gell was satisfied that without his help Nottingham would have been lost - "it will be adgudged by any councell of warr, that Nottingham towne and castle had been long since in the enemys possession, had they not had the assistance of Sir John Gell in driving the enemy from them at every tyme of neede, as the Colonells and Committee of Nottinghamshire did ever acknowledge"[36]. Colonel Hutchinson did not in fact agree completely and Gell clearly felt the need to justify himself, but his main point was undoubtedly right - he had saved Nottingham.

The Earl of Newcastle's advance

The last months of 1643 saw the advance into Derbyshire which had been expected and feared for most of the year. It came when Gell's force was widely scattered. Wingfield Manor was garrisoned by a detachment from Thomas Gell's company and there were garrisons at Chatsworth, vacated by the Earl of Devonshire, who had fled to France, and at Wingerworth, home of the royalist Sir Henry Hunloke. In addition Gell was under pressure to lend men to Sir Thomas Fairfax to assist in a march into Yorkshire. Gell asked Fairfax for help in another attempt on Tutbury Castle, but Fairfax, who spent several days in Derby with his cavalry force, not only refused to help but instead requested four or five hundred musketeers from the Derby garrison to march to Chesterfield and then to Yorkshire[37]. Gell was characteristically prickly and suspicious at this encroachment on his authority and developed a grudge against Fairfax which he harboured for the test of the war. He pointed out the danger to the town from Hastings if the troops which Fairfax wanted were taken from the garrison and offered instead to raise the five hundred by taking men from Wingerworth, Wingfield and Chatsworth. Fairfax and his cavalry moved off to Chesterfield, accompanied by Thomas Gell and Nathaniel Hallowes, who were joined by the men from the three garrisons. At this point Newcastle moved and was soon within two miles of Chesterfield. Not for the first time Gell was was left to his own devices, when Fairfax, after conferring with his commanders, retreated south. What men were left at Wingerworth and Chatsworth were now drawn back to Derby. In November royalists from Bolsover entered Derby and tried to raise a riot. They were driven away, but the position in Derby was sufficiently bad to persuade Gell to guard the way out of Derby by St Mary's Bridge and post a lookout on the tower of All Saints church. He was running short of gunpowder and asked Colonel Hutchinson for ten barrels. He was given only five - Nottingham too was in danger, and Hutchinson wrote to Gell protesting at his attempts to persuade the Nottingham garrison's "powder maker" to come over to Derby[38]. The reports that Nottingham had a large store of gunpowder were wrong - "we have been so exhausted that we have not sufficient for our owne defence" - and the five barrels were a favour.

Deserters

In spite of the guards and lookouts there were desertions from Gell's troops, including three officers who followed the example set by Sanders at Burton. These were two infantry officers, Captains Samuel Clarke and Samuel Taylor, with their men, and a troop of cavalry under Captain Randle Ashenhurst of Glossop. Clarke later claimed that he had made the decision to leave Gell at the time when Sir Thomas Fairfax's troops were in Derby and Sir John had told him that if Fairfax's troops collected any money in Derbyshire without the Committee's permission, Clarke "should pistoll them and charge them as open enemies"[39]. These desertions were a serious blow. Clarke and Taylor moved first into Nottinghamshire and Gell wrote to Colonel Hutchinson in Nottingham on the 2nd January 1644, asking him to arrest them and either send them back to Derby or hold them until Parliament and Essex decided what to do about them[40]. On the same day he wrote to Essex for warrants for their arrest, making a point which was clearly important to him, then and later - "if some speedy course bee not taken herein other Captaines and officers will doe the like, so that we are sure to bee undonne by raiseing forces to goe away at theyre owne pleasure"[41]. Clarke and Taylor joined Fairfax and Gell wrote to him several times in an effort to retrieve the men in their companies, with their horses and arms - "both these captaines have been in our pay, theyre companies raysed, armed and payd for by us"[42]. Ashenhurst joined the Staffordshire force, in which his brother was a colonel. The ability of junior officers like Taylor, Clarke and Ashenhurst to switch commanders, taking their men with them, and the willingness of commanders such as Fairfax to receive them, illustrate the confusion which prevailed on both sides during the early part of the war, making decisive action impossible for either.

The lowest point

Gell's main concern was to strengthen the Derby defences in case of attack and, in addition to employing the citizens of Derby itself, he sent out to the villages for labourers. Some of them found themselves caught between the two sides. Sir Andrew Kniveton, commander of the Tutbury garrison, wrote to the Constable of Hilton, noting that Gell "or some others in actuall rebellion against his Majestie" had instructed the villagers to go to Derby "to make bullworks for the defence of them"[43]. He ordered the Constable to make sure that they did no such thing and instead demanded that he send a working party by seven o'clock the following morning to Tutbury, each man bringing "either a wisket a scuttle a hack or a spade". The fact that Kniveton's letter was in Gell's possession probably means that the people of Hilton ended up labouring at Derby rather than Tutbury.

Gell did not restrict himself to defence. Newcastle found himself up against a vigorous and enterprising enemy. Sanders was sent to South Wingfield and captured two captains and forty soldiers in a skirmish. A few days later he again came off best in an encounter with a second detachment, capturing a major and ninety men and all their horses and colours. Molanus was sent to help the Staffordshire Parliamentarians oppose an advance by Newcastle's forces from Bakewell towards Hartington and the Staffordshire border. He arrived too late to help them, however, as Newcastle's troops had already defeated them at Hartington, killing many and capturing, among others, Randle Ashenhurst. Molanus had a skirmish with royalist troops, killing five and capturing thirty-six, before retreating to Leek, where he waited in vain for help from the Staffordshire force. In mid-December he returned to Derby, capturing another twenty-six royalists at Ashbourne on his way. On the 15th December a detachment of Newcastle's army surrounded Wingfield manor and forced the garrison to surrender, allowing the one hundred and sixty men to march out but seizing their provisions and ammunition. With the arrival in Derby of the defeated Hartington garrison, Gell had now lost all his North Derbyshire outposts and Newcastle's army had the run of the county, as far south as Derby itself.

There was no help to be had from Lord Fairfax or his son, who were not satisfied that Gell had provided them with as much help as he could have done. He did his best to persuade them of his difficulties, and in a long letter to Lord Fairfax he explained why he had not responded fully to his request for help by describing the situation in Derbyshire[44]. A troop of Hastings's cavalry, led by "a desperate and bloudy malignant" was camped three miles from Derby and more were within five miles. Hastings had promised to "put Gell out of Derby" and burn the town. The dragoons were all at Chesterfield since Newcastle's "fyrebrands & insendyaries" had created tumult in the Peak. They had been asked to help at Ashbourne with an uprising by "many papists". Derby's fortifications were incomplete, and Gell called poetic imagery into play to describe the danger - "our works for the defence of the Towne are now in the budd, & like to be blasted for ever, if we use not our best endevour to promote them with speede". There is no help to come from "the towne & countrie from whence we have received al our mayntenance & suplie hytherto", presumably meaning that the presence of Newcastle's troops in the county was preventing him from collecting taxes. Gell wrote several times, appealing for reinforcement - "We once more presume to press your Lordship to step in for our succour. We are much threatened ... if you desert us we are forlorne, & beseech you now to make no delays, but with some considerable force to march unto us. Our men upon news of your Lordship's approach will be coragious beyond exspectation. Consider our destruction will be the sorest blast the cause ever had, and the protection by your Lordship's succour wil renowne you through the nation"[45]. When no help came Gell appealed to Essex in a letter written on 8th December 1643, painting a desperate picture - "we have yet no certaine tyme appointed by Sr Thomas Fairfax, when he wil come to us; in the meane tyme the enimie increaseth his forces exceedingly, & our country myners flock into hym dayly, & though we cannot certainely know theyre strength, yet we are persuaded that theyre nomber for men is doubled since they came out of Yorkeshire"[46].

Allies' quarrel

The rift with Nottingham provoked an angry exchange of letters. Hutchinson and his committee wrote on the 12th January 1644 complaining about the behaviour of the Derbyshire troops in Nottinghamshire[47]. Horses had been stolen from Stapleford and elsewhere and a list of them was supplied, so that Gell could arrange for their return. This provoked a furious reply the next day - "Gentlemen, I assure you our Captaines of horse take this so ill that future help from them you can no more exspect ... How you will answer that inveygling & entertaining of Captains Clarke & Taylor, who have robbed our country of 140 horses at least, we knowe not"[48]. Since they were defending an open market town they were scornful of Hutchinson's retreats to Nottingham Castle - "And since you bid us defiance we as much slight you, though you have advantage of us, quitting a poor Towne upon each alarum & mewing up yourselves, up in your supposed invyncible forte". They suspected that the help they had given Nottingham would not be matched when they themselves needed help - "We suppose you pick a quarrel with us lest you shoulde pay your debt of helpe you owe us & promised. Thus loath to have uttered such expressions, had not your unexspected bitterness exstracted them from us". On top of every other irritation with his neighbour, Gell clearly thought that Hutchinson could have sent the fugitive captains back. The letter of 13th January was signed by Sanders, Mellor and Swetnam, and by Gresley, Wigfall, Hallowes and the Gell brothers.

CHAPTER 7

Dissidents

Gell and the opposition

Gell's heart was in the fighting. At home he was finding it increasingly difficult to maintain a united effort to support the regiment. He aroused resentment among townspeople as well as Sanders and his allies. The aldermen, burgesses, merchants and citizens of Derby had welcomed Gell and his regiment when they provided safety from the enemy. The soldiers were also spenders, as Thomas Gell's account shows. However, the townspeople soon realised the disadvantages of being a garrison town and Gell found himself in the position later occupied by the sheriff in the Western film who, having cleared out the gun-men, discovers that the respectable citizens cannot abide his rough ways. In addition to opposition caused by the natural friction between soldiers and civilians Gell was finding that some of the townsmen were less enthusiastic for the cause than he was and treated them roughly because of that. An example was a draper called John Dalton, imprisoned for a while for suspected "malignancy"[1]. Dalton, a future Mayor and MP, had given £20 in 1642[2]. Gell later took £10 worth of cloth for his soldiers in August 1643 and, in spite of promises, did not repay it[3]. When Dalton was faced the following year with a demand for a levy of £10 he told the collectors that Gell still owed him £10 and, in spite of being called before the committee and imprisoned five days in a rain-sodden room at Wingfield Manor, stood his ground.

Another enemy was George Bainbridge, owner of a gunpowder factory in Derby. He aroused Gell's anger by taking equipment from the Derby factory to one which he had set up for Sir William Brereton at Stafford[4]. Bainbridge maintained that Gell had given permission for this transfer, but he was visited in November 1643 by Gell and Molanus, who checked everything in his house. Three or four days later the Town Marshall came with soldiers, broke into his malthouse, and stole some of his malt. There were more confiscations, his new malthouse was destroyed by soldiers and he had three men quartered on him. He was eventually unable to provide for his wife and family, who went to live with friends. The background to this episode must have been the difficulty which Gell was having at the time in keeping his troops supplied with gunpowder, after he had failed to steal Colonel Hutchinson's powder maker and had been sent five barrels from Nottingham when he needed ten.

Two tradesmen, Thomas Youle and John Dunnage, both members of the town council, supplied goods to Wingfield Manor at the time it was garrisoned by the royalists[5]. Both had their original assessments of £3 increased to £10. Youle claimed to have noticed that those most loyal to Parliament received the largest demands from Gell and the Committee. He also complained that Gell entered the council chamber and threatened the members. Gell exacerbated the resentment of such as Youle and Dunnage by protecting his favourites. When one of his officers, Captain Robert Greenwood, called on a Mrs Colledge, the wife of an absent royalist, he found his Colonel in her chamber[6]. Mrs Colledge had been assessed to provide a third of the cost of a trained soldier, and Greenwood had called to collect this tax. Gell told him that Mrs Colledge was not to be assessed and in her presence said "that if hee would not obey his command hee would command [him] with powder and bullet". The violence of Gell's language, and sometimes of his actions, when confronted by any opposition, aroused and sustained a growing feeling in the town that he should somehow be curbed.

Northern opposition

There was also increasing opposition in the north of the county to Gell's way of doing things. In April 1644 he wrote to Essex reporting on his troops' actions against Hastings and making one of his frequent pleas for more help[7]. He also told Essex that he had heard that there were some, "no true freinds to theyre countrie", who had attempted to turn Essex against him. He asked Essex to "consider what we have donne, with whom we have grapled, what a handful we are, how barren of pay & of what concernment our garison is" and to ignore "some discontented spyritts, none of which (2 only excepted) that have ever appeared in this cause, but at best lived newtrally".

One of the two whom Gell agreed had been supporters of Parliament was Emmanuel Bourne, who had suffered at the hands of both Parliamentarians and royalists and had modified his opinion of Gell since he was urging him to action against the King in 1642. Bourne's revised opinions were expressed in a letter written in 1646, in which he had "a long tale to tell of my losses and misfortunes"[8]. Ashover had been afflicted first by Sir Francis Wortley's soldiers, who drank the alehouses dry and threatened to burn the place down if Bourne and others did not pay up for the king. Wortley "thought it best to retire" when Gell arrived, but the village was next visited by Gell's Captain White, "a man of mean birth and education, but glib of tongue, and making a great show of piety". White was on his way to Nottingham and called at Ashover "on purpose to spite his betters, and he demanded twenty pounds eache from me and Hodgkinson". The next soldiers on the scene were Newcastle's, "who like demons destroyed all they came neare, and left the poore to starve". Bourne's experiences seem to have affected his memory of Gell as he wrote that he "never could bear the sighte of him" since he had distrained Stanhope's cattle and then starved them in 1635, forgetting that he was still writing friendly letters to him seven years later. Gell had "also become a great braggart", and Bourne echoed an accusation made by Lucy Hutchinson, that Gell had paid Parliamentary journalists to praise him in the newspapers. The other Parliamentary supporter who had become a "discontented spyritt" was an influential merchant from Brampton, near Chesterfield, called Ralph Clarke. Clarke was the father of Gell's runaway captain[9] and, possibly because of his son's clashes with Gell or, more likely, because of a very high tax assessment placed on him, he was destined to be second only to Sanders in his hostility. Gell conceded that these two men were on Parliament's side but claimed that neither had contributed to the soldiers' pay, though both were men of means.

The problem of Major Sanders

Gell's position was greatly strengthened in January 1644 when Essex appointed him Governor of Derby[10]. The commission placed Derby "together with all officers & souldiers therein, to be under your commands". It instructed "all officers & souldiers under your power, & all other the inhabitants of the said towne, and alsoe all others whom it may concern to obey you as their Governor". Neither the agreement between Gell and Sanders nor the unambiguous terms of Gell's commission as Governor could prevent conflict between them, and Essex was soon aware that his arrangement was not working. On the 21st February 1644, two months after Gell had signed his submissive letter, Essex was writing to Sanders, reminding him of his military duty - "I would have you yeild all due obedience unto Sir John Gell as Colonell of that regiment of horse to which you are major"[11]. The appointment of Sanders to the committee and the inclusion in Gell's regiment of Sanders's company, officered by Sanders's own appointees, certainly "curbed and hindered" him. Sanders, like Gell himself a small man[12], was described by Lucy Hutchinson as "a very godly honest country gentleman, but had not many things requisite to a greate souldier"[13]. She was wrong about his soldierly qualities, since he proved a very successful commander "of one of the bravest regiments of horse in the North"[14] but, being "godly", he was continually offended by Gell's earthy language and behaviour. There was mutual loathing between him and his Colonel. When, in September, Sanders mentioned the agreement that Gell had signed on his appointment the previous year, Gell "spoke in a great deale of anger and said, I wish that clubb law were lawfull & in fashion, speaking in a threatening manner"[15]. However, in spite of his impatience and frequent angry outbursts at dissenters, Gell respected his officers' opinions on military matters and tried to take care of his soldiers. Sanders himself agreed that Gell consulted him and the junior officers, in a "loveing & amicable" manner, before undertaking any operation[16].

Newcastle's retreat

With enemies now within the camp as well as outside, Gell was once again saved by events outside the county when Newcastle, who had been far too cautious and had held back from attacking Derby, was compelled to withdraw from the county and march north to face an attack by a Scottish army. This army, paid and supplied by Parliament, was the result of long negotiations between the Scots and the English Parliament, who were anxious to obtain an anti-royalist alliance. The Scots had a natural loyalty to their own Stuart dynasty and none to the English Parliament, but they were Presbyterians and feared the effect on their religion of a royal victory as much as Parliament did. In the Solemn League and Covenant, signed on the 23rd September 1643, the "league" was Parliament's view of the alliance and the biblical "covenant" the Scots' minimum requirement for agreement. The English agreed to set up a church in England similar to that in Scotland, and signing the Solemn League and Covenant became the test of loyalty to Parliament. On the 19th January 1644 the Scots moved into England and by the end of the month Newcastle was on his way north, reinforced by over two thousand of the new recruits mentioned by Gell in his December letter to Essex.

He left behind him a reinforced garrison at Bolsover and new ones at Wingfield Manor, Chatsworth and Tissington. He had also created five regiments, commanded by Derbyshire royalists to whom he granted Colonel's commissions. The new Colonels were Rowland Eyre of Hassop, John Shalcross of Shalcross, John Frecheville of Staveley, Sir John Fitzherbert of Norbury and John Milward of Snitterton Hall. Milward was Gell's partner as chief barmaster of the Wirksworth lead mining liberties and, typically for this war, the two enemies continued their business partnership - a note in Gell's mining accounts records that he had received £30 from an ore-buyer "betwixt Mr Millard & myself about 8 Oct 1644"[17]. Gell had tried to enlist him for Parliament. Frecheville fortified his own Staveley House, Fitzherbert garrisoned Tissington and Wingfield Manor and Eyre, Milward and Shalcross garrisoned Chatsworth[18]. In the south Sir John Harpur had fortified Burton Bridge and Hastings had taken advantage of the improvement in the royal fortunes to place a garrison in a fortified place called Kingsmill, protecting the Trent crossing at Wilne Ferry.

On the 6th January Molanus was sent with a force of dragoons and cavalry to remove Harpur from Burton This was a comprehensive success, and Molanus returned with five hundred prisoners, including fifteen officers. The removal of the garrison at Kingsmill, "a place exceeding troublesome & burdensome to these parts of our county though it stand in Leicestershire" is described in a letter which Gell wrote to Essex on the 8th February[19]. The place was protected on the north by earthworks as well as by the Trent and on the south by a steep hill and by trenches filled with water from the river. "Our ordynance beinge but small did not much execution", so Gell picked a number of men from each troop of the cavalry, who were on the south, to form an assault force. Their attack was successful -"its thought to be as desperate a peece of service as any such a petty business hath beene in the North. Our men beate downe the windows & stormed in, & so forced them to give quarter". At a cost of five dead and twenty wounded, the Derbyshire troops captured two officers and fifty-two men.

The letter also told Essex of the five Colonels and their regiments whom Newcastle had created and left behind in Derbyshire. In the north of the county these troops plundered the area's farmers for provisions. The task of clearing them away was given to Sanders, who took five hundred dragoons and cavalry. He executed a pincer move on the royalists, who had hoped to surprise him in his quarters at Ashbourne. Sanders learned of their approach and attacked their front with his dragoons while his cavalry charged the rear. They were routed and pursued into Tissington, with many killed and a hundred and seventy taken prisoner. This defeat forced the royalists to abandon garrisons at Tissington and Bakewell and fall back on Staveley, Chatsworth and Wingfield.

Defeat at Newark

These successes in Derbyshire were spoiled for Gell by a disastrous reverse at Newark. This garrison had been a menace to Nottingham since the beginning of the war and a determined effort was made by the Parliamentarians to subdue it. Gell was ordered on the 24th February 1644 to send all his dragoons and cavalry to join a beseiging force of troops from Nottingham, Leicester and Lincolnshire. By early March the parliamentary forces had taken an area called the Spittle, to the south-west of the town, and fortified the Muskham Bridge in the north. Gell's horse, under Molanus and Sanders, guarded the men building the fortifications there, while his dragoons were in the Spittle, attacking the garrison with artillery and small arms fire. Newark was sufficiently important to the king to require the attention of Prince Rupert. On the 21st March the Prince engaged the Parliamentary cavalry and after killing more than two hundred of them and leaving Sanders with only thirty or forty men[20], he drove them back over the Muskham Bridge, trapping a large force in the Spittle. These men were offered the chance to leave with all their weapons but were disarmed as they left. Gell lost over two hundred men and their arms and ammunition in this action, though he had an immediate chance to show his resilience. Men from the Prince's and Hastings's forces were plundering the countryside around Ashby during Rupert's return to Oxford and Gell sent his Captain Rhodes to stop them at Egginton Heath. There were about six hundred of the enemy opposed to three hundred and fifty of Gell's cavalry. Gell called up Molanus with infantry to support Rhodes but by the time he arrived the cavalry had driven the royalists into the river Trent, where many of them drowned. Two hundred prisoners were taken.

New guns and a cavalry skirmish

Gell had never had enough artillery for his purposes, and had lost some of it at Newark. His problems in this regard were lessened in April 1644 when Parliament was able to supply him with forty guns. They were conveyed from London to Peterborough and from there to Derby, protected from the royalist cavalry at Newark and Ashby by a combined force of Molanus's and Lord Grey's cavalry and dragoons. In the same month Gell wrote to Essex reporting clashes with Hastings at Burton, and with the cavalry commander George Goring, who was marching with Prince Rupert to the relief of the Earl of Newcastle, beseiged in York[21]. Goring was pursued to Ashby, losing thirty prisoners and many dead and wounded. During this skirmish the Derbyshire cavalry captured a royalist flag "on which is the kings picture, crowned, with a drawne sword in his hand & this motto, Melius est mori in bello quam videre mala gentis nostra [It is better to die in battle than to see evil done to our nation]". Gell complained in a later letter that if he had had the extra thousand cavalry which he had requested several times from the Earl of Manchester, he could have destroyed Goring[22]. As it was, Goring drove north through Tutbury and the Peak, taking with him Derbyshire reinforcements for Prince Rupert

Marston Moor

With his new artillery Gell had a better chance of subduing the garrison at Wingfield Manor, which, together with the Bolsover men, was a constant thorn in his flesh. Wingfield, however, was a real stronghold and, although Gell used most of his regiment, plus help from Nottingham, the siege he mounted in June 1644 failed to take it. As on earlier occasions he was helped by events elsewhere, this time by the result of one of the decisive battles of the war. The armies of Lord Fairfax and the Scots which had been besieging the Earl of Newcastle in York since the end of April were joined in June by the Earl of Manchester's army, making a combined force of thirty thousand men. Prince Rupert, in spite of commanding a greatly inferior force, met the Parliamentary army on Marston Moor on 2nd July and was heavily defeated. The Derbyshire royalists Eyre, Freschville, Milward and Shallcross had moved north with Goring and fought in this battle under his command. Their forces were badly mauled and depleted, but the Colonels themselves escaped. Freschville was given Fairfax's protection after he had promised to surrender his commission, and returned to his house at Staveley with about two hundred troops. He defended himself defiantly against harrassment by Parliamentary troops from Chesterfield and complained about these attacks to the commander there[23]. Gell appealed to Fairfax on the 7th August to withdraw his protection and disarm him, pointing out that Frescheville had not laid down his arms and remained a potential danger[24]. Fairfax responded and informed Gell on the 15th that he had just heard that Freschville had surrendered his house to General Crawford[25]. Crawford was Manchester's second-in-command[26]. Rowland Eyre's regiment fell into Gell's hands. In a move to defend his southern flank against Hastings, who was preparing to reinforce the garrisons at Tutbury, Ashby and Lichfield, he despatched Sanders to Burton. On his way Sanders came across Eyre and two hundred exhausted survivors from Marston Moor, resting in Boyleston church. His dragoons surprised and captured the whole force and their arms. Moving on to Burton, he attacked a royalist force which had just entered the town, driving them out and capturing more prisoners to add to the two hundred at Boyleston. Sanders returned in triumph to Derby with his prisoners and trophies.

The taking of Wingfield Manor

The Parliamentary victory in Yorkshire removed the menace posed by Newcastle's garrisons, particularly the one at Bolsover, of which Sir George Gresley wrote later "It is impossible to relate our continuall and almost daylie incounters with the earl of Newcastle's garison at Bolesover"[27]. General Crawford was dispatched to take Sheffield, Staveley, Bolsover and Welbeck, which he did in succession[28]. Wingfield was taken in August after Sanders had returned and Gell had been able to leave Derby and resume his seige. After several days of ineffectual bombardment Gell called for help to Crawford who brought four demi-cannon, firing a thirty-two pound shot. The heavy guns were positioned on the west side of the Manor and on the 14th August breached the walls. The garrison surrendered. Two hundred and twenty men were allowed to leave and return home while Gell captured twelve guns, two hundred and fifty muskets and a hundred and fifty pikes[29]. To make sure that this fort remained in the right hands he left a detachment of two companies of foot and a troop of cavalry, and began to requisition supplies from the neighbourhood. He ranged far from Wingfield in his demands for provisions for the garrison and met with an absolute refusal when his warrant was produced over the Nottinghamshire border, in Mansfield[30]. The Nottingham garrison protested on the

18th August that after sending him men "we should bee persuaded oute of our meate too", denying sarcastically that "the libertie you have at home be likewyse taken abroade".

The Bolsover garrison

While Marston Moor ended the external threat in the north, the opposition to Gell in his own camp increased, reinforced by the new Parliamentary garrison which replaced the royalists at Bolsover. In a move which was a blow to Gell's authority, Lord Fairfax garrisoned Bolsover with a regiment recently raised by Randle Ashenhurst, exchanged after his capture and commissioned as Colonel by Fairfax. There had been a coolness between Gell and the Fairfaxes since Sir Thomas had been in Derby in 1643. He had been irritated at what he saw as Gell's reluctance to supply troops for his march into Yorkshire, in spite of Gell's explanations, and Gell himself resented Sir Thomas' refusal to send help to Derbyshire after he had left the Derby force in the lurch during Newcastle's invasion in November of that year[31]. Lord Fairfax had also incurred Gell's dislike by accepting former Derbyshire officers such as Ashenhurst into his own force. Ashenhurst himself had become an enemy when he left Gell's regiment and was later to join the opposition on the Derby Committee. Among his commanders were the two Captains who had deserted Gell in late 1643, now promoted to Major. Soon after the Bolsover garrison was established Gell sent arrest warrants for Clarke and Taylor, presumably the ones which he had requested from Essex[32]. Clarke was imprisoned for a month and only released after Fairfax had intervened.

It is little wonder that Gell, who was in any case intolerant of any challenge to his authority in Derbyshire, should be intensely irritated by the Bolsover garrison, officered by deserters from his own regiment. Lord Fairfax had already written to the Committee on the 16th April 1644 requiring them to take measures to pay Ashenhurst's regiment, using sequestration money[33], and on 30th August he wrote that he had heard of "the greate want my souldyers are in at Bolesover Castle" and asked them to help[34]. Gell's reply to this makes it plain that as far as the Derby Committee were concerned the Bolsover men were a liability[35]. He was sure that Fairfax would be unpleasantly surprised to hear that the garrison "you are pleased to call your men" consisted of about twenty officers and sixty men and that "so soone as these forces were wythin the doors at Boulsover they sent forth warrants for monyes, beds &

victualls, commanding that our warrants should not be obeyed". Because of their behaviour, the people would refuse any attempt he might make to raise provisions for them.

Fairfax, clearly baffled by the animosity in Derbyshire, wrote again in September, lamenting that the Bolsover soldiers "should fare the worse for acknowledging some dependancy upon mee"[36]. He assured Gell that he was only concerned to "joyne with them to the publique service" and asked again for his explanation of why he would not cooperate with the Bolsover men "which may be a ground of my further desisting in commanding in that county when I know the Parliaments pleasure", a reference to the fact that it was being proposed that Derbyshire should be put under his command. Gell in fact continued to do his best to prevent the garrison getting any provision from the surrounding area and went so far as to issue a proclamation to that effect in Chesterfield[37]. This was at a time when royalist troops under Sir Marmaduke Langdale were approaching, on their way to attack Lord Fairfax and relieve the beseiged town of Pontefract. The garrisons at Wingfield and Bolsover competed for provision from the same area, a chaotic situation which prompted a letter from Taylor in November in which he sensibly pleaded "let us not destroy the country under pretence of saveing it"[38].

Divided loyalties

At this time Gell was trying hard to persuade Parliament not to transfer Derbyshire to the Northern Association, a proposal which would place him under the command of the Fairfaxes and which was being pushed by William Wolley, Lieutenant-Colonel of the Bolsover garrison, and others of the anti-Gell faction[39]. On the 20th September the Leicester Committee wrote to Derby proposing a joint letter to the Speaker supporting their continued association[40] and Gell's main argument to Parliament was that, with the Earl of Newcastle's army gone, he and his regiment were more urgently needed in Nottinghamshire and Leicestershire. Privately, the last thing that Gell wanted was to serve under the Fairfaxes.

Unlike his Colonel, Sanders badly wanted to serve under Sir Thomas Fairfax. He proposed joining with the Nottingham cavalry under Colonel Thornaugh in an expedition led by Fairfax to relieve the Lincolnshire town of Torksey, then being beseiged by troops from the Newark garrison. In a scathing letter to Sanders written on the 25th September, the day after Sanders had been asked to join the Torksey expedition[41], Gell showed himself to be a wiser man and better commander than his rival[42]. He rebuked Sanders for the Torksey proposal, suggesting that Thornaugh's reason for going was simply that the enemy were near his estate. The Derby forces should undertake nothing without the order of "those that wee are under" and should "associate ourselves southwardly". Gell went on to insist that there should always be consultation before any operation was undertaken - "I beinge strange to the busines, doe desire to confere with those capts and officers that should go upon the servis, before I order them upon servis. It concerneth theyre lives, and the treuth is I am very tender of those brave and valiant frends that have been so faithfull in our servis". Gell finally condemned the enterprise as dangerous to the safety of the county - "If once routed beyond Trent it may prove the lose of our County". Sanders should have conferred - "I shall say litle more but leave it to a Councell of Warre and your selfe". Sanders made a sarcastic annotation - "Sr Jo: Gell his loving letter to me".

Gell also remined Sanders that the soldiers he was proposing to take to Lincolnshire had not been paid - "Further you know that our souldiers doe expect monies, which if they have not I can not expecte further servis from them ... I doe thinke it exceedinge harde to leave of gettinge of monies for our souldiers". Gell was always very serious about paying his soldiers. "The pathwai to martiall discipline" warned him to ensure that "the good souldier be not anie waies hindered of his paie, which would do so much hurt to his good nature, without whom the Coronell can availe little or nothing". The serious shortage of money for the soldiers' wages, and the likely dangerous consequences of not solving the problem, prompted Gell and the Committee to petition Parliament at about this time[43]. "Your petitioners have for a long tyme kept together the souldyers here with hopes of pay, of which they now grow weary & press your petitioners for some present money, more than we know how to raise, & in case of faylor, we are in danger to loose our souldyers (as being many thousand pounds in arrears unto them) which would be very prejudiciall both to this & divers other neighbor counties". They asked Parliament for £2,000 immediately and the proceeds of sequestration in the future.

The garrisons at Barton and Coleorton

In October, with the menace of the royalist garrisons in Derbyshire gone, Gell returned to the attack on another persistent drain on his resources, Tutbury Castle. On this occasion, instead of attempting to capture the place, he sent Captains Barton and Greenwood of Sanders's cavalry to set up a garrison at Barton Hall, about three miles from Tutbury, from where they attacked the defenders' supply columns and made continual raids against them. Gell was able to report to Essex on the 16th November 1644 that the force at Barton "so curbs that garison that on Thursday last the souldyers there laid downe theyre armes & refused to serve any longer without present money"[44]. In November Gell sent Sanders himself to help in setting up a similar operation at Coleorton, near Ashby, to nullify the effectiveness of the garrison there. In the poisonous atmosphere caused by his attempt to join Fairfax Sanders went off to Coleorton with five troops of his cavalry. The Coleorton garrison was to be manned jointly with troops from Leicestershire, the arrangement specifying Derby dragoons as well as cavalry, and Sanders was soon complaining that they had not been sent[45] . He also complained about the conditions and threatened to leave - "we this night lie horse and men in the fields ... pinched with cold". The infantry failed to arrive, though letters from Gell did come, provoking more complaints - "we expected mouskets, & not papers yesternight"[46]. Gell must have accused Sanders of cowardice for proposing to leave Coleorton, as Sanders' reply protested that his soldiers were brave men - "our horse have not been slow to ayd others upon the least alarum". A Leicestershire force of horse and foot was on its way to join them "and that you wil engage none of your foote after such importuning is strange". In spite of all the acrimony the Coleorton garrison succeeded in its objects of impeding the royalist lines of communication and keeping the parliamentary ones open.

The Burton garrison

In his letter of the 16th November Gell proposed to Essex that a garrison at Burton, added to Barton and Coleorton, would nullify the three royalist strongholds of Ashby, Tutbury and Lichfield and prevent the men at Tutbury getting the money they had been promised to persuade them to give up their mutiny. He asked for permission to provision the proposed garrison from two areas of Staffordshire then under royalist control which "we doubt not but presently to bring them to obedyence". Sir George Gresley had a personal interest in this plan, as his estates were all in the area in question[47]. Gresley was honest enough to tell Essex that a Derbyshire garrison at Burton would enable his daughter to collect the rents from her estate there.

Essex persuaded a doubtful Staffordshire Committee to contribute two hundred cavalry and a hundred infantry to a joint garrison and, well aware that acrimony had been a persistent characteristic of Parliamentary collaborations, hoped that "there may be no division amonst you, but accord (it being for the generall good of the kingdom) as becometh neighbours and loveing freinds"[48]. This proposal met an instant rebuff from the commander of the Staffordshire forces, Colonel Lewis Chadwick[49]. Gell had added a postscript to his letter to Essex on the 16th November saying that as Staffordshire had "many commanders & few souldiers" they were not able to maintain garrisons themselves, and Chadwick confirmed this. Stafford was by this time back in Parliamentary hands and Chadwick wrote to Gell on the 28th November to say that his total cavalry was only two hundred and that to take them and a hundred infantry would leave Stafford undefended. He had no objection to Gell garrisoning Burton himself, for Derbyshire's benefit, and would help when asked, if he could. Chadwick, however, was about to be deposed. He was a supporter of a disgraced Parliamentary commander, the Earl of Denbigh, and was dismissed after Denbigh's fall[50]. Gell himself was involved in Chadwick's removal. He and Brereton, with a detachment of infantry and cavalry, entered Stafford on the 3rd December and arrested him. The Burton garrison got its Staffordshire contingent.

Success in the Vale of Belvoir

By December Fairfax had become persuaded that the Bolsover garrison should be disbanded. He wrote to Gell on the 13th noting that the Derbyshire force had been instructed to help in setting up a garrison near Newark and and agreed that the men at Bolsover and Wingfield would be better employed there[51]. Gell replied on the 16th December that he had sent four hundred cavalry and dragoons to join Fairfax's troops at Newark but could not "dismantle" Wingfield Manor without the permission of the Earl of Pembroke, its owner[52]. In the same month hostility to the Bolsover garrison was carried to extremes. Gell sent troops to prevent it collecting taxes or provisions from the locality and Henry Wigfall, speaking as if the Bolsover men were enemies to be blockaded, said that if the Derby troops "quarter in Sutton House or Old Courte they might piss against the walls of Bollsover"[53]. Gell ended 1644 with a victory. The troops he had sent at Fairfax's request to join Sir Thomas Fairfax and troops from Nottinghamshire in blockading Newark came upon a large force of royalists in the Vale of Belvoir, commanded by the governor of Newark, Sir Richard Byron. Gell's cavalry charged and routed the enemy, driving many into a brook, capturing prisoners and horses, and sending Byron himself running on foot to Belvoir Castle, losing his wig as he ran.

The Recorder election

Gell's quarrels with Sanders and some of the townsmen became more venomous late in 1644, when the post of Recorder at Derby became vacant in November and Gell proposed his brother. Thomas was a barrister and must have seemed the obvious man for the job. Sanders, however, did not agree, and his characterisation of Thomas Gell in a letter written from the garrison at Coleorton throws grave doubt on his objectivity. Thomas Gell, "sweet Tom Gell", according to the Countess of Rutland, for whom he had worked[54], and faithful ally of his brother in all his causes, including the Parliamentary one, was, as far as Sanders was concerned "unfit for the place... in respect of his mean estate, want of learning, law and honesty, his conversation being so scandalous, for unclean swearing and hating all honest men; that he favoured malignants and enemies in arms and was not to be trusted or confided in"[55]. Gell, predictably was furious and gave Sanders a verbal beating at a meeting in Derby Town Hall.
Sanders, unrepentant, wrote to Gell from Coleorton - "I wonder at your slanderous words spoke of me in the open hall at Derby. I desire our actions may be compared and weighed, then it will appear wheather I be a brownist, a coward & a knave or noe. What I am & what I have don ... moste in these partes know: but to call me a knave, malice & envy itself (& I perseave there is enoffe in you towards me of both). I am confident my integrity will defend me. I confesse (as Mr Wigfall could tell you, for I spoke it to him at Dronfeald) I think the Lieutenant Colonel unfit to be Recorder and I will hinder it all I can. For two brothers and two sons-in-law solely to rule a county, all honest men resent. I seek not the place of governor or colonel. Rather than hinder the public, I will sit down from arms and seek to do the kingdom service in another way & if I be not called (for I will not by unlawfull meanes seek it) I will returne to a private life & soe end my dayes ... I desire that personal dislikes and grudges may not hurt the public"[56]. Sanders's reference to the Gell family control of the Committee indicates personal jealousy and his last sentence is an unlikely declaration of self denial from an ambitious man. To admit to being a "Brownist" or

Independent would at that stage to have been admitting to political extremism and Gell had clearly drawn blood with his gibe.

Brother Thomas, Lt. Col. Gell

Youle and Dunnage were concerned that Thomas Gell's election was rushed through, giving no chance for them to propose a Derby man. Another tradesman, Exuperius Fletcher, attracted Sir John's attention merely by criticising his brother[57]. He had reported Sanders's opinion of Thomas Gell to one of his supporters who had passed it on to the town Marshall, John Wright, who had in turn told Sir John. Fletcher too was imprisoned and his wife and friends refused permission to visit him. On his release Gell struck him, "laying his hand on his sword, swearing it were a good deed to run [Fletcher] through, and so badd [Fletcher] goe like a rogue as he was". Thomas was elected Recorder and, according to Fletcher, Sir John ordered the Mayor and Clerk of the Council to give him a list of those who had not voted for Thomas, which was contrary to a secrecy rule and designed to overawe the members.

The Committee enlarged

Parliament's division of responsibility between Gell and the Committee was always likely to cause conflict between them, as similar arrangements did in other counties, including Nottinghamshire. As Colonel of the Derbyshire regiment, Gell was responsible for military operations in the town and county, while the Committee was responsible for raising the money to finance them. At first the conflict was muted and Gell was able, up to the end of 1643, to conduct his war without challenge to his authority. The Committee, which was dominated by his relatives and his ally, Sir George Gresley, rarely met and allowed him to get on with things[58]. Even this Committee, however, was a necessary evil, and there are many reported expressions of Gell's impatience with it. As early as June 1643, according to one of his enemies, he called the committee men "base fellowes", who would "undo" the soldiers, and wished that there were no committees[59]. Sanders was probably accurate when he described Gell's method of conducting business - he regarded the Committee "as being a meanes to curbe & hinder him of sole power & rule, which he aimed at. When there was none of the Committee but himselfe, Sir George, his brother, 2 sons in lawe & Capt Mellor & myselfe he did what he pleased, wee two left standing for sifers - the rest did what he would have done.We had noe sett tyme, noe place but his chamber, noe chare & noe order entered but entered in an arbitrary way. When any person or cause came to him that he favoured he would then make an order & send it aboute to our houses for us to signe without any debate at all, but if an honest man came aboute a busines he affected not, were it never soe just, he would delay and tell him, I am but one and can not doe any thing, except the Committee were here"[60].

Parliament, alerted to the trouble in Derbyshire by a petition from the discontented, agreed to increase the size of the Committee. Gell tried to organise opposition to it among the officers of the regiment, all of whom he invited to a dinner in December 1644[61]. After the dinner Thomas Gell proposed to them that they should join in opposing the new committee's work. Gell had earlier said that Mellor and others were trying to "procure authoritie to the Committee & they would have me ruled by a Committee but I will not, and they that cross me I will cross them"[62]. It is clear from his brother's proposition that he imagined that his hostility to a committee controlling the military was shared by the soldiers. He was disappointed. The captains of horse, Sanders's men, all refused Thomas's proposal.

Resentment against Gell in his regiment was greatest among Sander's officers, though it was not confined to them. He was accused of unfair distribution of money as between his own and Sanders's troops and of welcoming any who consequently deserted into his own company. This perceived discrimination resulted during 1644 in Sanders's officers supporting the petition to Parliament for additional members to be put on the committee to break the Gells' grip on it[63]. One of the officers signing the petition was Robert Cotchett, Captain-Lieutenant in Gell's own troop of cavalry[64]. Cotchett objected both to the unfair distribution of money and to having to accept deserters into his own troop. Gell was furious at this disloyalty, calling Cotchett "a factious foole and knave". A year later, perhaps remembering this, Gell imprisoned him on the 12th May 1645 and ordered him out of town on the 14th, saying that "he was his enemie, and a Companion to all the enemies he had in this world, instancing Ma: Saunders and Capt Mellors".

Among the new Committee members were John Mundy, of Derby, Ralph Clarke, Rowland Moorewood of Alfreton, Captain Swetnam and Sir Samuel Sleigh. Clarke, described as a merchant, was placed on a committee of accounts and proved to be particularly assiduous in bringing to light any financial short-cuts which Gell had been taking. Mundy and Moorewood, gentlemen, and Sleigh, one of the gentry who had refused to accept the warrant when offered the deputy-lieutenancy in 1642, were to give evidence against Gell's conduct at Derby and Moorewood had been one of the advocates of Derbyshire's joining the Northern Association. The year ended with the first meeting of the newly-enlarged Committee invaded by the Captain-Lieutenant of Gell's infantry company, Drinkwater, leading a mob of officers and soldiers. These troops, in a move which was to be repeated, demanded that the committee should make good their unpaid wages. If this was not done they threatened to desert en masse. Gell himself was present, but did not intervene[65].

The death of Elizabeth

Under attack by his own side as well as by the enemy, Gell had suffered a further blow when his wife Elizabeth died in October 1644. Elizabeth seems to have been a sympathetic and compassionate figure. All the Willoughby letters suggest that she and her family were considerably more civilised and humane than the hard-bitten Gell and evidence that this was generally recognised comes in a letter written to her by an eighty year old minister oppressed by Civil War taxation and the expense of providing for soldiers quartered on him[66]. This was "H. Coke", "a poore distressed minister, and preacher of the gospell ... blinde of one eye, my wyf aged a 90 yeares and blinde of both eyes". Apart from his quarterly stipend of £16 he had no income, not "soe much as an egg at Easter", and the £16 had not been paid him. In addition to having soldiers living off him "since theis broiles began", he had been presented with a tax demand from the Derby Committee. He had written to the Committee, summarising his case for relief, but had received no reply. He hoped that Elizabeth would use her influence with Gell because "the generall report of your goodnesse hath incouraged me".

William Gell's letter of June 1638 is evidence that his mother was chronically ill, as her own mother's letters had suggested while she was still a young woman, and Elizabeth lived for only about five years after William's letter. This was long enough for her to have become Lady Gell on the award of Gell's baronetcy, and to have suffered the loss of her son in 1642. She was probably about fifty at the time of her death in 1644[67]. Elizabeth was buried at Wirksworth on the 26th October 1644 and, while Sir John's funeral twenty-eight years later was to be a grand affair, the only document which survives from the arrangements for Elizabeth's is a note of expenditure on cakes and on spice for the wine[69].

Precautions

Conscious of the growing weight of opposition to him, and of the danger that this posed to his family's fortunes, Gell took the step in December 1644 which was to save them seven years later, when his enemies came to sequestrate his estate. His son's marriage to Catherine Packer was followed by a comprehensive settlement, dated the 28th December. The bride's dowry was £3000, of which £2000 had already been paid, and all Gell's estates, including the lead ore tithes in Bakewell, Tideswell and Hope, were transferred to the younger John Gell and his wife. The third parties to this agreement between Gell and his son included John Packer and Sir John Curzon, and it was witnessed in Derby by Gresley, Luke Whittington, John Wigley and Molanus.

CHAPTER 8

Mutiny

The New Model Army

The course of the war was fundamentally altered in 1645 by the formation of the New Model Army. It had become apparent that the king was unlikely to be defeated while the operations of the different Parliamentary armies were imperfectly coordinated and while confusion often reigned at local level. In addition, the military competence of the commanders did not match their social rank and by the end of 1644 the Earls of Manchester and Essex were seriously at loggerheads with Cromwell, who was serving under Manchester. The military confusion in Derbyshire was typical. Here, the disruption caused by local commanders such as Sanders, who had raised their own forces and regarded themselves as entitled to serve under the superior officer of their choice, was compounded by the army commanders. Essex had failed to make clear who was in command of the Derbyshire cavalry and Lord Fairfax had first formed a regiment of deserters from the Derbyshire regiment and had then installed it in Bolsover Castle, where it competed for funds and supplies with Gell, who had a commission from Fairfax's colleague Essex to defend Derbyshire. Coordination was also hampered by the fact that militias such as Gell's force always placed local defence needs first. A centrally commanded, properly equipped and provided army was necessary if the king's own divided armies were to be destroyed and prevented from reforming. In February 1644 the House of Commons, recognising the need for coordination, had set up a Committee of Both Kingdoms to run the war, and in the autumn it ordered this Committee to consider the formation of a new army.

The Committee presented its proposals on the 6th January 1645. The new army was to consist of twenty-two thousand men, drawn from the existing armies, and by April Sir Thomas Fairfax had been appointed its commander. As second-in-command, with the rank of Lieutenant-General, Parliament appointed Oliver Cromwell, whose own regiment, nicknamed the Ironsides, had proved itself the best trained, best disciplined and most enthusiastic unit in the Parliamentary armies. Soon after Cromwell, who was an MP, was given his new command, Parliament passed the Self-Denying Ordinance of the 3rd April 1645. This disqualified members of both Houses of Parliament from serving in the army and had the effect of removing the Earls of Essex and Manchester from their commands. Cromwell was exempted from the new ordinance and kept his post. The appearance of this efficient national army, while not ending the existence of others, inevitably diminished the chances of commanders such as Gell to distinguish themselves by local heroics. Gell's position had already been weakened in September 1644 by the transfer of Derbyshire, along with Nottinghamshire and Leicestershire, to the Northern Association, done in spite of two joint petitions sent by the Derby Committee and the other two counties, asking Parliament to allow them to remain with the Midlands Association[1]. While he continued to take orders from Essex until the passing of the Self-Denying Ordinance, when Essex gave up his command, the link with the Northern Association increased the influence of Fairfax, against whom Gell nourished several grudges, as we have seen, and who had become weary of the quarrelsome Derbyshire force.

Presbyterians and Independents

Politically there were developments which were to end with Gell in the opposition, in spite of his commitment to the Parliamentary cause. His politics were determined by his membership of the smaller gentry class and by his Presbyterian beliefs. Like the majority in Parliament he believed in a centrally organised church governed by its own elders, on the model of the Scottish kirk. There was, however, a growing faction who demanded a church in which individual congregations decided their own form of worship - the Independents. While the Presbyterians were intolerant of other religious groups the Independents typically favoured toleration, though this did not extend as far as Catholics. Crucially, the Independents were especially strong in the New Model Army. Cromwell's famous plea to the Scots was typical of their religious open-mindedness - "I beseech ye, in the bowels of Christ, consider ye may be wrong". This religious division was sharpened by differing attitudes to the king. Like Gell, the Presbyterians in Parliament hoped that the old order would be restored after the war, with the King still on his throne, under Parliament's terms, and with the gentry in charge locally. The Independents, however, contained a strong democratic element and one reason for the success of

Cromwell's regiment lay in his appointing his officers on merit, rather than on their gentlemanly status - he was ridiculed for his rough captains. While Cromwell's attachment to the democratic aims of many of the Independents was to prove limited, he and they eventually reached the view that the king should be deposed. The quarrels between Cromwell and the Earls of Essex and Manchester were political as well as military and the ostensible aim of the Self Denying Ordinance was to remove politics from the prosecution of the war. It was, however, proposed by an ally of Cromwell's and was clearly not even-handed as between peers and commoners, since the former could not resign their seats in the Lords, while MPs could leave the Commons. In the event Cromwell remained both an MP and a general.

In what was ultimately a disaster for Gell, his own Major Sanders and his officers were Independents though, since the term was at that time still a term of abuse, they denied it. The Independents were the men now remembered as Roundheads, typically from lower in the social scale than country gentlemen such as Gell, more religious and disciplined than the generality of Parliamentary soldiers. It is noticeable that Sanders invoked the Diety far more often in his letters than did Gell in his and it is also significant that Sanders felt obliged to deny that he and his officers "go about to supress the gentry"[2]. The City Spectacles tract of 1648 abused Sanders and his officers in the vituperative style characteristic of the time - "In the next place I must needs unkennell a nest of Independent cowards and vermine. And first I must pluck out by the eares Sanders (that Diminiture of Alexander), Captaine under Sir John Gell; (the greatest act of valour that he ever did was to shoot a gentleman through the arme, and cut him after he was taken prisoner and disarmed): when he was to goe upon any service he had a trick to make his souldiers mutiny; which he did famously, when he should have gone with Colonel Gell to Naisby fight. His officers are like him"[3]. It is interesting that the pamphleteer repeated in 1648 the slander which had earlier been levelled against one of Sanders's officers by Hastings, that he attacked a soldier who had already surrendered. He went on to accuse Captain Hope of stealing a communion cup and being "pull'd out of his breeches" for it.

It was the new breed of Parliamentarians who came in 1646 to destroy Emmanuel Bourne's house, Eastwood Hall[4]. After blowing up the house with a barrel of gunpowder they sang a psalm and then marched to the church, where their commander preached a sermon. The cultivated Bourne was scornful - "Lord! what stuff and nonsense he did talke, and if he could have murdered the Kyng as easily as he did the Kyng's English, the war would long since have been over". After the service the troops destroyed the old parish registers, which were in Latin and therefore suspiciously "popish". These religiously and socially defined political divisions were eventually to cause a split between Parliament and the army. In the small world of the Derby Committee, where the arrival of Sanders in October 1643 had disturbed the hitherto unchallengeable alliance of Gell, his friends, his brother Thomas, his half-brother Curzon, and his sons-in-law John Wigley and Henry Wigfall, these large divisions were an element in the irreconcilable enmity between Gell and Sanders.

Gell versus Sanders

Gell's patience with his reluctant major broke in the early weeks of 1645. Sanders had refused to go with a force sent to Newark in December, instead going to London, where he was taking part in lobbying Parliament for the appointment of the new Committee members. On his return Gell wrote on the 5th January ordering him to join his cavalry, who were by then at Southwell, in Nottinghamshire[5]. Sanders ignored this[6], and Gell then wrote to Essex accusing Sanders of refusing to obey him.

Essex at last recognised the impossible situation he had engineered and decided to remove Sanders's commission and replace it with one which placed him unambiguously under Gell's command[7]. He sent Gell the new commission[8], and on the 29th January Gell informed him that Sanders refused to accept it and that he had therefore been placed under house arrest[9]. Sanders demanded to be allowed to resign his commission in person and "I refuse to accept a new one because I will not be under the command of him who desires my ruin more than any Cavalier in England"[10]. This was not the first time that Sanders had threatened to resign and Gell was characteristically sarcastic - "My Lord this Major hath usually upon discontent offered to lay downe his armes, which I conceive is no loss to the publique"[11].

Claiming that his officers and soldiers refused to serve under Gell, Sanders attemped to remove them from the regiment. While under house arrest he wrote to Colonel Sandes, commander of the Nottinghamshire cavalry, with whom his troops were then serving, asking him to send Swetnam to Fairfax to ask for a commission[12]. He also asked that Swetnam's troop should not be sent back to Derby, where "their horses and arms will be taken from them" and speculated that another troop of his company, Capt Hope's, might escape from Derby if Fairfax demanded more help from Gell.

There is nothing to suggest that Gell would disarm his own troops, and indeed all the evidence is that he was trying hard to keep these men on side. He wrote to them in Nottinghamshire on the 3rd February pointing out that Sanders had come to Derby not to get money for their pay, as he understood they believed, but with a pass from Colonel Sandes to go to London[13]. He said that the treasurer had no money but that he himself had borrowed some and would get more - "Some of you petitioned for a new committee but if it were not for the old, you would not have received one penny". However, the £400 or £500 he sent them was accompanied by a copy of a "protestation" which the reluctant officers were asked to sign, undertaking to remain in the Derbyshire regiment[14]. They wrote to the Committee asking whether, since they were not going to sign this undertaking, they should return the money. In an understandable fit of rage and frustration Sir John threatened the Committee men with his cane, which was clearly more than a ceremonial accessory. He told them that "if they medled with his souldiers or answered that letter hee would cracke the crowne of the proudest of them all (some Baronetts & knightts being then present) & he gave the committee most uncivile speeches calling them knaves & shitten stinking fellowes"[15].

While Gell was writing to the troops in Nottinghamshire, their Captain, Swetnam, was in York, pleading Sanders's case for a commission in Fairfax's army[16]. While "Sir John is extremely odious here", Fairfax could not give him one, "being loth to clash with Essex", but the commission would be granted "so soon as Sir Thomas is settled". On the 11th February Essex ordered Gell to release Sanders and send him details of charges against him[17]. Essex had at first intended to replace Sanders but had by then changed his mind. Gell was "not to put any other in his place, or remove any officer before you heare from me againe. But I intend he shalbe no longer your major than he shal obey you as his Colonel".

Thomas Gell was sent to put the case against Sanders, which was heard before the Council of War[18]. Sanders was accused of refusing to help in convoying the consignment of guns from Peterborough in 1644, of refusing to join a skirmish at Egginton Heath, of joining the party in London petitioning for addition to the Committee instead of joining Fairfax in blockading Newark and of refusing to go there on his return from London. In his answers Sanders denied being ordered to join the convoy, said he had failed to arrive in time at Egginton Heath because his stable was locked and he had no horse, denied refusing to go to Newark, saying that at the time he went to London it had not yet been decided who should go there, and said that he needed a rest for health reasons before joining his troops at Southwell when he returned. There were the story of Sanders's desertion at Burton, a claim that he had run away at a siege of Newark and another that he had never led his troops in person. He explained his conduct at Newark by describing the loss of most of his men, saying that he had been ordered to join the retreat with Major Molanus, and insisted that he had often led his men into battle. There were accusations and denials of subversion and Sanders insisted that he always obeyed reasonable orders from Gell.

Gell won a paper victory. Sanders and the cavalry remained hostile. Sir Thomas Fairfax wrote to Gell on the 7th February ordering him to send Sanders's horse from Nottinghamshire to assist Sir William Brereton, commander of the Parliamentary forces in Staffordshire and Cheshire, in a seige of Chester[19]. Still unpaid, the cavalry were posted to Chester. In a letter to the cavalry captains dated the 10th February conveying Fairfax's order, and in later ones, Gell gave vent to his anger at the subversion going on - "I am more beholden to Sir Thomas Fairfax than to you, for he acknowledges me to be your Colonel, but this I impute to that ungrateful fellow Swetnam rather than to the rest"[20]. He dismissed their refusal to accept the money he had sent to them - "if you refused the money I borrowed to send to you, it is no fault of mine". By May many of the soldiers had deserted and made their way back to Derby. Gell, instead of punishing these men, gave them £1 each on condition that they did not rejoin their company. At the same time he gave Captain Swetnam his opinion of Sanders in terms that echoed Sanders's own - "he had rather fight with Major Sanders than with any Cavalier in England and that he would have his pennyworth out of him"[21]. The expeditions to Nottinghamshire and Chester were, according to Sanders, part of Gell's malevolent campaign against him, as it put his troops to long winter marches, aggravating the discontent they already felt over lack of pay, while Gell's own troops stayed in the comparative comfort of Derby[22].

However, Gell's own soldiers, too, were in mutinous mood and, just as he used the cavalry's grievances against their officers, he exploited the Derby garrison's discontent against his enemies on the Committee. At the end of January 1645 Captain-Lieutenant Drinkwater and his had men invaded the committee-room, as they had done a month earlier[23]. Drinkwater said "that hee had as good bee killed before 5 as 500 & uttered desperate speeches", and presented the committee with a "warrant", presumably a statement of their grievances on pay. Gell signed it without either reading it or discussing it with the rest of the committee, some of whom followed suit. Clarke refused and said that Gell should punish Drinkwater and his men.

Bolsover dissidents

On the 4th April 1645 Gell, still anxious to get rid of the persistent Bolsover garrison, ingeniously supported a plea from the Earl of Newcastle's daughters that they should be allowed to live in Bolsover Castle, repeating that the local people complained about the garrison's behaviour and quoting General Crawford's opinion that Bolsover was not a suitable garrison town[24]. In a long letter sent to Essex on 16th May 1645 he explained that he had been instructed by the Committee of Both Kingdoms to pay the Bolsover men and had asked them to be mustered in order to know how many there were. They had refused to do so and, because of this refusal, and in spite of many requests, the Committee had since refused to order any pay for them[25]. He reported that the Derby Committee continued to receive many complaints against the Bolsover garrison, and that Mr Wolley had been arrested for requisitioning provisions without warrant. Wolley later described his actions as buying cattle and other provisions from the local people on credit, which he agreed alienated them, but which he said were forced on him by the garrison's lack of supplies[26].

Committee work

John Mundy made his first visit to the Committee in January 1645. At that time it had not yet changed much from 1643, when Sanders and Mellor had complained that "they had not the liberty of committee men"[27]. Mundy noted that Gell "ordered business himself", and thought at first that there was little service he could carry out there[28]. There was open hostility between Gell and the new members and John Wigley, writing on 5th March 1645 to his brother-in-law, John Gell the younger, "at Mr Packers house neare Westminster", expressed his worry at the situation - "I shall longe to heare what is done conserning our differences, and in the meane time pray to him who is only able to unite all harts and compose all our dissentions which, as in this soe in many other Counties, much advanceth the Cavelieres cause"[29].

Wigley had reason to be worried. In April Ralph Clarke and other Committee members went to to press their case against Gell with Parliament. Their party included John Withers, who was a Parliamentary solicitor for sequestrations in Derbyshire and, to Gell's disgust, Withers used his expertise to help draw up the Committee's papers for presentation to Parliament and to help Sanders with his defence[30]. Gell accused the new men of disrupting the work of the Committee. They were blamed for a failure to send income from the sequestered ironworks at Staveley and Wingerworth up to London, in May 1645 - "by reason of an Additional Committee for this County, who have not only questioned & opposed many of our former orders, but upon the receipt of your Honours letter, were soe averse, that they would not give care to it when it was read, nor meete to returne your Honour an answere, before theire goeing to London to Petition against our proceedings"[31].

Worse was to follow. Further candidates for the Committee were lobbying Parliament. Gell did what he could to discredit them, sending objections to particular nominees via Sir John Curzon and writing to the Speaker on the 15th April 1645[32]. The objections were that some had gone over to the enemy, some had fled at the enemy's approach and that none had served the cause faithfully from the outset as he and the original Committee had. Gell was explicit about his fears - that the new men would be "in such a nomber as quite to over vote those that have faithfully served you at all tymes".He pointed out that he and his colleagues had been declared traitors by the King "when those that now are so busie secured both theyre persons and estates from danger", valid points since unlike Gell and Gresley, who had lost a great deal, most of the new men did well out of the war. Gell exploded in frustration and fury at the subversion of his Committee - "he would not be thus used by a company of factious fellows soe long as hee was a souldier and had a sword in his hand"[33]. He could already be outvoted, and his position was further weakened when the new Committee secured the appointment of the extra members[34].

Gell's fears of being overwhelmed by opponents were realised. The new men were "Francis Mundy esq, and William Wolley esq, both of the commission of the peace, Robert Wilmott esq, a learned barrister, Edward Pegg, gent, an honest and able attorney at law, whose parts and breeding enable them to assist in the public service, more than ordinarily, Gervase Bennitt and John Dalton, two honest men and able burgesses of Derby, whose presence may help to clear and preserve the immunities of the borough". Francis Mundy was the father of John. Robert Wilmot had refused to pay a tax assessment of £1000 and Gell had been ordered by Parliament in August 1644 to sequestrate his estate[35]. He was a natural enemy. Bennett, who was to became mayor of Derby later in the year, was strongly opposed to Gell, and Dalton, as we have seen, had his own account to settle. Wolley was the Lieutenant-Colonel of the Bolsover garrison. Two other new members of the anti-Gell faction on the Committee were Robert Eyre of Highlow and Gell's old enemy Randle Ashenhurst. The Gell party was augmented by one. This was Henry Buxton, the comissary, who was nominated by Sir John Curzon[36]. Buxton and Henry Wigfall were both prisoners of the Newark garrison at the time Gell wrote to the Speaker in April, and Gell had written to the commander there[37] asking him to allow Buxton enough liberty to come to Derby to witness on Gell's behalf. The same letter includes an attempt to negotiate exchanges for Wigfall and Edward Charlton, another new Committee man. Buxton laboured under the accusation, levelled, according to Sanders, by Gell himself, of "being familiar with a whore and for disclosing to her secrets of the Committee"[38], but he proved a faithful ally during the difficult last year of the war and afterwards.

The Excise men

There is a picture of Gell's indulgence to his troops and of his high-handedness towards any rival authority to his own in an incident which took place in 1645, involving two excise-men, John Fatchett and John James. Acting under a Parliamentary ordinance of the 22nd July 1643, which had imposed an excise duty on tobacco, wine, beer and other products to raise money for the army's pay, the two sub-commissioners arrived in Derby in May to collect the duty from the townspeople[39]. They were armed with a letter from the Speaker and the origin of their visit lay in the petition which the Committee had sent to Parliament asking for a grant of £2000 to pay the troops. On the 22nd April 1645 Parliament had ordered that £1000 be paid from Excise receipts toward the Derbyshire force's pay[40], an order soon afterwards modified because, since the money was required urgently, it had been raised by loans. These were to be repaid by the Excise, with interest added[41].

Parliament had been made well aware by 1645 that its excise was universally hated, and the Speaker's letter instructed Gell, as Governor of the town, to help the officers to collect the money[42]. Gell's response was both disingenuous and typically sardonic. He told them that far from being able to help them he needed protection himself. When a crowd of townsfolk demonstrated against the tax-men, led by a small corps of female drummers, Gell was again asked for help. He avoided taking any action against the demonstrators, who included some of the wives and children of his soldiers, by his remark about not meddling with women unless they were handsome. When one of the commissioners' assistants was assaulted by an officer in Gell's regiment, he was asked to punish the assailant. At first he stalled by refusing to act without proof. When, however he was told that eyewitnesses were ready to testify he simply turned on his heel and went in to dinner.

While Clarke and the others were in London the Committee wrote to the Speaker on the 13th May 1645, after conferring with the excise men[43]. The letter was clearly written by Gell himself. The Committee felt that they should not have to pay the excise in view of their services to Parliament. They felt that no county had been "so cruelly tyranised" by royalist troops as Derbyshire had, and pointed out that though the enemy garrisons in the county had now been removed, there were several very close to the county boundary which maintained themselves by requisitioning in Derbyshire. They had themselves raised money for the New Model Army and the Derbyshire soldiers were being paid only 2/7d a week, "scarse enough to buy them bread, besides we are much indebted to them for service donne, when the Caviliers possessed in a manner al the countie". They had provided free quarter for the soldiers and had raised several sums for them, but the soldiers could see that the price of food and other supplies was rising while their pay remained the same. The Committee forcast trouble if the excise was added to their burdens.

If Gell was to retain the support of both the population and his own troops he could not be seen to cooperate with the excise men. The remarks in the Committee's letter about the service done by the soldiers and their deserving better pay expressed his own attitude to them and his success in maintaining control of a potentially mutinous regiment was achieved by a combination of discipline and indulgence. He demonstrated the discipline by his treatment of a soldier, Edward Barrow, who had spent four days helping the commissioners. The soldier was ordered by Sir George Gresley to report to Gell. Gell, having kept him waiting for some hours, simply said "Mr Barrow, are you turned excise?", and dismissed him. However, Barrow was kept on guard duty for the whole of the following night and, at 4 o'clock in the morning, was taken to the market square and chained to the bull ring there. This was on the orders of the same mutinous Captain-Lieutenant Drinkwater whom Gell so indulged that year and Drinkwater told Barrow that he could not be released without permission from Gell himself. Barrow spent eleven hours in chains and was stoned by some of the demonstrating mob while nearby, at the market cross, other defaulters were beaten. Barrow's punishment for stepping out of line was presumably intended to warn off any other potential supporters of the commissioners and would also gratify the majority of the troops and townspeople who were hostile to them

CHAPTER 9

The last phase

Missing at Naseby

While the threat from the north had been removed by Marston Moor, the garrisons to the east, west and south remained to harrass the Derbyshire force. It was during one such operation by the Newark garrison that Henry Wigfall and Henry Buxton were taken prisoner. Early in 1645 they and the rest of the Committee, escorted by one hundred and twenty cavalry, were in Wirksworth collecting taxes when the Newark troops mounted a night raid by two hundred and fifty cavalry. The Committee and their were escort were captured and taken back to Newark, along with £1,000 which they had collected[1]. There was one committee man who got away. This was John Wigley who, in his letter of the 5th March to his brother-in-law, described how the royalists marched through the night and surprised the garrison before sun-rise[2]. The Committee and the soldiers were roused out of their beds, while he was put to the indignity of escaping through a back door of his lodging.

Derby braced itself against a greater danger when the King's army moved as far north as Tutbury, threatening the garrison at Barton. This still consisted of troops led by Captains Barton and Greenwood, who sent urgent requests to Gell for powder and ammunition, which was not forthcoming[3]. The reason was probably that Gell had none to spare and no money to buy any. The King moved next against Leicester, sacking the town with the massacre of many of its garrison and, as part of a general concentration of Parliamentary troops to meet the danger, Gell withdrew the garrison from Barton. This was later held against him by Captain Barton, who claimed that the local villagers begged for the troops to be returned to defend them against the Tutbury garrison, which was now free to resume its marauding expeditions in the surrounding villages. After his success at Leicester the King turned south again and, although outnumbered two to one, engaged the New Model army at Naseby on 14th June and was heavily defeated.

Gell had been ordered to follow the King but in fact missed this decisive battle. Exactly why is difficult to determine. He had never before shown any tendency to avoid a fight and had been instructed by Fairfax to take command of the combined cavalry and dragoons of

Cheshire, Staffordshire, Nottinghamshire and Derbyshire at Nottingham and pursue the King. Gell claimed that this force took a fortnight to assemble and that by the time he moved off the King had already been defeated at Naseby[4]. Fairfax himself, in a letter to Sanders, talked of Gell's "unwillingness presented, but of disobedience cannot say"[5]. Although Gell was soon to be in favour of making peace with the King it seems unlikely that in 1645, with the war still undecided, he held back for political reasons. The answer may lie in the time which he claimed to have taken in assembling his troops at Nottingham. By the middle of 1645 he no longer had complete control of the either the committee or the regiment as the Sanders faction opposed him in both. Sanders's company was committed to him rather than to Gell and their discontent was aggravated by the usual difficulty in paying and feeding them.

The Scottish incident

The greatest of the indignities which Gell inflicted on Ralph Clarke, his biggest enemy on the Committee, came from an incident which took place during Gell's absence in June, before and after Naseby. A detachment of troops from the Earl of Leven's Scottish army in Yorkshire, under the command of a Colonel Stockdale, had moved into Derbyshire and were recruiting and requisitioning horses around Chesterfield. The committee, instead of complaining to Leven about the actions of these allies, took independent action against them. Stockdale was attacked and driven off, losing horses and arms in the process. Leven furiously complained to Gell[6], and Stockdale rode over to Derby in September with a troop of cavalry to demand satisfaction. He delivered a letter from Leven asking the Committee to make reparation, because "he had suffered a little before about Chesterfield" or to hand over Clarke and the two officers responsible for the attack, as Gell had said they should be "forthcoming to justice"[7].

Gell was not at the meeting and, after waiting until dark, the Committee sent Henry Buxton to Gell's quarters asking him to attend early in the morning. On receiving this letter Gell sent Buxton to ask Stockdale to come and see him. Stockdale called at Gell's quarters in the early evening and after half an hour's conversation the two men came out into the street together. Gell called for musketeers from the guard and he and Stockdale went to Clarke's house, where Gell shouted to him from the street. Clarke, who was preparing for bed, asked who was calling and Gell answered "A friend. I must needs speak with you". When Clarke came out Gell told him "I have received order from my Lord Leven to send you to him by this gentleman". Clarke, highly reluctant to trust himself to Stockdale, was marched through the dark streets by the Derby soldiers to Stockdale's quarters, where he was abused by the Scottish soldiers. He was refused permission to change his boots and get some money and was provided with a horse by Mundy, who had met Buxton on his way to Stockdale's quarters and had stayed to see what happened. For safety Clarke asked to be accompanied by the excise-man John Fatchett and one of Fatchett's collectors, Abraham Shockley. Both had been visiting Stockdale at the time of Clarke's arrest. Gell allowed this at first but changed his mind about Shockley just as the party was leaving the town.

Fatchett and Clarke, escorted by the Scottish troops, had gone about a quarter of a mile when they were met by Stockdale. Although Fatchett had been having supper with him a few hours earlier, Stockdale's demeanour had changed. He asked Fatchett how he dared leave Derby without Gell's consent, saying that he had offered Gell the greatest affront possible - "he could find it in his hart to tye [Fatchett] neck and heeles together and send him back to Sr John". Fatchett was allowed to stay with them as far as Duffield, where Stockdale stopped at an alehouse, took Fatchett's horse and sword "& badd him shifte for himselfe"[8].

In the morning Gell was asked by a committee member why he had handed Clarke over. His reply was that he was under the command of the Scottish general himself and would "rather venture Mr Clarke's neck than his owne"[9]. Unsurprisingly, Sanders wrote that the attack on the Scots had been ordered by Gell himself [10], in spite of the fact that it occurred during his absence and was highly embarrassing to him. Gell does seem to have been in danger, however, and Thomas Gell was later to claim that it was he who had saved his brother from being taken by Stockdale - "you know that it was onely my selfe that kept you from beinge sent a hostage to the Scots"[11]. In a letter to the Speaker dated the 4th October 1645 Gell explained that he had sent Clarke because he assumed that, being a civilian, he would not be harmed, and that he would be able to explain everything to Leven[12]. He ended with an apology - "If I have offended the House in this business, I am heartily sorry and beg pardon".

More mutiny

Mutiny by the troops of both sides was a common occurrence, almost always due to failure to pay the soldiers' wages. Gell constantly stressed, both to Parliament and to the Derby Committee, that he was not getting the money he needed to maintain the loyalty of his men. In fact he managed to keep his regiment intact, but there were many crises in 1645. The soldiers took their cue from their commanders, Sanders's men blaming Gell for their lack of pay, while Gell's own company blamed the Committee men. Rowland Moorewood, was told by some soldiers in July that if he did not pay them they would "serve him as the Protestants were served in Ireland. They would cut his throat [and they] threwe stones at [him]". Moorewood told Gell of this, without result. At the end of the month three or four of Gell's troops came into a sitting of the committee of accounts and one of them asked for "that rogue Clarke". This soldier accused Clarke of being the cause of their not being paid and "swore if hee had him there (laying his hand on his sword) hee would thrust him through"[13]. A third committee man to be harassed by the troops was John Mundy. He was stopped at the door of the committee room by one of Gell's men, who took Mundy by the arm, with his sword in his other hand and told him that he "would have money of him or els hee would have his harts-blood"[14]. On 20th July Ralph Clarke was walking through Allhallowes churchyard on his way back home from a committee meeting when he was surrounded by a large group of soldiers who jostled and manhandled him, demanding payment of their wages[15].

The most serious of the Derby mutinies took place in August, while Gell was at Wingfield Manor. About two hundred of Sir John's company marched through Derby, with drums beating and "matches lit", ie with muskets ready for firing. After unsuccessful negotiations with some of the Committee, who promised to raise some money, and after ransacking Sir Samuel Sleigh's chamber[16], the men marched out to Duffield, fully armed. Gell must have been told of this affair very quickly, and have successfully pacified the soldiers, as he marched back into Derby at their head the following day with Mollanus bringing up the rear. Instead of being punished for their mutiny the soldiers were rewarded with an issue of free beer for returning to their colours[17]. The postcript to Sleigh's story came the Friday after the mutiny, when Gell brought an order to the committee, already signed by himself and others, levying £400 or £500 on the townsmen of Derby. Gell told Sleigh that if he did not sign it "the souldiers will be at your chamber againe". Faced with this threat Sleigh signed. The problem persisted, however, and Gell told Clarke in October that if they "might dispose of the monies hee durst undertake there would bee no mutinies"[18].

Sanders persists

After the battle of Naseby, Fairfax ordered Gell to remain north of Leicester until the royalist garrison there was subdued and then dismissed him. Later in the month, in a confusion which was typical of this war, the Derby garrison received conflicting orders from Fairfax and the Committee of Both Kingdoms[19]. Fairfax instructed Sanders to take the cavalry to Gloucester. While the Committee at Derby wrote to Fairfax for confirmation of this order a second came from the Committee of Both Kingdoms addressed to Gell, instructing him to take his brigade to Worcester to join the Scottish army there. The disaffection among the cavalry officers errupted on the 5th July, when Gell was leading the regiment out toward Worcester. According to Sanders, who had gone to Gloucester, his troops heard that he was on his way back to Derby and immediately deserted Gell[20]. Gell's explanation was that they refused to go beyond Sinfin Moor because there was no money to pay them[21]. Whatever the reason the troops returned to Derby where they were not allowed to enter the town. The Derby Committee wrote to Sanders, asking him to collect these soldiers together as they were "scattered about in the country, to the great damage and oppression thereof"[22]. Gell's depleted expedition proved abortive and he too returned[23]. By the 8th July Sanders, who had been instructed to continue serving under Gell, had collected all nine troops of his company. He wrote to the Committee of Both Kingdoms - "You have commanded me to obey Sir John Gell as my colonel. I conceive it hard that I and those honest valiant captains should be engaged to observe the result of one mans absolute will while others have their commands from Parliament"[24]. If matters from then onward were to be properly conducted by a council, he was prepared to serve under Gell, "but if I am subjected to his sole will, I shall lay down my commission and sit down in some angle, spending the rest of my days in contemplation and devotion". The threat of resignation remained Sanders's favourite ploy. At the same time he wrote to a contact asking him to intercede with Fairfax and Cromwell to make him sole commander of the cavalry. He described quarrels among the Derbyshire regiment, where his own soldiers were wearing Fairfax's colours and Gell's own troops, wearing Gell's colours, were abusing them and threatening to pull the Fairfax colours out of their hats[25]. In a letter dated the 14th July 1645 Gell reminded Sanders about the order from the Committee of Both Kingdoms instructing him to obey him as his Colonel[26] - "I therefore command you to come to Derby and bring your own troop, Capt Swetnams, Capt Bartons, Capt Watsons and Capt Sleighs".

Fighting in the West

Whatever the reason for his failure to reach Naseby, Gell continued to fight during the rest of 1645. Barton was reoccupied and in August troops from there took part in harrying the king's army. The King moved north after Naseby, reaching Lichfield on the 10th August, Tutbury on the 12th and Ashbourne on the 13th[27]. During the royal army's march from Tutbury to Ashbourne Sanders attacked its rear near Barton and on the 14th Gell sent him instructions - "I desire you with the regemente to follow in the reare & to take all advantages that may be, but with this causion, that the regement be not too farr engaged ... when the enemie is to goe or passe thorrow any streete place or lane, then you may ingage so many as you thinke fitt for you to fall on with our horse, and doe your worke quickly. You had better to spare sum of Capt Greenewoods horse & send for the dragoons to make good your retreate for by this observation you will expecte a party to be sente against you speatially to drive you awaie. Take heede of ambuscadoes ... I pray you send to the Stafford horse to join with you. I have directed one troope to you that did com oute of Staffordsheare"[28]. This was sound and helpful advice, but probably the kind of detailed supervision that Sanders hated. However, he continued to follow the King and Gell reported to the Speaker on the 15th that a hundred of the Derbyshire cavalry, "more valient than discreet", had charged five hundred of the enemy[29]. Sanders had one killed and ten taken prisoner, against twenty royalists killed and sixteen captured.

Also during August the Barton garrison successfully raided Tutbury, after Gell sent reinforcements[30]. Greenwood and another cavalry captain, Villiers, took a hundred horsemen and, dismounted, made their way through Tutbury and captured the guardhouse. They came away with prisoners and about a hundred and twenty horses. In September Gell wrote to Sanders recalling Villiers's and a second troop to Derby and noting that "Mr Barton, your supposed captain" had quit the county[31]. Barton had made his long expected transfer to Fairfax's army, where he continued to press Sanders's case for a commission. Gell expected further defections and repeated his order to Sanders to send Villiers' troop to Derby, and "in case they do mutiny and will not return to spare their country, you are to imprison some of the chief, whereof Cornet Allen is one"[32].

Tutbury failure

At the beginning of September Gell was asked by the Staffordshire force to join in another attack on the garrison at Tutbury. By his own account he responded by sending Thomas Gell with four hundred infantry[33]. However he had been instructed by the Committee of Both Kingdoms to hold five hundred infantry ready to march to join Colonel-General Sydenham Poyntz, who had recently been appointed commander-in-chief of the forces of the Northern Association[34] in a blockade of Newark. According to Gell's account the Derbyshire and Staffordshire contingents met a mile from Tutbury and considered the situation. They decided that as any seige of the castle would take at least a month, during which time the Derbyshire force might be recalled to comply with the Parliamentary order, the operation should be abandoned. On the face of it this was a sensible decision. However it provided more material for the plotting going on at Derby, which this time involved Thomas Gell.

According to Sir Samuel Sleigh, Sanders had been sent to the rendezvous, accompanied by himself and Thomas Gell[35]. The Staffordshire force had withdrawn unilaterally when they heard that the Derbyshire troops were on standby, leaving Sanders and his men "to the fury of the enemy", who had been alerted by the troop movements. In spite of the obvious military reasons for the withdrawal Sanders branded this aborted operation as disgraceful and demanded to know why the orders had been changed. Gell was scornful - "What, do you prate?", and threatened to knock him over the head[36]. Sanders claimed that Thomas Gell had agreed with him that the return from Tutbury was a shameful desertion.

He went on to say that Thomas had told him that his brother was unworthy to command the regiment and had only kept his position through the efforts of Curzon and himself. Sleigh claimed that, after this episode, Thomas said that if the militia continued under his brother's control the country would be ruined and proposed that he and Sleigh should take a proposal to Parliament that the regiment should be run by a sub-committee of the county Committee. This plan was abandoned when news was received of the king's army approaching Lichfield. However, Nathaniel

Hallowes drafted an outline in a letter to Curzon, which Sleigh did not expect Curzon to accept, though Thomas was sanguine. Sanders's, Sleigh's and other stories of Thomas's disenchantment with his brother may be true. He was later to reveal that the constant loyalty he showed to Sir John concealed a growing resentment at his elder brother's complacent reliance on his support. The conflicting accounts of this episode, and Gell's apparent failure to communicate fully with his senior officers, suggest that the hostility between Gell and Sanders was damaging the effectiveness of the regiment. It was still, however, to play a valuable part in the last moves in the war.

The King's last stand

Six days after the withdrawal of Gell's troops from Tutbury the King's army appeared there[37]. The King had moved as far north as Doncaster before returning to Oxford and then marching west in an attempt to raise the seige of Chester. He had been defeated near there at Rowton Heath on the 24th September. He had then moved across the Midlands to Lichfield and repeated the march north through Tutbury and Ashbourne, through the Peak to Doncaster and from there joined the garrison at Newark. In this hazardous march the royal army was shadowed by Poyntz and, as it marched north from Tutbury, Gell's cavalry, presumably commanded by Sanders in his military role, again attacked its rear at Ashbourne, taking a Major and twenty-five others prisoner. On the 4th October the King reached Newark and reorganised the garrison.

On the same day Gell wrote to Sanders, informing him of a Parliamentary order to send the whole of the cavalry, with the exception of the Barton garrison, to join Poyntz, who was on his way to blockade Newark[38]. These troops however were still unpaid and were only persuaded to march to Nottinghamshire by promises that the Committee would send some money. Word came to them that Gell had prevented this money from being sent to them and the men mutinied. According to their commander, Captain Swetnam, Gell first asked to know the names of the ringleaders and threatened to try the officers for their lives if they did not tell him[39]. However, once he had the names of the mutineers Gell looked at them and said that for all he knew they were the state's best servants. When Swetnam imprisoned one of the ringleaders Gell released him, gave him a horse from Swetnam's company and protected him, saying that any mutineers against Swetnam were welcome to join his company.

Within a week the order to march east was altered, and the cavalry were sent off to rejoin the seige of Chester - on the 14th October 1645 Gell wrote to the Speaker, William Lenthall, "According to your command I gave order for my horse to march to Chester, and they went yesterday. I have only reserved three troops for defence of this county, in regard many of the King's horse quarter near our country"[40].

The final victory

Gell was involved in severe fighting in Nottinghamshire and the Vale of Belvoir in October and November 1645 and joined with a strong Parliamentary force in attacking Welbeck. The recently-installed Parliamentary garrison there had been taken by surprise by Colonel Freschville, who had justified Gell's suspicion of his promises to Lord Fairfax by changing sides again. Molanus was sent to besiege Chatsworth, which had been taken by Colonel Shallcross and garrisoned with men from Welbeck which, after its recapture by the royalists, had been held by men from the King's army at Newark. This siege ended when news came of the taking of Welbeck by General Poyntz, and Shallcross surrendered. Poyntz had taken the garrisons at Shelford and Wiverton, as well as Welbeck, and stormed Belvoir Castle on 17th November. Gell's men took part in this assault and lost eleven killed and twenty-seven wounded. The defenders fled into the castle, which surrendered in February 1646. Gell's men remained part of Poyntz's army which, with the help of Leven's Scots, beseiged the King in Newark The Derbyshire troops took part in much hard fighting there and in other actions in the last months of the war. On New Year's Day 1646, Molanus distinguished himself by remaining firm in a royalist attack on Poyntz's camp at Stoke, when most of the Parliamentary horse fled. The Derbyshire infantry fought a three-hour battle, losing four men killed and thirty wounded, including the Captain-Lieutenant Drinkwater who chained Edward Barrow to Derby bull-ring. The royalists fled, having lost seventy-two men killed or wounded. This exploit earned Molanus a public commendation from Poyntz on the battlefield[41]. In April Gell finally accomplished one task which had beaten him throughout the war. On 30th March he and Brereton returned to Tutbury, which was surrendered by its commander, Gell's old opponent Sir Andrew Kniveton, on the 20th April. Remembering Gilbert Kniveton's plunder of Hopton Hall at the beginning of the war, this final victory over his brother must have been a sweet one.

CHAPTER 10

A bitter victory

The record

At a time when desertions, caused by low pay and poor provision, were common in both Parliamentary and royalist armies, Gell had held together a force which had repeatedly fought off attempts by the King's forces to occupy Derbyshire, thereby saving the county from the devastation which a major battle would have brought. If he had not held Derby for Parliament the strong royalist garrison at Newark would undoubtedly have taken Nottingham and the King's armies would have had liberty of movement through the centre of the country. With energy and forcefulness he had used the Parliamentary Committee to control the county and ensure that enough money was raised from those who could pay to enable him to continue his war. The elimination of the royalist garrisons in the north of the county in 1644, the fall of Newark and the capture of Tutbury in 1646, brought peace to the county and Gell, as he was frequently, and sometimes plaintively to remind Parliament, had been the main instrument in keeping Derbyshire on the Parliamentary side.

Gell had undoubtedly been his usual rough self in money raising. He had also been high-handed and dictatorial in Derby. Percival Willoughby's opinion of his brother-in-law seems to have been changed by Gell's role in the Civil War. He was surgeon to the garrison and therefore in a position to observe the behaviour of Gell's soldiers[1]. In 1647 he wrote of "the unfortunate days when Sir John Gell, Baronet" was "Colonell of Derby" and his troops roamed the town, peeping through windows at night and intimidating juries. He quoted a case in which a jury acquitted a woman of infanticide because the soldiers pitied her. They had discovered the crime because "it was then the custome of Derby souldiers to peep in the night through windows, when they espied lights"[2].

There is also no doubt that Gell's troops were given considerable license in enforcing the Derby committee's tax demands. The letter from Henry Coke was typical. He had had troops compulsorily quartered on him from the beginning of the war and was being asked to pay more than his income. A surviving page from a letter which, from internal evidence, was addressed to Thomas Gell, from the owner of an iron foundry in the Chesterfield area, demonstrated what some of the gentry of the county contributed to the war[3]. £30 had been demanded from the writer "When Sr John Gell came first into Derbyshire with his forces". This was more than he could pay and Captain Stafford had been instructed to reduce the sum to £10. However Captains Stafford and Vermuyden had later ordered him to produce two iron cannon, which he had done, at a cost of £13-13-1d. He had paid £52-5-8d to maintain a horse in Captain Ashenhurst's troop and a further £20-18-9d to Captain Stafford, for which he had receipts. He had sent two men and horses to Bawtry to help guard arms sent from Hull, costing him 12/6d, and had paid for one of the muskets. He had also sent men on five occasions to Chesterfield and Sheffield and had had two of his men in the attack on Lord Deincourt's house and in a battle with the Earl of Newcastle's army. During the brief period when Newcastle had been in control of the north of the county he had been instructed to assess his parish for tax and had saved it £140 by delaying. For all this service he had been repaid only £6.

However, Gell's fall from grace and subsequent exile and tribulations in London were the result not of popular resentment but of a combination of politics and personal enmity. Parliament was bombarded with petitions protesting at Gell's conduct of the war, and Sanders presented the Commons Committee for Examinations with a long list of articles for his impeachment.

On the defensive

Sir John and Thomas vigorously defended themselves against charges that they had used the war to enrich themselves. In a printed pamphlet published in February 1645 Gell described the allegations and claimed that they had been proved false in accounts just presented at Derby [4]. His recruiting expedition to Hull and his subsequent actions had all been at his own expense - "When I went first to Hull with my brother, I went at my own charge, and raised my men without any penny of advance money. Since that time and in this service, I have sold my stock, laid out my whole revenue, which at that time was fifteene hundred pounds a year, borrowed money of my brother and others, married my only sonne, received part of his portion, all of which I have spent in maintenance of the Parliaments cause". He also reminded his critics that while he was about Parliament's business supporters of the king had plundered Hopton Hall. There is no reason to doubt that Gell had indeed spent his own fortune. At the beginning of the war he could have had no resources but his own and his protracted campaign to get redress from Parliament after the war is evidence.

The investigations - Sir John

Gell's enemies on the Derby Committee and in Sanders's company had combined to present the petition mentioned by Withers when he so enraged Sir John[5]. They asked that Gell, his brother and Molanus be called to answer to Parliament for their misdeeds, that Gell's and Molanus's "rough soldiers" be removed from Derby and given some other service and that the government of the town be transferred to Sir George Gresley and four others - "a committee of honest and able persons only, that they may see the desires of their souls in the advancement of justice, piety, lawful liberty and safety". On the 28th October 1645 Parliament gave Gell a month's notice to appear before the Committee to answer the charges against him, and Sanders, Swetnam and Greenwood a similar time to appear to testify[6]. The anti-Gell campaign was going well and at the beginning of November 1645 Bennett sent Sanders, serving with Brereton at the seige of Chester, a copy of a letter he had received from Mundy, Hallowes and Clarke[7]. They reported that the petition had been delivered, accompanied by a speech by Sir Samuel Sleigh, and had been well received. Bennett enclosed a copy of the indictment. Bennett, Coke, Sleigh and Clarke wrote again to Sanders on the 5th November, enclosing the Parliamentary orders for him and the others to appear, and telling him to get a pass from Brereton[8]. Careful organisation is revealed by the note that "Capt Hope and Capt Watson are not summoned because all cannot be spared at once", and the conspirators told Sanders "we go towards London this day sennight [a week]". Brereton issued Sanders with his pass on 10th November, noting that his regiment was left in the hands of Capt Watson, and that he was expected to return quickly - there was still a war on[9]. Beginning on the 5th December 1645, the Committee for Examinations heard a sucession of Gell's accusers, including the military men Sanders, Cochett, Swetnam, Barton and Greenwood, councillors Youle, Dalton and Dunnage, his enemies on the committee, Clarke, Mundie and Moorewood, and the excise-man Fatchett and sequestration solicitor Withers[10]. For many of its meetings the committee included Sir John Curzon and the former Derbyshire treasurer Nathaniel Hallowes. The allegations of Gell's dictatorial rule in Derby were damaging to him - among many similar outbursts he was quoted as wishing, with Molanus present, that "the devil cutt the throats of the new committee". However, the financial allegations were potentially the most serious and the ones he was at most pains to refute. They were elaborated mainly by Ralph Clarke and John Withers. Clarke had been the driving force behind the Derbyshire committee of accounts. He explained that the Parliamentary Committee of Accounts had asked for Derbyshire's accounts in July, 1645 and that it had been established by September that £50,000 had been received by "severall commisaries, officers and treasurers" employed by Gell. This, plus £2,000 of sequestered money, had not been accounted for. Henry Buxton, "kinsman and servant to Sr John Gell, and noe treasurer" had received £20,000 of which he had paid the treasurer £5000 and disbursed the rest without authority. Clarke further alleged that Gell and Molanus had received £2,200 from the committee's first treasurer, Hallowes, recorded in receipts which they had given and which had been presented to the accounts committee by Hallowes. This sum did not appear in Gell's accounts.

Among the detail of Clarke's evidence was Gell's continued conduct of the lead industry. 564 pigs of lead, marked "D" and belonging to the committee, had been sent from Hull to London. They were worth £1,100 and this money had never appeared in the accounts. 100 fother [approximately 100 tons] of lead, marked "Db" and also belonging to the committee, had been entrusted to a former delinquent and never accounted for. Gell had continued to enjoy the lead taxes in the Wirksworth wapentake, worth £1,000 a year, although he had leased them from a delinquent, Thomas Coke, while his partner in the lease, John Milward of Snitterton, had fought in the king's army. An ore buyer testified that he had paid £201 to Gell for ore which he collected from the barmaster and which he took to be tax ore since that was the only category of ore which barmasters stored. Another had paid £150-£200 for tax ore and had paid lead tax to the barmaster since midsummer 1645.

The Parliamentary authorities were concerned that all income from the property of their opponents which had fallen into Parliamentary hands, including lead, should be used for the war effort, and not for the private use of anyone who could get his hands on it. On the 3rd August 1644 the Derby committee had received an order from the Earl of Manchester forbidding any trading in lead within Derbyshire[11]. His reason was that "there is greate quantities of lead belonging to malignants [royalists] & persons disaffected to the Parliament in the County of Derby & partes adjacent, which leade divers persons under hand buy and convert to their owne private benefitt, by which meanes the state is exceedingly diminished & deceived". Any lead which had been mined was to be sent to Gainsborough, where any Parliamentary supporter could claim what was rightfully his, leaving the lead from mines owned by royalists to be seized by the state. This edict brought an immediate protest from Gell, conscious that he was collecting tax from all the mines in the Wirksworth Wapentake, irrespective of the allegiance of their shareholders, "with so many hartie expressions, which I may looke upon rather as a chardge than an information"[12]. Gell pointed out to Manchester that his order had caused a sudden drop in the price of lead, threatening the livelihoods of the miners[13]. He proposed a meeting to explain the mining industry's point of view. Manchester agreed to meet him[14] and presumably took his point, since the industry continued to flourish. Gell had, in fact, received detailed accounts from his barmasters of the amounts of lead ore produced at each mine, the tax paid and the amounts received from the sale of tax ore. The figures for the Wirksworth liberty have survived intact for the years 1639 to 1645 and there are fragmentary accounts for two further years[15]. They reveal, interestingly, that Molanus, who rented a smelting mill from Gell, managed to keep his business going in the intervals of fighting, buying his ore from Gell. With these accounts it would, therefore, have been easy to declare his income from this source to the assessors. What Ralph Clarke did not know was that the title to this income, and the rest of Gell's estate, had been vested in his eldest son, John, since 1636, a transfer confirmed at John's marriage in 1644. The point about the mineral rights being the property of a delinquent and therefore the property of Parliament was presumably invalid, as in 1651, when Coke's estate was sequestrated, John was able to retain the lease, for which he had paid £1,000 in 1648[16].

Gell was accused of keeping cattle and horses in Horsley Park, seized from the earl of Chesterfield, and of running an ironworks at Wingerworth, the property of the royalist Sir Henry Hunloke. Clarke alleged that the stock which Gell kept at Horsley was under the protection of the enemy garrison at Newark, and Withers reported that when Gell had been questioned about it he had sarcastically said that if they found any horses there he would eat their tails. At Wingerworth Hunloke's "servant, bailiff and agent", Thomas Gladwin, was now employed by Gell, and Clarke alleged that £500 worth of iron had not been accounted for. Gell and his allies on the Committee had in fact, in their letter in May, accused Clarke and his friends themselves of preventing this money being sent to London and had promised to send £1500. In addition to accusing Gell of seizing this royalist property for himself Clarke claimed that he had been lax in collecting sequestrated money for the committee - he had heard Withers ask him to send some of the committee to Scarsdale with the sequestrators to seize "many a £1,000", but Gell had put him off.

In addition to neglecting to declare his own estate for tax, Gell, according to Clarke and Withers, did what he could to protect others from paying it. He seems to have had the same impatient disregard for tax-gatherers as he had for committee men. When Withers asked him in September 1644 who the solicitors for sequestration and commissioners for excise were, Gell told him "they did not desire any such officers among them but rather to keepe them off from being there imployed". When, in the following month, he asked Gell for assistance in his work, he was fobbed off with "he and the committee would considder of it when they mett". Since the committee rarely met, and only then when Gell himself called a meeting, there was no help forthcoming. Withers described land in the Peak on which no tax was paid, including a grange at Youlgreave owned by Sir John Curzon. He gave this evidence on a day when Curzon himself was in attendance. He had discovered that certain of Gell's tenants paid no tax and had been told by the constable that, according to Gell's agent, Spencer, Gell had instructed that his tenants should avoid paying it for as long as they could. The constables of Hopton, Carsington, Wirksworth, Middleton, Ible and Weston Underwood refused to help Captain Swetnam requisition horses from their parishes even though he was armed with a warrant from the committee. These places were in Gell territory and Gell himself told Swetnam he was to leave them alone. Clarke testified that Gell had presented an order to the committee on the 28th January 1645 exempting Wigfall from paying tax for two years. He had refused to sign, though Gresley and others had. This evidence was corroborated by Thomas Curtis, treasurer and high constable of Scarsdale from May 1645. Curtis said that Wigfall paid no tax and owed £30 and that the soldiers collecting the tax always said that they could find nothing on Wigfall's land.

Coupled with the accusation that he and his friends were excused from paying any tax was the accusation that others were over-taxed.

Gell took "the best part of a thousand loads of hay & corne" from John Mundy's father Francis in the winter of 1643-44 and, in contrast to the protection given to Hopton, Carsington and the other Gell villages, those near Derby were made to pay. They were oppressed by "free quartering, hay, provender, other taxes and carriges, more then the neighbouring townes. This was done by warrant from Sr Jo: Gell & others of his kindred that are of the committee". In March 1645 Gell had ordered that absent inhabitants of Chesterfield were to be taxed double, contrary to a Parliamentary Ordinance of January 1644. There was evidence from one of them, however, that although he had been double-taxed, he had never paid it. This witness, Alderman Thomas Foard of Chesterfield, had been told by the assessors that those living out of town must pay double. He testified that Ralph Clarke's assessment had been quadrupled.

Ironically, just as Gell had accused the Bolsover garrison of refusing to muster their troops, thereby making it impossible for him to disburse the right amount of money to pay them, he was himself accused of ignoring an order of the 11th July 1644 to muster the Derby troops each month so that the Committee could distribute their money appropriately. Without muster rolls the Committee had no accurate lists of names and could not therefore distribute the money fairly, but Gell failed to respond to repeated requests to call a general muster. This accusation was linked to the general one that Gell disbursed money unfairly, and the particular one that he starved Sanders's company of money in order to persuade his troops to desert and join Gell's own company. Clarke testified that Gell spent large sums of money on the soldiers without accounting for it, an accusation that is easy to believe, considering the importance which Gell placed on regular payments to the troops. He, Clarke, had refused to approve some of Gell's orders in that respect. Gell always favoured his own troops and when, at Clarke's suggestion, the committee agreed that a sum of money received for convoy duties carried out by the soldiers should be divided equally between all the companies, Gell "went away & said, Do you vote what you will, I will do what I list".

The investigations - Thomas Gell and the election

At the same time as Gell's conduct was being investigated by the Parliamentary Committee for Examinations he was helping his brother in a Parliamentary election which was itself to be investigated by the Committee of Privileges. In September 1645 the split between the Gell and Sanders camps had been formalised by a Parliamentary election, one of the so-called "recruiter" elections held throughout the country to fill seats vacated either by the death of the sitting MP or by his allegiance to the King. The Derby vacancy was in the seat formerly held by the royalist Allestree, and the two factions in the county government put forward their candidates, Thomas Gell and, for the Sanders faction, Captain Robert Mellor. Electoral malpractice was normal then and continued to be so until the introduction of secret ballots, and each side behaved badly. Gell, however, as Governor and Colonel, had the advantage and made the most of it. A request from the recently-established Chatsworth garrison for reinforcement in the face of an enemy advance gave Gell the chance to include Mellor and his company in a force which was hurriedly sent off to help[17]. This not only meant that Mellor was kept busy, but that about sixty men of his company, who claimed to be qualified to vote, were also out of town. Thomas Gell and his company were now the only troops in Derby.

With Mellor out of the way, Gell began electioneering on behalf of his brother. He was accused of intimidating two of his old enemies, the councillors Youle and Dunnage. The two men were ordered out of the town and one, Thomas Youle, was marched out by a squad of musketeers[18]. Youle spent two nights imprisoned in Wingfield Manor on a charge that he had failed to provide a horse when one had been demanded by Gell. John Dunnage also had a similar demand for a horse and also failed to provide one[19]. On being ordered out of town Dunnage asked for time to prepare himself and found himself at the sharp end of Gell's sarcasm - "Sirrah if you bee not fine enough I will send you a couple of barbers". When Dunnage was brave enough to say that he was as good a Parliamentarian as any in Derby, Gell, clearly taking this as a personal insult, demonstrated his easy recourse to violence and his command of furious invective. "Sirrah, sayth Sr John, doe you make comparisons? With that [he] gave [Dunnage] a blowe on his nose that it did bleed, & said Sirrah, if you make comparisons, before God I will cane you. Get you gone, you stinking rascal". Youle lamented "it was hard that hee should bee turned out of towne for not sending a horse when hee had none & that those should stay in towne that had cursed [Youle] for being a meanes of bringing Sr John to the towne", a reference to the welcome which Gell had originally received from the townsmen at the beginning of the war. These events occurred after the writ for the election had been received[20], giving Gell's enemies the chance to accuse him of attempting to help his brother's candidacy by intimidating the opposition, but it is possible that Gell's treatment of Youle and Dunnage can be explained more easily by exasperation than intimidation, since both had opposed the war effort. Horses were urgently needed for the regiment's many commitments at the time and, according to Robert Cooper, one of Gell's soldiers, they had both said that even if they had been able to supply horses they would not have done so, since they refused to be commanded by him[21].

The mayor, Luke Whittington, complained to Gell that he was harrassing Mellor's supporters, asking him why he was sending townsmen away, terrifying the people and preventing a free meeting, which the Council had held to discuss the election[22]. Gell asked him whom he had sent away and Whittington answered "Capt Mellor & divers free men in his company, Mr Youle to prison and [you] came with musketeers to looke for Mr Dunnage to hinder our meeting". Gell was his usual dismissive self - "Sr John did answer, what, can you not have a meeting without Youle and Dunnage, and soe left them and left the musquetieres at Dunnages house". Whittington, whose term ended during these proceedings, was succeeded by Gervase Bennett, successor to Nathaniel Hallowes as treasurer to the committee and another Mellor supporter. Mellor himself returned from Chatsworth and was immediately ordered to join General Poyntz's force blockading the King at Newark.

Just as Gell's exactions on Parliament's behalf were matched by similar activities in royalist-held areas so any electoral misdemeanors were paralleled by those of his opponents. One Gell supporter, a councillor called Thomas Calver, was threatened by Nicholas Wilmot, who was Mellor's brother-in-law and the brother of the committee man Robert Wilmot, whose estate Gell had been ordered to sequestrate. Wilmot reminded Calver that he had influence with Sir Andrew Kniveton, who owed Calver a great deal of money. If Calver voted for Mellor he would use that influence to get Calver's money repaid but if he voted against Mellor and Mellor won the election he and Mellor would "take away all that you ever have away from you". Wilmot revealed his own motivation when Calver referred to Thomas Gell as "an honest gentleman" - "thou goest about to choose one to be burgess that may question mine and my brother's estate"[23]. Calver was also canvassed by John Dunnage. It is no surprise to read that when Calver said he intended to vote for Gell Dunnage cried "Why will you do so wicked a thing? He that stands for Mr Gell stands for the Devil, for he is a worthless man and a man of no trust. They that give their voice for him do damn themselves and their posterity to the Pit of Hell"[24].

The new Mayor, Gervase Bennett, did his best to prevent Thomas's election. According to Lieutenant Robert Ireland, of Thomas Gell's company, "when the precept was made at the crosse and the Mayor, beinge much Captaine Mellors freind, had declared himselfe, and spake to the people for him, the Recorder Mr Gell then offeringe to have spoake somethinge, the Mayor putt his arm to his throate, and forbad him to speake"[25]. This story was supported by Robert Cooper, who added that the Mayor had said that others should do the same as himself, and vote for Mellor "or it would be the worse for them if he were Mayor". There were shouts for both Mellor and Gell, the loudest being for Gell[26].

The voting took place on the 12th November in the town hall and was conducted by the Mayor. It was an open poll, in which each prospective voter gave his name, and the name of the candidate he favoured, to the two tellers, who were Henry Buxton and Roger Allestree, brother of the former royalist MP[27]. Each teller then wrote the voter's name in the appropriate column of his poll book and the two books were compared at the end of the poll. Controversy arose over who was or was not qualified to vote. One opinion was that the qualification was confined to those who had taken the "burgess oath", assuming both duties and privileges of a citizen of Derby, and that their qualification remained even if they lived outside the town. This was the Gell position, supported by a sizeable body of the burgesses themselves. On the Mellor side it was argued that the qualification extended to anyone who had been born in the town or who had served an apprenticeship there[28]. Each side was allowed to take "exception" to any voter presenting himself. According to Buxton there were "divers" exceptions to Mellor voters and the Mayor was asked to exclude them. Bennett insisted that they be included and told the protesters that they could make their exceptions to Parliament, after the poll. At one point Bennett asked the tellers how things were going[29]. When told that Gell at that stage had twenty-nine more votes than Mellor he went over to a window overlooking the market square, waved his hat and shouted "A Mellor, a Mellor". When voting appeared to be proceeding slowly he twice sent the town cryer into the streets to persuade the townsmen to come and vote.

Gell was accused of bringing soldiers into the hall to overawe the voters and, when the soldiers were removed at the insistence of the Mayor, of parading them in the market place, near the Town Hall, while he himself sat at the door noting the names of voters and which candidate they voted for. He was accused of preventing some from voting, for a variety of stated reasons - "vizt Robert Parr who came to give his voice for Capt Mellor but was put by for nonage [being under age]: to whom Sr John said, Sr you show your teeth although you cannot bite"[30]. Buxton and others described Gell as sitting quietly, writing down names as they were called, but not interferring with the poll, which was conducted throughout by the Mayor[31]. According to Robert Cooper, Gell was in fact present because the Mayor had asked him to attend. Gell himself admitted to Parr's exclusion, and his sarcasm, but denied any other influence[32]. In particular "I do expressly denie that I gave anie order for them [the soldiers] to be there in armes nor did I know of it untill the election was pursued".

Lieutenant Ireland was happy to take responsibility[33]. He explained that the reason for Thomas Gell's company being the only one in the town was that the five hundred troops sent to the siege of Newark at the request of Parliament could only be made up from the other three companies then in town, Thomas Gell's being only a hundred and twenty strong. This explanation was supported by Buxton, who said that the decision had been reached by the Committee, meeting in its usual place. He pointed out that since a Parliamentary ordinance of 26th May 1645 troops could not be dispatched without the consent of at least five Committee members. Ireland realised that the election proclamation would be known to the nearby royalist garrisons who might imagine the town's defences would be relaxed during the polling and choose that as a good time to attack. The guard was being mounted by "townsmen" and when he checked he discovered that, with the men away voting, the guard consisted of nothing more than a few boys. He decided "to secure the towne, the losse whereof he was to answer with his life", and called out his company. This was at 1 o'clock, four hours after the poll had opened, and the men assembled in their usual place, near the magazine, and molested no one. He had not told Sir John what he intended to do because, when he went to the town hall to do so, he had been ordered out by the Mayor.

When, some time after the town cryer had made his two expeditions to bring in more voters, it had become apparent that there were no more to come, it was agreed between the Mayor, the candidates and others present that the votes be counted. Thomas

Gell had 170 votes to Mellor's 149, a result greeted with dismay by the Mayor. Gell asked the Mayor to return him as MP and Bennett refused, saying "I know the penalty, am able to pay it, and will returne whom I list"[34]. Mellor was alleged to have told Bennett "It is strange, considering how you have carried the business, that Mr Gell should have one and twenty voyces more than I have, to whome the Mayor replied, if Mr Gells one and twenty had been one and forty more than yours I would not have returned him"[35]. Bennett and Withers, against the protests of Roger Allestree, pruned enough votes from Gell's list to make Mellor the winner, at which point the Mayor cried "A Mellor, a Mellor and fell a laughing and went his wayes"[36].

Parliament then received firstly a writ from the High Sheriff, who for 1645 was Sir George Gresley, declaring Gell returned by the councillors and later an indenture, also from Gresley, declaring Mellor returned by the Mayor and others. By the time that Bennett's indenture was received Thomas Gell had been admitted to Parliament and the matter was referred to the Committee of Privileges, who met in November 1646[37]. Both sides gathered their witnesses and submitted written evidence. Thomas Gell's case was organised in Derby by his servant, who wrote "To his honoured master Thomas Gell Esq at Sr John Curzons chamber in Caesars Buildings in the Temple Jury Yard" on 8th February 1646, giving names of witnesses prepared to testify and noting that he had given them £1 each to cover their expenses in travelling to London[38]. He was confident that the election "will bee proved very fayre on your part and as foul on theires". The Committee received written evidence from a group of fourteen councillors that Bennett's indenture was an invalid document, sent without their approval[39], and from a group of twenty that Bennett had approved Mellor voters who were not eligible and excluded Gell voters who were[40]. There was a petition from Mellor alleging that Sir John had intimidated voters and that there had been a conspiracy between him and Gresley to return Thomas Gell, ignoring the result of the vote, which was in his favour[41]. He asked that Sir John and Gresley be examined and punished. The Committee decided that it could not consider Sir John's alleged misdeeds, since these were being examined by the Committee for Examinations, that there were no allegations against Thomas Gell and that, since Gell had been admitted to Parliament the result should stand. The case was still continuing in June 1647, when Thomas Gell's servant wrote to his master to tell him that

Robert Cowper and William Cockayne had been "tampered with" but were nevertheless willing to come with him to London to testify again[42].

Thomas Gell revolts

In February 1646 Gell received a letter from Thomas in which his brother finally gave vent to what was clearly an accumulation of resentment[43]. The letter was provoked by John Gell's failure to reply to a letter from Thomas asking him to sign "a paper", which seems to have been a financial one, since Thomas had hardly enough money to buy clothes and food. He was unable to raise money from his own estate because "I have joyned my busines with yours onely for your advantage and to help forwards yours, and soe I have neclected my owne being of lesse valew". He had been surviving by making use of the money he had accumulated as Receiver of the Honour of Tutbury and "must now pay in the kings money, witch I cannot doe without". In fact he was about to get a letter from the Committee of Revenue demanding that he surrender this money[44] and remained in trouble over it for several years - in 1649 Parliament ordered the Committee of Revenue to take action against him because he had failed to clear a debt of £737 in 1646 and by Lady Day 1648 owed the crippling sum of £6000[45]. He reported a conversation with their half-brother Sir John Curzon, in which Curzon had said that he would be ashamed to have made such poor provision for his younger brother as John Gell had done for his - "that poore annuity after your death". This mean provision was unwarranted, and Thomas reminded John of his service to him over the years - "You know how for at least twentie years past I have bin continuallie imployed in your affaires, and that I have solissited all your causes". He listed some of the occasions when his help had been crucial - the struggle with Carrier, the help in John's appointments as JP and Baronet, help when Molanus and others had accused him of treason, help when "a sarjiant at armes waited two dayes together to fetch you a prisoner to London, witch if it had then bin donne you had bin utterly disgrased", and the occasion when he had saved John from being sent as hostage to the Scots.

When he had presented his "paper" for John's authorisation John had accused him of having designs on him, which Thomas thought was "verie discortios dealinge, when your owne heart tells you that I have ever labored all in my power both for your honor and profit, and if my designes had moare prospered the better it had bin for you".

Any stranger would have treated Thomas better if he had done half as much for him as he had done for John. If John refused to sign the paper Thomas threatened that he would break with him, which would be the worse for him - "all your enimies are mine and for your sake, and it will be noe wisdome in me to continue there malice to me, without anie satisfaction, when as I can have there love with my arrears if I desert". Curzon had lost his friends in Parliament "in stickinge to you" and because of this had failed in an effort to get soldiers removed from their quarters in his house. Thomas threatened that "if you refuse to grant me my request, then I will make peace with my adversaries, witch I doubt not will be moare to your prejudice than you are aware of, in manie severall respects, both in reviving the old and bringing new trobles upon you, to witch they will be encoraged when they shall know how busines goe betwixt us". The letter must have persuaded Gell that if he wanted to keep Thomas on his side he should do as he was asked since later correspondance shows that the old relationship was restored. Gell summoned his son back to Hopton in May 1646[46] and himself left for London to face his accusers. He was also still determined to fight for compensation for his war losses.

The Sanders paper

There were more complaints in the summer of 1646 and Sanders presented an indictment to the Committee for Examinations - "Articles against Sir John Gell, Baronet, Colonel of a Regiment, Governor of Derby and a Justice of the Peace for the said county"[47]. It was a summary of Gell's alleged high-handed and tyrannical behaviour toward the Committee and others, his financial misconduct, and his unfairness to Parliamentarians and favour to royalists. There were specific allegations that Gell had failed to supply Colonel Ashenhurst and the Bolsover garrison and that he had abandoned Ashenhurst to an enemy attack near Bakewell, the latter presumably a reference to Molanus's late arrival when the Staffordshire troops were defeated at Hartington in November 1643, and Ashenhurst captured. The indictment ends with a general attack on Gell's character. Gell, "besides other scandalous conversations, is a frequent swearer, jeerer and scoffer of religious men and practices, a protector of loose and disolute persons". Gell does indeed seem to have been skilled in the highly coloured invective in fashion at the time. While this seventeenth century abuse often sounds either quaint or exaggerated to twentieth century ears, the offence which it clearly caused to his enemies demonstrates its effectiveness. The large amount of religious material among his papers suggests that his jeering and scoffing was selective, directed, in the fashion of the time, against any whose religion differed from his own brand of Presbyterianism. He is also likely to have had a short way with any whom he considered hypocrites.

Scandal

The mention of "scandalous conversations" and "loose and dissolute persons" echoes Lucy Hutchinson's accusation that he was a "foul adulterer"[48]. Gell's own remark about his not meddling with women unless they were handsome lends some colour to this accusation. It is also supported by the fact that he was with Mrs Colledge, the wife of an absent royalist, when Captain Greenwood came to collect her tax[49]. The fact that Gell violently insisted that she be exempt, in spite of the fact that her husband was on the other side, suggests that his visit was of an amatory rather than a military nature. It was also Greenwood who "came into a roome where Sr John was & a Mrs Gibb who is reputed a scandalous woman". Mrs Gibb was abusive and Gell, said Greenwood, defended her by striking him across the mouth with his cane. Gell probably did take whatever sexual opportunities presented themselves and as squire was in a favoured position. The facts that he married before he was sixteen years old, and was the father of three children by twenty-one, indicate a degree of sexual enthusiasm which had probably not altogether died by 1644, the year in which Greenwood made the first of his ill-timed visits. There is other possible evidence of sexual emancipation in a short Latin poem among his papers celebrating the Roman enthusiasm for the amorous opportunities of the baths[50]. It has an English translation - "The heat of the Bath ... Here Cupid sporting dipt his darts/ With which hee fires loveing hearts" . The poem ends "scarce here breathes a guest/ But feeles loveticklings in his brest". The waters at Bath, to which Gell took regular visits for many years, may have had other attractions to him than purely medicinal ones. His enemies knew that accusations of immorality would strengthen their case with a puritanical Parliament.

Verdict

There is no reason to doubt the abundance of evidence that Gell conducted the finances of the war in a totally unprofessional way, and that the arrival of the new committee men at the end of 1644 saw a tightening of procedures and accounts, all opposed with disgust by Gell. He saw this as a slight on his conduct of the war and a disregard of the sacrifices he had made. He was driven by a mixture of conviction and ambition. Self-enrichment was not his motive for fighting the war and he suffered losses which contrasted favourably with the gains made by some of his enemies, who died rich men. His favouritism over taxation and soldiers' pay was unscrupulous and obviously unfair. However, it was also one of the devices - another was fear - which he had to use to maintain his position and continue to present an effective opposition to the royalist enemy. The way in which he waged the war can only properly be judged in the light of events and procedures elsewhere. His poisoned relations with committee men and officers of his regiment were similar to conflicts on both sides and in all parts of the country. Colonel Hutchinson's quarrels with the Nottingham committee were only the nearest example. Misbehaviour by Gell's troops was also typical. Neither Parliament nor the King were able to create and maintain paid and disciplined armies, and both sides oppressed the farmers and villagers of the areas they controlled. In the south and south-west of the country this indiscipline inspired the rise of a neutralist movement, the Clubmen, who opposed both sides and attempted to stop the war. The New Model Army was the first professional force in the modern sense of a properly paid and firmly controlled army, and with its arrival the Clubmen movement faded. The Derbyshire mutinies again were parallelled throughout the country and were caused by Parliament's inability to pay its soldiers. The Earl of Leven complained in July 1645 that his men had no food and no money and were regarded as enemies by the local people near Worcester. He warned Parliament that his force could not fight without provisions[51].

A failed counter-attack

Gell counter-attacked in the summer of 1646 by accusing five of his tormenters of delinquency and pressing for the sequestration of their estates. The five were Sir Edward Coke, grandson of the former Secretary of State and nephew of the royalist Thomas Coke, Sir Samuel Sleigh, Francis Mundy, Rowland Moorewood and Edward Pegge[52]. Between the 18th and 20th August the committee met in Chesterfield, where the five accused made their defences before two solicitors for the sequestrators. All were acquitted by majorities of ten to four. The Gell faction was without the two brothers, who were in London defending themselves before the Parliamentary committees. Curzon, Gresley, Wigfall and Wigley were outvoted by the five accused and their colleagues Colonel Randle Ashenhurst, John Mundy, Francis Revel, Clarke and Sanders. The defeated minority protested to their colleagues about committee procedures and to the Parliamentary Committee of Compounding about the alleged delinquencies, without success[53].

Post war

Having won his war, Gell had lost the peace, though none of the accusations made against him resulted in prosecution. With the war over, however, Parliament was anxious to return as quickly as possible to a peace footing. Among large-scale demobilisations throughout the country, in June 1646 the Derby garrison was ordered to be dismantled and the troops offered service in Ireland, the infantry to be commanded by Thomas Gell's former Lieutenant, Robert Ireland, newly promoted to Colonel[54]. Gell's Governorship was thereby abolished and Derby returned to the administration of the Mayor, Aldermen and Burgesses. Service in Ireland did not appeal to all the troops, however, and throughout 1647 there were still subversive officers at Derby leading unpaid and mutinous soldiers. Sir John remained in Derbyshire. In June 1647 Thomas Gell's servant, writing to him about his witnesses being tampered with, reported that Sir John had gone to Bath and that Sanders had gone to the army "with a petition from some of the horse of his faction"[55]. In November Henry Buxton, still disbursing money, reported to Thomas on his difficulty in raising £1200 which Thomas had demanded of him, since the Committee had ordered him to pay the soldiers' monthly wages[56]. This £1200 had been awarded to Thomas by Parliament, with instructions that it should be paid from money still held by Buxton[57]. In fact Buxton was short of money and the soldiers, whose officers still included Sanders, Swetnam and Hardstaffe, were angry at the suggestion that their pay be delayed in order to send Thomas his money. In the same letter Buxton promised to pass on to Sir John Gell a demand from Sir John Curzon for reimbursement of his expenses in quartering troops. Six months later Buxton wrote to Thomas to say that he had paid Curzon £60 and would pay the rest as soon as possible [58].

CHAPTER 11

Post-war London

Thomas Gell's letter had painted a vivid picture of his brother surrounded by enemies and it was indeed a time of danger for him. The first threat came from the attacks mounted by his enemies in Derby and, although the Presbyterian Parliament took accusations of corruption and immorality seriously, the charges did not stick and he was not prosecuted. What proved to be a greater danger lay in his attitude to the new political situation. By 1646 the defeat of the royalist armies had led to the expectation that the King, whom Parliament still recognised, would be reinstated with reduced powers and the authority of Parliament recognised. Charles, however, instead of making the best of a bad situation, retreated into an obdurate refusal to accept any infringement of his powers and played off Parliament, the Scots and the new power, the army, hoping to profit from their disagreements. After his capture at Newark the king was taken by the Scottish army to Newcastle. As King of Scotland, as well as England, he hoped that he would be able to go with them when they eventually went home. The Scots, however, while favourable to this, knew that Charles would not be accepted in Scotland unless he signed the Solemn League and Covenant. For the rest of 1646 he was subjected to the harangues of Presbyterian ministers and the earnest pleading of Scottish and English royalist politicians, all hoping to persuade him. Even Queen Henrietta Maria thought that the throne was worth a Covenant. By the end of the year they had all reluctantly accepted that Charles was indeed a man of principle. He would not accept a Presbyterian Church of England. As soon as the Scots had agreed a Parliamentary payment to settle their soldiers' arrears of pay, they moved back over the border and the king was taken under guard to Holmby House, a remote country house in Northamptonshire.

Gell, as a moderate Parliamentarian, hoped for an agreement between the King and his adversaries which would see stability restored and the king on his (reduced) throne. He took the position powerfully expressed by the leading Presbyterian minister Stephen Marshall, two of whose sermons are among his papers[1]. Marshall preached that Parliament's victory was a righteous one, but that it was being imperilled by the winning side's infighting - "it is not long since this poore wretched kingdome was cast into very deepe distress, a heavy yoake lay upon our state, upon our liberties, upon our consciences; we were allmost swallowed up with tyranny and popery ... what admirable things have beene done by our armies especially this time twelve month: he hath (as it were) made the sun stand still, and dryed up the sea, and made the walls of Jericho to fall downe, the Lord hath so brought it about, that if our owne devisions doe not undoe us, it will be well with us". Gell agreed too with Marshall's main theme - that the root of their success was the Solemn League and Covenant, and that they should stick to it.

Army coup

Gell's warming toward the king was accentuated by the increasing bitterness which he felt against Parliament because of his failure to persuade it to recompense the losses he had suffered during the war. However, the King remained obdurate. In June 1647 he was removed from the custody of Parliamentary commissioners at Holmby by the army in a famous coup carried out by a junior officer, Cornet Joyce. The reason for this drastic step was the army's growing antagonism to the Presbyterian faction in Parliament, who had attempted to disband the soldiers without paying their arrears. This foolish move had provoked the army into organising itself as a political force and Parliament was forced into a step-by-step retreat. The more extreme Presbyterians had become so alarmed by the growing power of the army that they were planning to send the king to Scotland, hoping for his return with a Scottish army which would crush the New Model. The army advanced on London and impeached eleven of the Presbyterian MPs for treason. Cromwell, who had been in retirement since the end of the war, was told that unless he returned to lead it, the army would carry on without him. He resumed command as Lieutenant-General under Fairfax. Cromwell and the senior commanders were by then alarmed at the rapid spread of democracy in the army, and hoped to thwart it by negotiating the King's restoration on their terms.

Talks

On the 5th July 1647 Parliament published a broadsheet announcing that it had set up a committee to negotiate with the City of London and the Army Council concerning a settlement with the king[2]. The army set out its own views in a pamphlet published in the same month[3]. This was strongly against the "Scottish-Presbyteriall Partie" in Parliament and reported that the army, having impeached this party's leaders, at first thought it wise to camp near London "till satisfaction were given in all particulars". This intention was conveyed to London causing great alarm. The impeached members tried to have Parliament dissolved, hoping that the Army would be blamed for it. However Parliament agreed to send negotiators and the Army changed its mind and moved further from the capital. There would now be an agreement between king, army and Parliament so that the country would "now be freed from all Scottish Incroachments" and the king be restored "into his throne through Parliament". These hopes collapsed when, in December 1647, the king reached an agreement with the Scots that they would invade England and restore him. This alliance was made in the mistaken belief that the quarrel between the Presbyterians in Parliament and the Independents in the army, and an apparent outbreak of indiscipline in the army, meant that he and the Scottish Presbyterians would be accepted by Parliament. The Scots, for their part, were dismayed by the political power of the army and the religious toleration preached by the Independents. Charles's adventure ended in disaster, with the rout of the Scots by Cromwell and his own capture and imprisonment on the Isle of Wight.

Incognito

Gell moved permanently to London in 1648. That his own position was well-known by then is apparent from the City Spectacles pamphlet published in that year which used the term "Independent" to abuse Gell's enemies[4]. He was showing dangerously royalist tendencies, as was shown later when his brother Thomas argued that an offence which he committed in 1648 could not be punished in 1650, because of a one-year limit which had been placed on prosecutions by Acts of Parliament passed in 1649[5]. In a series of letters between September and December 1648 Gell kept his son up to date with the progress of the army, which was at that time completing its suppression of a series of royalist risings, and with the negotiations between Parliament, the army and the King[6]. Gell was clearly concerned to hide his activities since these letters are addressed not to "His loving son" in the fashion of the time and in the style of letters which he wrote later, but simply "For John Gell Esqr". The letters are also unsigned, ending "from your servant", and references to his own visits to Hopton are put into the third person -

"Sr John wilbe downe presently & so will his brother Thomas". In one of them Sir John gave his son the classic instruction of surreptitious letter writers - "burne this letter lest you lose it".

In spite of the collapse of his hopes of a settlement after the King's disaster, the letters described the comings and goings optimistically, always expecting harmony to break out. From the Isle of Wight the King continued to plot and there were royalist risings in several parts of the country. The Presbyterian majority in Parliament took advantage of the absence of the army to attempt to conclude an agreement with the king, whereby he would give up most of his power in return for his throne. Determined to yield nothing, the king temporised, giving audience to a succession of his former enemies who now hoped for peace and preferment in a new court. According to Thomas Coke, giving evidence in 1651, Gell was one of these[7] - "Sir John Gell sent thither to tender his service and to desire a pardon from the late king for his former actions. The king gave him something to that purpose under his hand and signett. One Bowring, a servant to the Lord Commissioner Lisle, came down to sollicite the business. What money was given for it, he best knows". Gell in fact handed over £300 in gold[8].

John Lisle was one of the parliamentary commissioners carrying out the vain attempt to make a treaty with the king. On the 3rd October Gell sent his son a copy of a royal negotiating document which had been rejected by Parliament for its tolerance of non-Presbyterians. A week later he reported hopefully that it was "howerly expected the kings concent for a finall conclewsion", and on the 17th that "the Treaty goeth on fayrely no rub but a little concerning Bishopes". Gell's hope of a successful agreement between King and Parliament was generally shared at that time, but the army had more stringent terms in mind and was by then of a mind to exert its authority over Parliament. Gell was referring to tension between Parliament and army when he commented "there is no jarniment [adjournment] of the howses [of Parliament] though much spoke of". On the 14th November "there is like to be a peace if the souldiery interpose not & whether they will or not I can say nothing".

By November 21st the army had in fact "interposed" and sent a statement of its demands to Parliament, which had not yet answered them. Parliament had sent further propositions to the king and "there may yet bee a peace". Clearly Gell's hopes were getting weaker. A week later the king had not replied to Parliament's propositions and "the Armie is dayly expected heare". Hampton

Court was already garrisoned and one regiment had seized money in Suffolk for the seige of Pomfret "& for ought that I perceave no body will say wronge that they doe". A week further on Gell reported that Parliament had "voted the kinges consessions sufficient for a well grounded peace & have appointed 6 of there members to repare to the Generall [Fairfax] to treate with him, whom is now at White Hall in his head quarters". The army, however, had realised by then that the king would never compromise and planned to dissolve Parliament, call elections for a new one, and proceed to try Charles for treason. The Parliamentary vote to continue negotiations, taken on the 5th December, stung the army into action. The Independent MPs urged that their Parliamentary enemies should be expelled, and on the day following the vote Colonel Pride earned his place in history by standing with an armed detachment at the door of Parliament, arresting or turning away those MPs who had voted to continue treating with Charles. One of them was Sir John Curzon[9]. This "Pride's Purge" left a much reduced House of Commons, soon christened the "Rump Parliament".

The tide was now strongly against Gell's brand of religion and politics and in the last letter of this series, sent to Hopton on December the 12th, he reports arrests, nothing being done in Parliament and "a great expectation of a new Moddled government. What the isshew wilbe time will shew". The arrests were of people of Gell's own persuasion, and his son's mother-in-law, Mrs Phyllis Packer, writing to Hopton on the same day as Sir John, told his son that " your father Packer and I went to see our good frends that are imprisoned by the Armie. We found them very cheerfull and I hope will continew constant in a good cause"[10]. Gell mentioned the arrest of a "sherive Browne ... the famous souldier" and Mrs Packer also reported "this morning they have taken major general Browne". Browne was a Presbyterian like Gell and, also like him, had fought for Parliament[11]. Mrs Packer "dare not venture to goe into London it being now full of the Armie".

Among Gell's papers is a series of six letters written between the 25th December 1648 and the 11th January 1649 and copied into a book without the names of sender or addressee[12]. They were from a political insider with an intimate knowledge of the comings and goings in Parliament and the army. Their standpoint was the same as Gell's - " Nor are the feuds of this faction relating only to the publick, but besides their petty subdivisions in opinion about government and interest, they have their particular camisados [trivial quarrels], as between Fairfax and Cromwell, Ireton and Lambert, Hus and Rich; and the only binder, that holds these heterogeneous parties in a body, is necessity of self preservation, against an universall odium, in enjoying the present sweets of power and proffit ... this devilish faction is cloven as well as their Masters foote". The "devilish faction" prevailed and the Rump voted to try the king for treason. He was found guilty and was beheaded on the 30th January 1649. It was at this point of his life in London that Gell found himself in opposition to the authorities and Parliament ordered on the 23rd February that he should be dismissed from "all commissions of peace and other commissions"[13].

An unhappy marriage

The chief domestic topic of the London letters of the autumn of 1648 was the relationship between Gell and his recently married second wife. While it was not surprising that Sir John remarried after Elizabeth's death, the identity of his second wife certainly was. She was Mary Stanhope, widow of Sir John Stanhope of Elvaston and, from the bitterness of Stanhope's relationship with Gell, the woman it might be supposed least likely to want to marry him. Lucy Hutchinson described Gell's defacing Stanhope's monument in Elvaston church and his destruction of Dame Mary's garden, all done under the pretext of searching for arms, and concluded that Mary was "deluded by his hypocrisies" when he wooed her[14]. The charge of vandalism was probably exaggerated. It seems unlikely that Gell's wooing would have been successful if he had indeed wrecked her garden, whatever his charm. The marriage took place at the end of December 1647[15] and, according to Mrs Hutchinson, Mary then "found that was the utmost poynt to which he could carry his revenge, his future carriage making it apparent, he sought her for nothing elce but to destroy the glory of her husband and his house".

In a way typical of the intermarriage of prominent seventeenth century families, this marriage made another connection between the Gells and the Radcliffes, his daughter-in-law's family, since Mary was the daughter of Sir John Radcliffe, of Ordsall, in Lancashire. Common sense, however, and Gell's proven interest in wealth and self-confessed interest in women, suggest that his motive in marrying Mary Stanhope was neither dynastic nor vengeful, but simply that he found either her or her property attractive. He certainly lost no time in putting Mary's real estate to his own use. In February he arranged that her manor of Toton, in Nottinghamshire, should be made over to trustees, who should then make certain payments[16]. All his debts, including one of £800 to John Milward, his old business partner and war adversary, should be paid, and £1500 each be paid to his grand-daughters Katherine and Elizabeth Gell. However, Gell discovered that Mary had put most of her fortune beyond his reach before their wedding and the two were soon at loggerheads.

The quarrels between the two are apparent from the first of autumn 1648 letters to his son. Clearly Sir John and his new wife were not a loving couple. On September the 5th 1648 he notified his son that Mary was about to visit Derbyshire and instructed him to collect the rents and tell her that he had been told by her husband to give her £100. The tension between the two is evident in the detailed instructions on the attitude which the younger Gell was to adopt toward his step-mother. If Mary should question him about the estate he must tell her he had been instructed to write to his father who would then write to her, "and then shee shalbe fully acquainted with the state of all things". It seems that Gell was being as secretive about his estate as he later accused her of being about hers. If Mary showed any sign of wanting to get her hands on the rents John should make sure that his agent payed them to him personally. Anxious to avoid further trouble Gell told his son "give her good words".

On October 3rd he asked him "how your mother entertayned you at Elvaston wheather she would speake to you or not". The picture of a broken marriage is confirmed in a letter of November 14th - "your mother is gone from me & hath left me utterly without any just groundes or cause at all that I can conceave or know my selfe. But it is a thing that I have expected, & doe not looke for reconsileation. The dispositions of many are so veterate [long-standing] that noe reconsilement wilbe admitted. I doe vow there is no such cause as to parte that is knowne to me". Bearing in mind the history of the relations between himself and the Stanhopes and the animosity between himself and Mary which was to be revealed after her death, it is less surprising that the marriage failed than that it took place at all. Gell was surely being disingenuous in his last sentence. Mary had in fact left after the couple, with the help of mediation by their friends, had worked out a separation agreement[17]. Mary was to have £200 a year from the proceeds of the Toton estate. On December the 5th Gell told his son that he had passed on his letter to Mary. By then the separation was complete. A week later Gell reported that

"Your mother & my selfe is like to accord", and John seems to have been representing his father in a division of property - "loose not the fine ovall table I sent you by Fran: Lockoe of Spondon. The table was carried to Elvaston". John was told to be ready to hand over the deed concerning Toton manor.

Money grievance

Apart from his marriage break up, Gell was still preoccupied in 1648 by his attempts to reclaim the money lost during the war and by the need to defend himself against accusations still being made by his enemies. On September the 5th he had had no success with the former - "I do not know how to get the monies returned as yet", but hoped that the fact that the renewed war was almost over, with the Prince of Wales having left the country and Cromwell and others having only small pockets of resistance to clear up, would enable Parliament to settle his case. However, Thomas Gell's letter had noted in 1646 that "now the busines wilbe harder then befoare it was, for now both howses must concurre to the grantinge of money witch befoare the howse of comons did aloane, and this happened within this weeke". The business continued to be hard for many years. Gell presented a petition to the Committee of Revenue early in 1650 asking for two years of arrears of his rent of the mineral rights in Wirksworth to be discharged or respited "untill such tyme as itt shall please ye Parliament to give him some recompense for his said service"[18]. The petition summarised Gell's war service and claimed that he had lost above £5000 in rents and had received only £56 in recompense. The Committee asked the auditor to certify Gell's arrears and Nathaniel Hallowes and a Colonel Crompton were asked to investigate his war service and expences. Significantly, these two were substituted for the men originally given the task - Sir John Curzon and Thomas Gell. Sir John's claims were partly met in 1653, when Parliamentary commissioners for Derbyshire certified that Gell had spent £3,000 between November 1642 and September 1646 and should be repaid this sum, plus interest at eight percent[19].

Sir John, giving the lie to accusations that he had done well from the war, was short of ready money and relied on regular payments from his son. On October 3rd he told him "all my monies is gonn I pray you returne me some more" and on November the 21st "I pray you to returne me so soone as you can the £100. I hope now that I shall not spend so fast as formerly". At Hopton, John Gell the younger seems to have been in some difficulty himself since, although his father told him on December the 12th that he had received the £100 and given a receipt for it, the letter sent to Hopton by Mrs Packer on the same day reveals that it was his mother-in-law who had raised the money. She too seems to have been short of cash - "Your father himselfe upon Saterday last rec: heere the £100 for which he gave mee a note of his hand. The times are such now that I could by no way get returnd but £50 and I found a frend which did lend me the other £50".

Managing Hopton

Sir John remained concerned about the running of the estate during all the years he lived in London and at this time his main preoccupation was with the fact that after the upheavals of the war, when he had been unable to collect his rents, the tenants were refusing to pay them to his son. In the course of instructing John on how to conduct his meeting with his step-mother, in the letter of Sept the 5th 1648, Gell tackled the problem - "comand the fellow Jaques to pay all the rentes to you or if they pay to any other they are sheure to pay them over agayne". The younger Gell seems to have needed his father's authority as by the time Gell was writing to Hopton on October the 3rd he had had a letter of complaint from Jaques - "Jaques playneth [complains] that you expecte reall [honest] dealing from him, & so from all the rest, or they shall beare the burden & be worse dealt withall if they be not reall to you, & you may informe them that the power is in you & that I wish you to deale pleanely with them". A week later he quotes his lawyer brother Thomas "that let all the world say & doe what they can, you may have, & so intend to have, all the rentes. Of those that refeuse to pay you you will make a short worke, & make such as refeuse to know them selves". There was further advice on October the 17th. Jaques should be told that any tenants refusing to pay their rent could be compelled to do so, at great cost to them. John should avoid any personal confrontations - "take not much paynes your selfe but send sum one that can say onely what you desire to bee sayd"

Old acquaintance

Thomas Gell had referred in his 1646 letter of that year to the fact that the last letter he had received from John was delivered by "Vanduran". Marcellus Vanduren was a lead merchant who had helped finance his Dutch colleague Cornelius Vermuyden's draining of the Dovegang at Wirksworth there are enquiries in the letters to

John old allies such as Vermuyden, Vermuyden's son Cornelius and Johannes Molanus. In 1648 Molanus was still a mine-owner and smelter in Wirksworth, where the younger Gell was the chief barmaster, and seems to have kept his rough ways. In a case brought against four men for stealing "eight whetstones of lead" from John Gell's smelting mill at Wirksworth their defence was that they were taking goods to the value of debts which Molanus had incurred with them and not repaid[20]. The letters make it clear that the relationship between Gell and Molanus had soured, presumably because of the betrayal described by Thomas, when Molanus had almost succeeded in having Gell arrested on a charge of treason. It must have been particularly crushing to have such an old ally turn against him and the two were no longer friends - "Mollanus would not let me have ether wa[t]ch or ring but sould them at lese rates to others. Doe him the like for ore". The "others" to whom Molanus had sold the watch and ring may in fact have been Dame Mary, as her son was to say in 1653 that his mother had given a silver watch to his daughter and a ring to his son[21]. If Molanus was in fact joining in the conflict between Gell and his wife it is not surprising that Gell should want his son to hurt him commercially in Derbyshire. As barmaster, mine-owner and owner of the mills at which Molanus smelted his ore he was in a position to do him harm.

Father and son and their hawks

Gell commiserated with John on an injury which he had sustained to his hand, reported that he had not yet made up his mind whether to make his usual trip to take the waters at Bath, and frequently let John know that there was something on its way to Hopton by the "Ashbourne carrier". There were several consignments of books and, when he had not confessed to having forgotten them, or the carrier was not going that week, barrels of oysters. He sent John a lance to let blood, probably for veterinary rather than medical use. The traffic went both ways, of course, and on one occasion Gell asked his son to "get sum partriges & cakes & bake them & directe them to me at Major Blethes a linen draper at the Bell nere Temple Bare & so your letters". He asked regularly for news of the horses and dogs, and on October the 3rd he warned John that it was too late in the year to keep the newly castrated geldings in the open, that he should have them "often stopte [bandaged] & greased or they will founder in the stable" and that he should not allow the servants to use them on outside work. However his pressing concern was always with the hawks. Almost all of Sir John Gell's letters to his son, including the ones written in the autumn of 1648, mention what was obviously his great passion - falconry. He was constantly advising John on the care and training of the hawks. With a revolution going on around him, one in which he was personally concerned and one which was almost to cost him his life, beset by determined enemies and struggling to retrieve a lost fortune, Gell still worried about his hawks. He asked his son to "send me word what you want for the hawks & you shall have it", and on December the 5th he told John how it did him good to hear of one of the young hawks attacking a heron and looked forward to the day when, fully trained, it would be pleasing John by taking on a duck or a drake

CHAPTER 12

Treason and pardons

The aftermath of the Civil War, up to and after the execution of the king in January 1649, and the establishment of the Commonwealth government, was a time of plots and fear of plots. The new authorities took precautions against any attempt to install the exiled Prince of Wales in his father's place, setting up the Council of State to deal with counter-espionage and the High Court of Justice to try accused traitors. On the execution of the king his son Charles, then in France with the Queen, was immediately proclaimed King in Scotland. Being much more flexible than his father, he signed the Solemn League and Covenant in 1650, enabling him to travel to Scotland, where he was crowned on the 1st January 1651. Faced with the threat of a Scottish invasion to place Charles on the English throne, Cromwell mobilised. Charles invaded England and reached Worcester, where his forces were defeated by Cromwell and he fled the country once more. In this climate of fear and uncertainty the Council of State employed agents who, in addition to unearthing genuine plots, had the Council's approval in encouraging perceived royalists to incriminate themselves. Gell was suspect because of his contacts with the King in 1648, his vehement disatisfaction with Parliament's failure to recompense him for his war losses, and his sympathy with the expelled members of Parliament. In 1650 he was the victim of a manufactured conspiracy.

Eusebius Andrews and his plot

The chief target was a former Colonel in the royal army called Eusebius Andrews. Andrews, a barrister by profession, had joined the King early in the Civil War and had remained with him until the fall of Worcester to Parliamentary forces in 1646, when he returned to practising law[1]. While despairing of the royal cause he did not recognise the new government and refused to sign the Solemn League and Covenant or take the tests which followed it. He was therefore carefully observed by the Council and its agents, whose record of his movements was "as if they had kept a diary for him". It was unfortunate for Andrews that one of his regular acquaintance, a former Major under his command, had by 1650 entered the service of the Council of State and was ready not only to betray Andrews for any overt hostility to the Commonwealth, but actively to provoke him into anti-government action. This man, John Barnard, introduced his old comrade-in-arms to two other royalist sympathisers, a Captain Holmes and a clerk called John Benson, who were hoping to exploit the guilt and discontent felt by many Parliamentarians after the execution of the king. They proposed that Andrews should revive an old plan of his to take the Isle of Ely as a first step in bringing in the Prince of Wales. However the failure of royalist movements in Scotland and Ireland persuaded Andrews to abandon the idea and, since there was by then a Parliamentary ordinance that all who refused to sign the Covenant should leave London, he made arrangements to live abroad. Barnard had to move quickly to prevent his prey escaping and delayed Andrews's departure by inventing a forthcoming rising in Kent, Dorset and Buckinghamshire. Barnard initially succeeded in inducing Andrews to subscribe to this but he quickly discovered that there was to be no rising and set off for the Continent. Barnard had delayed arresting Andrews only in the hope of drawing in more disaffected royalists and once it became plain that he was determined to leave England, the agent acted. Andrews was arrested at Gravesend on 24th March 1650.

He was imprisoned in the Tower of London and charged with treason, the evidence being a letter setting out plans to take the Isle of Ely and Lyme Regis, among other places, and to instal the Prince of Wales as King. Andrews sent four petitions to the Council requesting either a pardon or a speedy trial. All were ignored and he then petitioned Parliament itself. Parliament's answer was to arraign him before the High Court of Justice and, although he argued that this was not a proper court to try a man for his life, since it had "power only to condemn, not to acquit", the point was dismissed by the prosecutor, the Attorney General, who argued that the only item of importance before the court was the incriminating letter. The judge was the Lord President, John Bradshaw, who had spent the previous eighteen months condemning first the King, and then a succession of royalists to death. Bradshaw had been appointed by Parliament to the parliamentary commission to try the king and, though he expressed reluctance through a sense of his inadequacy for the role, had been elected their president and given the title of Lord President. He was a fervent republican and, once in office, was merciless in tracking down and condemning royalists for treason to Parliament. During Andrews's trial he repeatedly cross-examined him in an attempt to get him to incriminate himself. Bradshaw condemned Andrews to death on the 6th August 1650 and after a final petition to Parliament had been turned down on the 19th August he was beheaded on Tower Hill three days later.

The Andrews letter

Sir John Gell was one of the potential enemies of the state whom Barnard had hoped to bring down with Eusebius Andrews, and it is probable that Gell and Andrews had met. Gell, however, was too shrewd a man to have committed himself and Barnard's method was to persuade Gell to subscribe to the letter in which Andrews had supposedly outlined his plans, and which Gell later argued was in any case a copy. Barnard brought the letter, addressed to "Sr John Barronet", to Gell's house late on the night of the 23rd March and, according to him, left it with him after Gell had read it. Thomas Gell, preparing his brother's case, noted that there was another witness, Henry Ashley, in the room and that he "saies upon his faith he saw it not delivered"[2]. Furthermore, while Barnard alleged that Gell had read the letter in his presence, he said nothing of Gell putting on his spectacles to do so. By 1650, at fifty-seven years of age, Sir John's eyesight was failing. He could only have read the letter by candle-light with the help of spectacles and Thomas reasoned that Barnard would have mentioned this if he had in fact watched Gell read the letter. In any event the letter, as in the trial of Andrews, was the only evidence that Barnard had and he had shown it to the Council before taking it to Gell. Gell was arrested on the 25th March, imprisoned in the Tower and arraigned before the High Court on the 11th September, under an Act of Parliament of the 26th March 1650, on charges of treason and misprision of treason. His misprision was to conceal the letter which Barnard alleged that he had delivered and which by then had disappeared.

Petitions and pamphlets

Gell's first attempt to get himself out of this very tight spot was to address a petition to Parliament[3]. This was a not only a vigorous rebuttal of "the treacherous designe of one Barnard" but also a restatement in the strongest terms of his service to Parliament at a time when it most needed defending, and of the money which he maintained was still owing to him. In order to put the greatest pressure on the MPs he had this petition printed and circulated. He estimated that the pay which he had never received, plus the money which he had paid from his own pocket during the war, amounted to a debt of £20,000 and that it was now time for Parliament to pay him. Gell stressed that he had spent five years fighting for Parliament, "notwithstanding many temptations from the late king and his party", while Barnard was a cavalier, "that hath been in Armes against you". It would be a dangerous precedent for "the Parliament of England" to be seen to be questioning the lives of loyal servants on the testimony of its enemies "who having failed by power at treachery, now by policie endeavour to create jealousies among you, that being divided, they may destroy you".

Calling in aid his service to the Parliament during 1642-1646 was not in itself likely to impress the Parliament of 1650, whose record included the execution of the king and which was well aware that war-time supporters like Gell had long parted company with it. Gell therefore protested that he had done nothing to harm the present government and took care to acknowledge that "extraordinary proceedings" were justified against irreconcilable enemies of the state. However he claimed that faithful friends of Parliament would be discouraged to see that "for the least pretended miscarriage you give them up to be proceeded against in the same extraordinary way used to the worst of enemies", especially as Parliament had promised that the ancient laws and liberties of England would still protect its people. He asked Parliament, once it had settled its money debts to him, to allow him legal help for a trial at common law, if there were any crime for which he could be tried - "it being not onely the Englishmans birthright, but also the price of that blood shed in the late Warre, against those that would have subverted the same".

This was an age of pamphleteering, even by men awaiting trial for their lives, and Gell managed to produce and circulate an eleven page pamphlet putting his case, damning Barnard and denying charges that he had enriched himself during the war. This came out in August, entitled "The true state of the case of Sir John Gell, Prisoner in the Tower"[4], and was immediately countered by another from Barnard - "A true confutation of a Fals and scandalous Pamphlet, entituled, The true state of the case of Sir John Gell, Lately published to deceive the People, by John Bernard, Gent, Captain of a Troop of Horse in the Service of Parliament"[5]. Gell's pamphlet had painted Barnard as a royalist, a Catholic and a conspirator against Parliament, making it obligatory for Barnard to stress his Parliamentary connections. Gell's contention was that the whole conspiracy was an invention of Barnard, that the Lord

President, Bradshaw, had kept the letter from Andrews to "Sr John Barronet", sending a copy to Gell, that he had refused to sign it and had burnt it. He alleged that he was arrested the following morning, on Sunday, and since no work was done on the Sabbath the warrant for his arrest must have been prepared before the letter was taken to him.

Barnard's pamphlet denied each of Gell's points in turn and alleged that Andrews, who by then had been executed, had said in evidence that he had met Gell several times - "About the midst of December 49 I was invited to give Sr John Gell a meeting, and amongst other discourses, Sr John Gell did take notice of his requital for his service and his losses, and the misapplication of his and others' services to an end they intended not, and that hee desired to bee so understood, and when oportunitie should bee, to bee so represented to the Prince, and did intimate, that if hee took up arms again, it should bee for the Prince, and at several other subsequent meetings the discourses were general, and much to this purpose ... that Sr John Gell had twice or thrice in March last bespoken to him to beget a good opinion of him in the King; and was not satisfied in the waie hee had taken formerly, and that hee was sorrie for what he had done against his Father ... also Wednesdaie 20 March last I wrote to Sr John Gell to meet mee at dinner, hee promised to cum, but came not, and sent his man to excuse him and defray the charge, and that afternoon I saw him by chance, and hee told mee that hee had not subscribed, nor would, but what hee had said to mee as touchinge his realitie to the Prince, I might ingage myself for". By stating that Gell had refused to "subscribe" Andrews supported him in denying any involvement in the conspiracy, but the description of his opinions rings true. Gell was indeed bitter at his losses, at his treatment by Parliament, and by the outcome of the war.

The trial

When his efforts to avoid the High Court by petition and pamphlet had failed, Gell, for the time being, abandoned further stirring appeals to Parliament and applied himself to the legal battle, helped by his brother. At his first appearance before Bradshaw in the High Court he pleaded not guilty and asked for time to prepare his case. He was given a week, and at the second hearing, on the 18th September, he produced witnesses, who were heard, and argued "divers small matters of Lawe"[6]. A further week was granted and on the 25th September he produced "his Councill learned in the Lawe".

Thomas Gell's draft of the legal arguments put to the court shows considerable ingenuity[7]. The arguments were that (1) the Act under which the charge was brought refered to messages brought from abroad to members of the former royal family, whereas the letter in question came from Gravesend and was addressed to a baronet, (2) Gell could not be guilty of both treason and misprision since misprision consisted of hiding evidence of another man's treason, not his own; hiding evidence was not itself treason but if Gell were nevertheless found to be party to treason he could not be condemned for hiding evidence of it, (3) the offences were Common Law offences and should be tried by a jury under oath, (4) the indictment accused Gell not of concealing treason but only of concealing knowledge of "wicked practises and designes", which were general terms - "now as 20 trespasses shall not make one felony, nor twentie felonies one treason, so 20 wicked practises and designes shall not make one misprision of treason", (5) the contents of the letter were not mentioned in the indictment, which did not say that it "did tend to the raisinge of insurrection or a newe warre within the nation", in the words of the Act, (6) to be effective the indictment should use the words of the Act in describing the concealment of the letter, namely that Gell "did not forthwith reveale the same to the Speaker of the Parliament, or the Counsell of State, or unto two of the members thereof, or to two justices of peace", (7) the alleged offence was committed on March 25th while the Act making it an offence did not become law until March 29th, (8) according to the evidence the Council of State knew about the letter before Gell did, and he could not therefore be accused of concealing it from them.

The court, arbitrary as it was, seems to have come to a fair verdict. While Gell had been careful to avoid joining in Andrews's schemes, such as they were, he had certainly kept them to himself. The court ignored all but one of Thomas's "small matters of Lawe", as it had brushed aside Andrews's arguments and was not impressed by the absence of Sir John's spectacles in Barnard's testimony. However, it accepted the point that misprision could not be brought as evidence of treason because the two offences were different in nature, one being punishable by death the other by imprisonment, unlike, as Thomas said, murder and manslaughter, which were both (at that time) punishable by death. Gell was acquitted of the treason charge but found guilty of misprision.

His punishment was life imprisonment and the confiscation of his estate. Ashley, Benson and three others were found guilty of treason, but only Benson paid with his life. He was hanged and the rest pardoned. Justice was eventually to catch up with Barnard too. After receiving money and promotion for his efforts in 1650 he was hanged at Tyburn in 1654 for robbery. Gell remained in prison and, with his brother's continuing help, composed a series of petitions to Parliament during 1651, concentrating on the retrospective nature of the charge against him and the fact that Ashley and other condemned traitors had been pardoned, while stressing his long imprisonment and the debt, financial and moral, which Parliament owed him[8]. With Charles II crowned in Scotland and invading England, Gell acknowledged "the unreasonablenes of the time for this petition in regard of present plotts" but offered security for his future good behaviour[9].

Frustrated predators

The execution of Gell's sentence was moved from the High Court to the Exchequer, which directed the Derbyshire High Sheriff to investigate the extent of Gell's estate[10]. The Commission for Compounding, set up in September 1643 to punish delinquents by seizing their estates, met in the Goldsmiths Hall[11]. On the 11th March 1651 it ordered its commissioners for sequestration in Derbyshire to seize the Gell estate. The commissioners were Gell's old enemies Robert Mellor, who had been mayor of Derby in 1647, Gervase Bennett, who served as an MP for Derbyshire during the Commonwealth, and Ralph Clarke[12]. They were no doubt eager to complete his ruin and must have been frustrated when, in the course of carrying out the Committee's order, they came up against the difficulty posed by the 1636 indenture, which had been found during the Sheriff's searches[13]. While it had "lyen dorment ever since", and had not affected Sir John's possession of his estate, it had legal force. They had also learned of the 1644 marriage settlement, though they had not yet succeeded in having sight of it. This, unlike the earlier indenture, certainly had substance, since Gell's son was in possession. They reported all this to the Commission who asked the Exchequer for directions for further action[14]. Thomas Gell submitted a motion to the Commissioners on his brother's behalf and on the 20th May they reversed the sequestration order, ordering sequestators in Derbyshire, Nottinghamshire and elsewhere to "forebeare to intermedle with any of the said estate by vertue of the sequestration or by any act done by the said Sr John for which he was tried by the High Court of Justice"[15].

Freedom

The family fortune was safe, then. Perhaps in recognition of his part in saving it, and of his continuing help, Thomas was given a part of it in 1651. In a deed of gift dated the 4th June Sir John and his son gave annual rents of £100 from the estate, for the duration of his life[16]. Sir John, however, was still in the Tower and, with help from his brother and others he continued to plead his case for release. His pleas were addressed to Parliament and a petition of September 1651 contrasted his continuing imprisonment with the pardons granted to some of the others found guilty of treason - "Your petitioner languisheth under a heavy sentence of the High Court of Justice and hath noe meanes of releife but the favour and mercy of the parliament. Hee most humbly prayeth that in regard of his long imprisonment being above eighteen moneths, a greate parte whereof he was a close prisoner in the Tower, and that since you have pardoned all those whoe were found guilty of treason in that very busynesse whereof your petitioner stands guilty of misprision onely, you wilbe pleased to release and pardon your petitioner of that sentence"[17].

By the time he delivered this petition Gell was not in fact in prison. In August he had been allowed out of the Tower for three months "to go to the Bath, for recovery of his health", on security of £5000[18]. This parole was renewed in October until January[19] and in January until April[20]. On the 1st April, two years after his arrest, he entered into an agreement with John Bowring, by now an MP, whereby Bowring, acting by himself or with "others in the Parliament of England", should present his latest petition, since "he being in restraint is not able to manage that Petition and affayre in his owne person"[21]. Gell was presumably calculating that Bowring's association with Lisle would be enough to get him a hearing. Lisle had prospered since 1648. He had taken a prominent part in the trial of the king and in 1649 had been placed on the Commission of the Great Seal and the Council of State[22]. If the pardon was duly granted Bowring was to receive a minimum of £300 and a maximum of £400. Gell must have thought that inside help was what he needed, but in fact, and presumably without Bowring's involvement, Parliament resolved on the 13th April that "Mr John Gell be discharged of his imprisonment and that the Lieutenant of the Tower do take notice hereof and release him accordingly"[23].

By then Parliament had abolished titles granted by Charles I after the 4th January 1641. Gell had the draft of a petition to Cromwell on this subject[24], claiming that while many titles had been granted with the object of ensuring their recipients' allegiance to the Crown, the baronets named in the petition had all in the event been faithful Parliament men. In April 1653 he was finally pardoned and his estates officially returned to him[25]. In this pardon document he was named as Colonel and on the cover of a deed dated the 20th April 1656, by which Gell formally revoked the 1636 arrangement between himself and his son, a later hand has written "Sir John Gell Bart stiles himself John Gell Esq his title of Baronet having been taken away from him"[26].

The death of Mary Gell

In April 1653, at about the time that Parliament finally pardoned him, Gell received news of the death of his second wife, Mary. The reasons for the break up of their marriage in its first year were soon made public. Gell entered a Bill of Complaint against the children of Mary's first marriage to Philip Stanhope in an effort to win some of the money he had hoped for when he married her[27]. According to this, Mary had claimed at the time of their marriage that she had an estate worth £10,000 but that, once they were married, she had refused to let him know the extent of her fortune and had conspired with her children and her estate managers to keep him in the dark. In order to have a plausible reason not to cooperate with him she had left him. A year after the marriage, she had conveyed the estate, in trust for some of her children, to her brother Alexander Radcliffe and Sir John Curzon, whose daughter Jane had married Dame Mary's son John[28]. Without the knowledge of Curzon and Radcliffe, Mary had back-dated the deed to five or six days before the marriage. Clearly the couple were at loggerheads from the moment they were married and it is unnecessary to believe Gell's conspiracy theories to understand that this was a quarrel between a wife who wanted her own children to have their rightful inheritance and a husband who demanded his rights to his wife's property. In answering Gell's complaints, and denying most of them, Dame Mary's son John told the court that Curzon had told him that Gell knew of the deed before he married Mary[29]. The reason Gell had given for Mary's leaving him was false. She had gone "upon more just grounds which are well knowne to the said Complainant".

Death threats

In 1657 a ghost from the past, in the shape of Lieutenant-Colonel Humphrey Mathews, late commander of the Hull contingent of volunteers in Gell's regiment, came back to haunt him. Without Mathews's own story it is impossible to know what his grievance was, but he seems to have blamed Gell for the loss of his company and there seem also to have been accusations that Gell had stolen money from him. Whatever the reason he bore a grudge and "protested that if ever he mett Sr John Gell he would be the death of him". William Thomas, who seems to have been exceptionally loyal to his old commander, reported this to a magistrate at Lincolns Inn in October 1657, submitting a certificate in which he described the circumstances at Derby in November 1642[30]. These included the fact that Mathews had left a sum of money with his landlord, which was overlooked by Captain Aldridge of the Hull garrison when he seized Mathews's belongings. Thomas testified that Mathews wrote to him from Gloucester asking him to go with a Thomas Harriman, brother of Mathews's landlady in Gloucester, along to his old landlord at Derby and collect the money. Thomas and Harriman did so and the money was sent to Mathews, who told Thomas in 1647 that he had received it. The faithful Thomas gave his reason for submitting his statement - "To acquitte and cleere Sr John Gell (as far as truth and my conscience assure mee) from all aspersions and reproachfull scandalls cast uppon him by any malevolent or malitious person whatsoever as that hee should bee guilty or accessary of takeing the moneys goods or chattles of Lt Col Mathews or to deceive or deprive him of his Company" Thomas's story gives names and details and seems watertight, and the magistrate put out a warrant in June 1658 for Mathews's arrest for disturbing the peace[31]. Whatever the truth, the war was continuing to cast a long shadow in Gell's old age.

The death of Thomas Gell

John Gell had continued to rely on his brother's help and Thomas had been one of the main agents in his release from prison. Thomas, in addition to his legal expertise and the wide acquaintance among the "great ones" which he had built up during a life largely spent in London, had also been re-elected to Parliament for Derby in 1652. He was thus able to continue to keep John informed about political developments and to exercise influence in Parliament on his behalf until 1653, when the Rump Parliament was dissolved. Thomas made his will in 1653, leaving his estate to Sir John and his son, apart from the £50 "that my servant Thomas Gell of Derby oweth to mee"[32]. Tom Gell was left this £50 , plus another £100, and also "all my apparrell and wearing cloathes linnen and woollen and all other cloathes belonging to mee". This gift of clothes was reduced in a codicil of 1656 by the clothes "that I now weare", which were left to another servant, William Spicer. Thomas died in that year, leaving his brother to fend for himself. He was buried in Wirksworth church with his ancestors, carried there from London in considerable style. The coffin's velvet pall, the hearse and the four plumed horses were adorned with his coat of arms and the funeral was arranged and supervised by two heralds from the College of Arms[33].

Aches, pains and taking the waters

John Gell, sixty-three years old at his brother's death, continued to live at his house in St Martins Lane and kept out of trouble during the reign of the Lord Protector, Cromwell, who had assumed power in 1653, after forcibly dissolving the Rump Parliament. Though disgraced and out of office, he still had clout, as a letter from his cousin Henry Sacheverel demonstrates[34]. It was written in March 1653 and was a request that Gell sign a certificate which Sacheverel's cousin Jacinth Sacheverel of Morley needed to recover money lost in the war, which would no doubt include the £3000 "brought from Mr Sacheverell of Morley" to Nathaniel Hallowes in 1642. A new Parliament, elected under new rules, was called in 1654 and the younger John Gell was elected as one of the Derbyshire MPs, maintaining his father's source of Parliamentary information[35]. Gell appointed deputies to carry out the duty of collecting the rents of the Honour of Tutbury which he had inherited from his brother[36] and carried on his custom of spending three months of the year at Bath, starting at Whitsuntide, which he thought "a prime time of the yeare to bathe in"[37].

Bath was not the elegant, fashionable spa that it became in the eighteenth century, but the town was thronged during the seven months of the bathing season. Gell visited Bath for over twenty years, hoping for relief from "a stupor and dullness sometimes in the head and a seeming clout about his tongue, and a kind of creeping and sleepiness (as they call it vulgarly) upon arm, leg, sometimes one, sometimes another, and a kind of clumsiness whilst it remained there"[38]. This description of Gell's symptoms was by a local doctor who went on to say that they had made him afraid that he was about to become palsied. Gell's remedy for his problems, which may have been caused by restricted circulation, was typically root-and-branch. The authorities at the baths provided a service called "pumping", which consisted of pumping hot medicinal water at affected parts, at a charge of 2d for 100 pumps. This was done in the centre of the King's Bath, watched by the throng of bathers and spectators. Gell, dressed in the special bath costume of yellow canvas drawers and waistcoat, yellow because the water discoloured white linen, took these jets of hot, sulphurous water on his bare head, starting with 700 or 800 on his first day, gradually increasing to 2000 and then gradually decreasing. Whether or not these drastic assaults were necessary, we can be sure that Gell enjoyed his extended Bath holidays. In addition, he was never palsied, and comfortably survived his three score years and ten.

Pardon

The last crisis for John Gell came in 1660. The death of Cromwell in 1658, followed by the ineffectual performance of his son Richard produced a climate in which the return of the king began to seem inevitable. During Cromwell's reign England had become a major power in Europe and he and his army had removed all danger of invasion by the Scots as well as suppressing the Irish rebellion in an infamously brutal campaign. However, rule by soldiers and Puritans was unpopular and once the genius of Cromwell had gone an irristible yearning took hold among the gentry for a return to the old order and rule by King and Parliament. Richard Cromwell had neither the inclination nor the ability to exercise his authority and the Army Council, dominated by republican Independents, assumed effective power in England.

The man who displaced them and managed a peaceful return of the old order was the commander of the army in Scotland, General George Monck. The English commanders broke with Parliament and expelled its members, a move which Monck opposed. He advanced into England in early 1660, supported by petitions from every part of the country supporting the restoration of "a full and free Parliament", ie one which restored the members expelled in Pride's Purge. Gell collected dozens of these petitions and joined Henry Buxton, Edward Pegge and others in sending one from Derbyshire, "humbly desiringe your consideration and promotion, according to your capacity, of these our desires for a free and full Parliament according to the fundamentall lawes of this Nation"[39]. Monck, who had been a royalist during the war but had served Parliament faithfully since 1646, had resisted several attempts which Charles II had made to recruit him. At this point, however, with his army in control in London, he recalled the excluded MPs and ordered a dissolution and new elections. The Parliament thus elected was christened the Convention Parliament. At the same time Monck was in touch with the King in Holland and on his advice Charles made a declaration promising religious toleration and pardon and indemnity to his enemies. Monck presented this and other letters from the King to the new Parliament who voted on the 1st May 1660 for the restoration of the monarchy.

Gell had known that the restoration of Charles II was potentially dangerous for him, as for many others who had supported Parliament. Having survived the shifting ground of politics in 1650 he had prepared for the King's probable return by drafting a plausible picture of loyalty to the Crown. He did it by reinventing his war[40]. He explained his decision to fight in 1642 as a defence against his local enemies, who had plundered his house and seized his rents, making it impossible for him to survive unless he fought back. As soon as he realised that the king was losing the war he had lain down his arms. At the battle of Naseby his failure to intercept the king's army was deliberate. He was commanding a brigade and could easily have done so - he inflated the size of his brigade to 100,000 cavalry. He and Cromwell were enemies and Cromwell had taken his command from him after Naseby. He had refused to pursue the king to Worcester. After the war he had given the king £300 in gold in three separate amounts, for which he had the receipts "in small peeces of paper". He had later been tried for treason after he had helped Charles II, had been imprisoned and had lost his estates. Gell also prepared for a renewed attempt to retrieve his war expenses and losses. He had lost £11,000 during the war, had received only £20 in wages and £3000 in compensation and asked the King to order the Speaker of the House of Commons to repay his money.

In the event this elaborate and totally unconvincing account was not needed. Charles had already shown good sense by signing the Solemn League and Covenant, and his Declaration of Breda, signed on Monck's advice, granted pardon to those who had fought against his father, though not to those who had taken part in his execution. Charles crossed the Channel soon after the vote of the 1st May and on the 18th published a list of those "who sate in Judgement upon the late King's Majesty when sentence of Death was passed against him", with an order for their arrest[41]. Among these names was John Hutchinson, Gell's counterpart at Nottingham during the war. Hutchinson, who had been elected to the Convention Parliament, escaped execution by pleading that he had helped in bringing about the restoration, and repented of his part in the King's death. He was released from the Tower, but subsequently imprisoned again for suspicion of taking part in an anti-royalist plot, and died in 1664.

Gell fared better. On the 4th June he presented his plea for pardon, quoting only the king's Declaration - "I Sr John Gell of Hopton in the County of Darby Barronett doe with most humble and hearty thankfullnesse lay hold upon his Majesties free and generall pardon by his said Declaration graunted And I doe hereby publiquely declare that I doe lay hold upon that his Majesties grace and favor And that I am and will continue his Majestyes loyall and obedient subject"[42]. The document was witnessed by his son and by the Speaker of the House of Commons, and the pardon was granted three months later. The pardon document, dated the 17th September 1660, is written in Latin on parchment, headed by the royal coat of arms and decorated by a very good engraved portrait of the king in the top left corner[43]. The reconciliation with the king seems to have been complete. "A list of gentlemen in Derbyshire and how they stand affected", drawn up in 1663, summarised the political loyalties of thirty-two survivers of the Commonwealth[44]. While his son was described as "the most rigid Presbyterian in the county", Sir John was clearly in favour with the King - "His parts are well knowne. Hee is sworne a gentleman of the Privy Chamber Extraordinary by my Lord Chamberlaine".

Father and son

There were to be no more upheavals in John Gell's life. An honoured member of the royal household, he lived quietly in St Martins Lane and, if a printed list of preachers for February, March and April of the last year of his life is an indication, was a regular churchgoer[45]. He kept in close touch with home. His son valued his advice and help in business and pleasure and with family matters. Among other preoccupations Sir John was giving his best medical advice to John's wife, Catherine. In a letter of the 3rd February 1663 he translated some "wordes your wife did stumble at"[46]. Malagogon was for treating melancholy, diaforalica was to be taken for sweating. He advised against depending on apothecaries. She should take "20 graynes of pille Rawdie, 15 graynes of Allhandall & nothing else". She should also take the "spleene pill every forth or fifth day so much as will ocation three loose stooles". Catherine was clearly not a well woman. This letter mentions two of his grandsons, "Jacke & prittie Franck". Jacke was the eldest, and was to become that generation's lawyer member of the family, and Francke, or Francis, was three years old in 1663. Sir John ended by hoping that "your wife will have sum good by her groves" - she was a mine-owner and among the family papers are "Mrs Gells acct for Gray Mare Arse 1657"[47].

The early 1660s were a time of plague and in a letter of the 10th February 1663 Sir John told his son that he had given "all the phisick notes" to his brother-in-law to translate into English and send on to his wife[48]. He had given John's servant a recipe and some medicine for the plague. He had a remedy prepared by a Doctor Burgess which consisted of boiling up sage and rue in malmsey or muscadine wine, straining it and adding pepper, ginger, nutmeg, mettredate, treacle and a quarter of a pint of "white Angellico [angelica] water"[49]. Mettredate, or mithridate, was itself a universal antidote against plague and poison and Dr Burgess must have felt justified in claiming that one or two spoonfulls of his concoction, taken daily, would not only be good for plague victims, but would cope with smallpox, measles and "surfitts" too.

Sir John sent supplies of all sorts from London. On the 3rd February he commented "it is well the pipins and orringes did com to your hands without broosing. They are very good of theyre kind". In a letter of the 1st June 1669 John Gell asked his father to organise the supply of pewter plates and dishes to Hopton "notwithstanding anything my wife hath written" to the supplier[50], and a week later thanked him - "For the dishes wee are much engaged to you, that you are pleased to take such care about them"[51]. He also had a family scandal to report. His cousin Esther of Alsop-in-le-dale had had a baby daughter, for which a Mr Trot had admitted responsibility. The couple had since married and the whole affair had caused great upheaval in the family. It was "a sad disaster", presumably because by marrying Mr Trot Esther had married beneath her.

The end

On the 4th May 1671 Sir John signed his will, witnessed by his son-in-law John Wigley[52]. It seems, in the fashion of the time, to have been drawn up only when Gell, by then seventy-eight years old, felt that his time had almost come. The main business of passing on his estate had been accomplished twenty-six years before then, and he was concerned only with the usual token gifts to the poor of the parishes at home, and with more useful ones to his relatives, friends and servants. The poor people of Wirksworth were left £20 to share among them, those of Hopton £10 and of Carsington £5. His daughters Bridgett Wigley, Elizabeth Wigfall and Eleanor Allsop all received small sums of money. The fact that his eldest child, Millicent Radcliffe's name is missing presumably means that she was already dead by then. Two of his London servants were left £50 each while a third, "my servant Elizabeth", got £5. Elizabeth's receipt for this legacy has survived, revealing her to have been Mrs Elizabeth East of St Martins Lane, either living in Sir John's house or a neighbour of his[53]. She signed her receipt with her mark. One old friend was given a gold ring, engraved "momento mori" and two "speciall good freinds" a gold ring apiece. Plans had been made for Sir John to return to Wirksworth to be buried with his ancestors, a journey which would take several weeks, and "I give to every Towne where the Corps doe staye all night forty shillings to the poore of the parishe". A codicil added on the 31st July left his clothes to his servant Thomas Smedley and his household goods in London to Smedley's wife Anne, "excepting my gold Watch and my pendulum Cloke". Sir John's grandsons Phillip Gell and Daniel Wigfall were left some money and his grandson Francis Gell "the little Welch mare". Nicholas the falconer got all Sir John's hawks and the roan mare which he had wanted to shoe in 1669. In the last sentence of the codicil there seems evidence of a last-breath quarrel - "I doe revoake the guift of those two Rings given in my will to Mr Edward and Mr William Hortone", special friends no longer apparently.

The peaceful last years of Sir John's turbulent life ended when he died on 26th October 1671. According to plan he, like like his brother, was buried in Wirksworth church, and his body was carried there in stages and with pomp and ceremony similar to Thomas's funeral[54]. The hearse and horses were draped in buckram cloth decorated with Sir John's coat of arms. Norroy King at Arms accompanied the funeral procession as it moved slowly up from London, making sure that the body was accomodated at "every days jiourneys end" in a manner suitable for a baronet, with his coat of arms displayed. By the end of November the cortege was nine miles from Market Harborough, with another fifty miles to go[55] The King of Arms was responsible for displaying Sir John's coat of arms in Wirksworth church and for the proper performance of the funeral. He was assisted by the Arms Painter, who was also to see that funeral baize was supplied at each stop and at Hopton Hall. An extra set of coverings for the hearse and horses was provided at Derby to replace those which started the journey and were by then worn and defaced. Gell's standing in London by the end of his life is indicated by the fact that among those attending his funeral were the widows of Sir Thomas Viner and Sir Thomas Adams, former Lord Mayors, and of Rowland Wilson, who had been Sheriff of London[56]. Sir John's grave remained unmarked for eighteen years. His son, however, made provision in his will for £100 to be spent on a memorial and on his death in 1689 a tablet was set into the wall of Wirksworth church near Ralph Gell's tomb[57].

BIBLIOGRAPHY

ABBREVIATIONS

BDHS Bakewell and District Historical Society
BM Add MSS British Museum Added Manuscripts
DAJ Derbyshire Archaeological Journal
DAS Derbyshire Archaeological Society
DLH Derby Local Studies Library
DRO Derbyshire Record Office
DRS Derbyshire Record Society
HCJ House of Commons Journal
HMC Historical Manuscripts Commission
MLS Matlock Local Studies Library
PDMHS Peak District Mines Historical Society
PRO Public Record Office, Chancery Lane, London
RGO Royal Greenwich Observatory
TA A true account of the raysing and imployeinge of one foote regiment under Sir John Gell from the beginning of October, 1642, (by Sir George Gresley) (printed in Stone,1992).
TR A true relation of what service hath beene done by Colonell Sir John Gell... from October, 1642, till October, 1646, (by Sir John Gell) (printed in Stone, 1992)

PRINTED WORKS

Auden, M. Barton Blount and the Civil War. DAJ, 43, 1921, 1-18
Barker, S.A. Civil war and civil strife in south-west Derbyshire 1500-1650, Derbyshire Miscellany, 9, pt 5, Spring 1982, 118-122
Bill, E.G.W. Calendar of the Shrewsbury papers in the Lambeth Palace Library. DAS, 1965
Brighton, J.T. The Gell family in the sixteenth and seventeenth centuries: a case of the rising gentry. BDHS Journal, 7, 1980, 4-33
Brighton, J.T. Royalists and roundheads in Derbyshire. BDHS, 1981
Brighton, J.T. Sir John Gell, Governor of Derby, 1642-46. BDHS Journal, 9, 1982, 1-53
Cox, J.C. Three centuries of Derbyshire annals. Volume 1. 1890
Craven. M. The Curzons: 2. Derbyshire Life, 52, no 3, 1987, 60-62
Dictionary of National Biography
Fisher, F.N. The Every family and the Civil War. DAJ, 74, 1954, 112
Fletcher, A.J. Petitioning and the outbreak of the Civil War in Derbyshire. DAJ, 93, 1973, 33-44
Gell, P.L. The Gells of Hopton. DAJ, 35, 1913, 103-110
Glover, S. History and gazetteer of the county of Derbyshire. 2 volumes. 1829
Hill, C. God's Englishman: Oliver Cromwell and the English Revolution. Penguin, 1972
Hill, C. The world turned upside down: radical ideas during the English Revolution. Penguin, 1975
HMC. 12th report, the Cooper MSS, volume 2, 1888
HMC. 13th report, the Portland MSS, volume 1, 1891
Hutchinson, L. Memoirs of the life of Colonel Hutchinson; ed. H. Child. 1904
Ince, T.N. and Sleigh, J. Pedigree of Gell, of Hopton. Reliquary, 11, 1870-71, 225
Innes-Smith, R. The Gells. Derbyshire Life, September 1980, 58-60
Kiernan, D. The Derbyshire lead industry in the sixteenth century. DRS, 1989
Kiernan, D. Twenty thousand miners can't be wrong. PDMHS Bltn, 11, no 5, 1992, 249-253
Newton, S.C. The gentry of Derbyshire in the seventeenth century. DAJ, 86, 1966, 1-30
Pendleton. J. History of Derbyshire. 1886
Petitions, grants, and declarations, concerning Derbyshire miners, 1641-2. Reliquary, 23, 1882-3, 113-115
Sherwood, R. The Civil War in the Midlands, 1642-1651. Sutton, 1992
Sitwell, G. The Derbyshire petition of 1641. DAJ, 19, 1897, 20-23
Slack, R. The Dovegang plot. PDMHS Bltn, 12, no 3, 1994, 102-107
Sleigh, J. The family of Sanders. Reliquary, 11, 1870-71, 166
Smith, E. Sir John Gell. Derbyshire Countryside, 20, Oct-Dec 1954, 80-82
Stone, B. Derbyshire in the Civil War. Scarthin Books, 1992

Taylor, S. Percival Willoughby: a 17th century Derby physician. DAJ, 59, 1937, 67-94
Turner, E.S. Taking the cure. Joseph, 1967
Verity, L. Sir John Gell of Hopton, 1961. (unpublished typescript, DLH).
Waldo, M. The Gells of Hopton. DAJ, 34, 1912, 145-152
Wedgwood, C.V. The king's war, 1641-1647. Collins, 1958

REFERENCES
(DRO archives D...)

Chapter 1. The Gells and Hopton
1 D258/59/13a
2 D258/7/5a
3 Ince, 1870-71. This genealogy was challenged by P.L. Gell in 1913. Gell quoted Inquisitiones Post Mortem in support of John (d.1471) being succeeded by his son Ralph (d.1508) and Ralph by his son John (d.1526). However surviving deeds in the Gell papers support the pedigree by Ince and Sleigh. They establish that John (d.1471) had a wife called Elene and a son Ralph in 1453 (DRO D258/54/17b) and that Ralph must have reached his majority by 1441, when he took part in a land transfer (D258/7/5c). In 1467 a Ralph Gell, described as being "of Ible" bought land there (D258/53/2l, o, q). A Ralph Gell, residence unspecified, was identified in the same year as the eldest brother of a Thomas Gell, both men being sons of John Gell of Hopton (DRO D258/53/2v) The description "eldest" may imply a third brother, and there was at the same time a John Gell Junior of Hopton (DRO D258/53/2l,m). P.L. Gell makes this John Gell Junior and Ralph Gell of Ible the sons of Ralph and grandsons of the John who died in 1471 and, assuming that he was twenty-one in 1467, when he witnessed two legal documents, and had therefore been born in the mid-1440s, John Gell Junior could have been Ralph's son, rather than his much younger brother. However, that Ralph succeeded his father in the possession of Hopton is not borne out by later deeds, which name John Gell, not Ralph, of Hopton in a number of the years at the end of the fifteenth century and early in the sixteenth. Further evidence that the successor to the Hopton estate in 1471 was John Gell lies in statements made in 1615 by the future Sir John in defence of his right to Hopton manor (D258/59/13a-g). Gell claimed that the manor had been in the family's possession since the time of his grandfather Ralph's father John, and that when the case had been argued in 1608, during his minority, it had been supported by court rolls from 1471.
4 D258/53/3a & 38/14a
5 Gell, 1913
6D258/53/2a-c
7D258/7/1d(1418),Gell,1913(1432),D258/53/1f(1200),D258/53/2e(1439),D258/53/2k(1457),D258/54/1 7b(1453).D258/53/2v(1467)
8D258/38/10
9D258/53/3b(1517),D258/53/3a(1537),D258/64/9ab(1546),D258/64/9a(1546),
D258/35/113(1534),D258/65/2c(1540),D258/42/11f(1537),D258/38/14a(1550),
D258/64/10a(1550),D258/7/5b(1552),D258List25,no46(1553),D258/65/2d(1562),
D258/47/15a(will,1564), Kiernan,1989(1564)
10 Kiernan, 1989
11 Kiernan, 1989
12 D258/64/1g
13 Kiernan, 1989
14 Kiernan, 1989
15 Brighton, 1980
16 Gell, 1913
17 Brighton, 1980
18 D258/60/1
19 Kiernan, 1989,D258/42/2h,D258/44/2i
20 D258/41/30v
21 Bill, 1965
22 D258/44/27, 27a
23 D258/41/30ba
24 D258/41/30p
25 D258/41/30aa

26 D258/41/30ga
27 D258/41/30la
28 Brighton, 1980. There are a number of Gell documents which refer to Thomas Gell as being "of Bakewell" from the death of Ralph Gell to that of Anthony Gell, 1564-83, including D258/29/26b, and letters between Anthony Gell at Hopton and Thomas at Bakewell, including D258/41/30w & /30z
29 Ince, 1870-71
30 D258/66/4
31 Gell, 1913
32 D258/60/38a
33 D258/31/29
34 D258/47/19d
35 Craven, 1987 & Kedleston Hall brochure
36 Ince, 1870-71
37Gell, 1913
48 Ince, 1870-71
39 D258/44/5,D258/31/75,D258/31/64e, D258/64/23d,e,D258/47
40 D258/59/13a-g
41 D258/44/30,D258/41/31u,D258/31/1,D258/31/1v, D258/47/19l
42 D258/59/2a
43 D258/47/3
44 D258/44/42
45 D258/41/31j
46 D258/44/42
47 Craven, 1987
48 D3287/1043/4 (note by L.A. Verity)
49 Gell, 1913
50 D259/60/50
51 D258/28/5i
52 D258/31/16
53 D258/28/5i
54 D258/60/26
55 PRO State Papers Charles II, CLXVI, 35. Printed in Reliquary, 6, new series, 1892,112
56 D258/31/21
57 D258/64/36
58 D258/64/35a

Chapter 2. The miners
1 Kiernan, 1992
2 Kiernan, 1989
3 D258/31/88za
4 D258/59/13h -j,D258/47/17i
5 D258/47/19n
6 D258/59/13m
7 D258/47/17i
8 D258/59/13l
9 D258/41/31z
10D258/41/31ea
11 D258/31/88za
12 D259/54/19ja
13 D258/31/91e
14 D258/31/64f
15 D258/42/14g
16 D258/30/11h
17 D258/42/25
18 D258/42/15
19 D258/47/17h
20 D258/60/78o

21 D258/61/40b
22 D258/58/18f
23 D258/58/18b
24 RGO33 (Microfilm in MLS)
25 DRO XP 1091
26 D258/35/5
27 D258/56/52i
28 D258/54/19p
29 D258/42/29e
30 D258/67/35b
31 D258/31/91b
32 D258/28/13m
33 Slack, 1994
34 PRO E101/280/18
35 D258/58/47

Chapter 3. Royal favour
1 D258/60/42
2 PRO State Papers, 1630, p346 - copy in D3287/1043/4
3 D258/44/2s
4 Cox, 1890
5 D3287/1043/4
6 D3287/1043/4
7 D258/60/60
8 D3287/1043/4
9 Verity, 1961
10 D258/60/26c
11 D258/58/11
12 D258/58/8
13 D258/58/5ag
14 D258/56/5a
15 D258/28/6c
16 D258/58/31
17 D258/31/87
18 D258/28/6c
19 D258/42/28
20 D258/56/27a
21 D258/56/27c
22 D258/56/27b
23 D258/59/14s
24 D258/46/22
25 D258/56/5b
26 D258/28/6c
27 D258/56/6
28 Hutchinson, 1904
29 D258/41/31e
30 D258/60/78h
31 D258/60/78f
32 D258/41/31d
33 D258/47/19h
34 D258/28/6c
35 D258/58/31
36 D258/28/6d
37 DNB
38 D258/60/78l
39 D258/28/6e
40 HMC 12th report, 170
41 D258/58/18p

42 D258/59/14t
43 Hutchinsin, 1904
44 D258/60/52
45 D258/58/31
46 D258/60/78k
47 D258/60/52
48 D258/31/33n
49 D258/31/10ab
50 Cox, 1890
51 D258/61/10a
52 D258/65/18
53 Craven, 1987
54 D258/56/28b
55 D258/58/18e
56 D258/41/36
57 D258/28/2d
58 D258/41/31ta

Chapter 4. Family matters
1 D258/58/18e
2 D258/67/35b
3 DNB
4 Ince, 1870
5 D258/41/31pa
6 D258/41/31b
7 Brighton, 1980
8 D258/59/2t
9 D258/41/31ha
10 D258/41/31ta
11 Ince, 1870
12 DNB
13 D258/31/10ma
14 D258/56/2
15 D258/31/30x
16 D258/S/16f
17 D258/46/22
18 D258/47/19k
19 BM Add MSS 6680 ff132-135
20 D258/28/20a
21 D258/58/18j
22 Kiernan, 1989
23 Kiernan, 1989
24 D258/52/6b
25 Kiernan, 1989
26 D258/61/50b
27 D258/28/20aa
28 D258/28/20aa/1
29 D258/54/5a
30 D258/59/6
31 D258/44/4 - legal procedings against Thomas Birkett
32 D258/60/26c
33 D258/60/68a
34 D258/47/19k
35 D258/60/26c
36 D258/41/31g
37 D258/41/31n
38 D258/60/68b
39 D258/58/18e

40 DRO XM 1/111 - Wirksworth burial register (microfilm)

Chapter 5. The coming of war
1 Stone, 1992
2 Stone, 1992
3 D3287/1043/4 - printed broadsheet
4 D3287/1043/4
5 D258/60/59
6 Fletcher, 1973
7 D258/56/25a
8 D258/31/10ha
9 Sitwell, 1897
10 D258/56/25b
11 D258/44/45
12 Fletcher, 1973
13 D258/66/2c
14 Brighton, 1982
15 BM Add MSS 6677 f48
16 BM Add MSS 6677 f47
17 Petitions, grants and declarations...,1882
18 D3287/1043/4
19 HMC, 13, vol 1, 1891, p66
20 Fletcher, 1973
21 D258/56/28h
22 D258/34/10 - evidence of Sir Samuel Sleigh
23 D258/34/10 - evidence of Thomas Curtis
24 D258/60/61
25 D258/56/7
26 D308/Z9/f53
27 Fletcher, 1973
28 HMC, 12, vol 2, 1888, p326
29 D803/Z9/f56
30 HMC, 13, vol 1, 1891, p78
31 TA
32 D803/Z9/f137
33 D803/z9/140
34 Fisher, 1954
35 TA
26 D3287/1043/4
37 Glover, vol 2, 1829
38 TR
39 D258/60/16a
40 D258/56/28i
41 Smith, 1954
42 D803/Z9/f46
43 Hutchinson, 1904
44 Glover, 1829
45 HMC, 13, vol 1, 1891, p78
46 HMC, 12, vol 2, 1888, p328
47 D803/Z9/137-8
48 D803/Z9/F140
49 D803/Z9/f138
50 D803/Z9/f41
51 D803/Z9/f47-8
52 D803/Z9/f49
53 D803/Z9/f46
54 D258/60/39
55 D3287/1043/4

56 D258/34/10 - evidence of Ralph Clarke
57 D258/30/9
58 D803/Z9/f57

Chapter 6. Into action
1 D803/Z9/f55
2 DNB
3 D803/Z9/f55-6
4 DNB
5 Glover, 1829
6 DNB
7 Stone, 1992 - the sequence of marches, sieges and battles follows Stone's count
8 HMC, 12, vol 2, 1888, p328
9 HMC, 13, vol 1, 1891, p66
10 D803/Z9/f52
11 TR
12 HMC, 13, vol 1, 1891, p103
13 TR
14 TA
15 Glover, 1829
16 Glover, 1829
17 Waldo, 1912
18 Auden, 1921
19 TA
20 TR
21 TA
22 D1232/030
23 D1232/033
24 Hutchinson, 1904
25 34R
26 351232/032
27 361232/032
28 D1232/056
29 D1232/032
30 D1232/04
31 Brighton, 1981
32 D1232/01
33 TR
34 Hutchinson, 1904
35 Stone, 1992
36 TR
37 Glover, vol 2, 1829
38 D803/Z9/f67
39 D258/34/10 - evidence of S. Clarke
40 D803/Z9/f72
41 D803/Z9/f74
42 D803/Z9/f78-9
43 D258/60/16d
44 D803/Z9/f51
45 D803/Z9/f61
46 D803/Z9/f69
47 D803/Z9/f80
48 D803/Z9/f81

Chapter 7. Dissidents
1 D258/31/33l
2 D258/60/39
3 D258/34/10 - evidence of John Dalton

4 D258/34/10 - evidence of George Bainbridge
5 D258/31/331
6 D258/34/10 - evidence of Thomas Youle, John Dunnage, Robert Greenwood
7 D803/Z9/f83
8 Pendleton, 1886
9 Brighton, 1981
10 D258/60/32
11 D1232/06
12 Sleigh, 1870
13 Hutchinson, 1904
14 D1232/015
15 D258/34/10 - evidence of Thomas Sanders
16 D1232/033
17 D258/58/18j
18 Brighton, 1981
19 D803/Z9/f77
20 D1232/030
21 D803/Z9/f83
22 D803/Z9/f85
23 D803/Z9/f94
24 D803/Z9/f91-2
25 D803/Z9/f96-7
26 DNB
27 TA
28 DNB
29 Stone, 1992
30 D803/Z9/f96
31 D803/Z9/f82
32 D258/34/10 - evidence of Samuel Clarke
33 D803/Z9/f92
34 D803/Z9/f100
35 D803/Z9/f100
36 D803/Z9/f122
37 D258/34/10 - evidence of Samuel Clarke
38 D803/Z9/f115
39 D804/Z9/f103-4
40 D803/Z9/f102
41 D803/Z9/f115
42 D1232/08
43 D803/Z9/f105
44 D803/Z9/f110-111
45 D803/Z9/106
46 42 D803/Z9/107
47 D803/Z9/f109
48D803/Z9/f111
49 D803/Z9/f112
50 Sherwood, 1992
51 D803/Z9/f116
52 D803/Z9/f117
53 D258/34/10 - evidence of John Withers
54 Waldo, 1912
55 D258/34/10 - evidence of Exuperius Fletcher
56 D1232/09b
57 D258/34/10 - evidence of Exuperius Fletcher
58D258/34/10 - evidence of John Withers
59D258/34/10 - evidence of Robert Greenwood
60D1232/056
61 D258/34/10 - evidence of Nathaniel Barton, Robert Greenwood

62 D258/34/10 - evidence of Nicholas Wilmot
63 D258/34/10 - evidence of Joseph Swetnam
64 D258/34/10 - evidence of Robert Cotchett
65 D258/34/10 - evidence of Rowland Moorewood
66 D258/60/78b
67 Verity, 1961
68 DRO XM 1/111 Wirksworth burial register (microfilm)
69 D258/58/18h

Chapter 8. Mutiny
1 D803/Z9/f102-3
2 D1232/025
3 Auden, 1921
4 Pendleton, 1886
5 D1232/010
6 D803/Z9/f123
7 D803/Z9/f125
8 D1232/125
9 D803/Z9/f126
10 D1232/015
11 D803/Z9/f126
12 D1232/012
13 D1232/013
14 D1232/043
15 D258/34/10 - evidence of Ralph Clarke
16 D1232/014
17 D1232/126
18 D1232/024-033
19 D1232/016
20 D1232/020
21 D258/34/10 - eveidence of Joseph Swetnam
22 D258/34/10 - evidence of Thomas Sanders
23 D258/34/10 - evidence of Ralph Clarke
24 D803/Z9/f133
25 D803/Z9/f134-5
26 D258/34/10 - evidence of William Wolley
27 D258/34/10 - evidence of John Withers
28 D258/34/10 - evidence of John Mundy
29 D258/66/2i
30 D258/34/10 - evidence of John Withers
31 D258/59/2w
32 D803/Z9/f131-2
33 D258/34/10 - John Withers
34 D1232/037
35 D258/60/33
36 D1232/063
37 D803/Z9/f132
38 D1232/063
39 D258/34/10 - evidence of John Fatchett
40 D1232/035
41 D1232/036
42 D258/30/12
43 D803/Z9/f134

Chapter 9. The last phase
1 Stone, 1992
2 D258/66/2i
3 D258/34/10 - evidence of Nathaniel Barton, Robert Greenwood

4 TR
5 D1232/054
6 HMC, 13, vol 1, 1891, p281
7 D258/34/10 - evidence of John Mundy
8 D258/34/10 - evidence of Ralph Clarke, John Fatchett, Abraham Shockly
9 D258/34/10 - evidence of John Mundy
10 D1232/040
11 D258/67/35b
12 HMC, 13, vol 1, 1891, p280
13 D258/34/10 - evidence of Rowland Morewood
14 D258/34/10 evidence of William Leech
15 D258/34/10 - evidence of Thomas Curtis
16 D258/34/10 - evidence of Sir Samuel Sleigh
17 D258/34/10 - evidence of Exuperius Fletcher, John Withers
18 D258/34/10 - evidence of Ralph Clarke
19 D1232/038
20 D1232/040
21 TR
22 D1232/039
23 TR
24 D1232/038
25 D1232/040
26 D1232/042
27 Auden, 1921
28 D1232/044
29 HMC, 13, vol 1, p251
30 D1232/045
31 D1232/046
32 D1232/047
33 TR
34 DNB
35 D258/34/10 - evidence of Sir Samuel Sleigh
36 D258/34/10 - evidence of Thomas Sanders
37 D258/34/10 - evidence of Thomas Sanders
38 D1232/052
39 D258/34/10 - evidence of Joseph Swetnam
40 HMC, 13, vol1, p289
41 Glover, 1829

Chapter 10. A bitter victory
1 Brighton, 1982
2 Taylor, 1937
3 D258/56/28j
4 D258/31/10ga
5 D1232/058
6 D1232/060
7 D1232/059
8 D1232/061
9 D1232/062
10 D258.34/10
11 D803/Z9/f88
12 D803/Z9/f89
13 D803/Z9/f90
14 D803/Z9/f99
15 D258/60/11
16 BM Add MSS 6686 ff132-135
17 D258/30/5m
18 D258/34/10 - evidence of John Withers

19 D258/34/10 - evidence of John Dunnage
20 D258/34/10 - evidence of Thomas Youle
21 D258/30/5m
22 D258/34/10 - evidence of John Withers
23 D258/30/5b
24 D258/30/5a
25 D258/30/5c
26 D258/30/5m
27 Brighton, 1981
28 D258/30/5j
29 D258/30/5d
30 D258/34/10 - evidence of John Withers
31 D258/30/5m
32 D258/56/8b
33 D258/30/5c
34 D3287/1043/4
35 D258/30/5m
36 D258/30/5d
37 D258/30/5f
38 D258/30/5l
39 D258/30/5h
40 D258/30/5i
41 D258/30/5f
42 D258/41/31f
43 D258/67/35b
44 D258/56/28g
45 HCJ, 6, 31st May 1649, p220 - copy in D3287/1043/4
46 Brighton, 1982
47 D1232/057
48 Hutchinson, 1904
49 D258/34/10 - evidence of Robert Greenwood
50 D258/59/12
51 HMC, 13, vol 1, 1891, p234
52 D258/31/33r
53 D803/Z9/ffxx & xxiv
54 Glover, 1829
55 D258/41/31f
56 D258/59/14v
57 HCJ, 5, 22nd October 1647 - copy in D3287/1043/4
58 D258/41/31p

Chapter 11. Post-war London
1 D258/60/14a
2 D3287/1043/4
3 D258/45/1
4 Auden, 1921
5 D258/60/10
6 D258/56/14b
7 HMC, 13, vol 1, 1891, p593
8 D258/56/28h
9 Newton, 1966
10 D258/31/10h
11 DNB
12 D3287/1043/4
13 HCJ, 6, 23rd February 1648 [1649], p150
14 Hutchinson, 1904
15 D258/41/1e
16 Committee for Compounding 18th March 1651 - copy in D3287/1043/4

17 D258/41/1e
18 D258/31/30g
19 D258/30/16
20 D258/31/10b
21 D258/42/14e

Chapter 12. Treason and pardons
1 DNB
2 D258/60/10
3 D258/56/9
4 D258/58/1d
5 D258/58/1e
6 D258/56/12b
7 D258/60/10
8 D258/56/10b
9 D258/60/31
10 D258/31/30x
11 Fisher, 1954
12 Cox, 1891
13 D258/31/30x
14 D258/31/30i
15 D258/31/30h
16 D258/35/114
17 D258/66/2d19
18 HCJ, 6, 7th August 1651, p681 - copy in D3287/1043/4
19 HCJ, 7, 31st October 1651, p33 - copy in D3287/1040/4
20 HCJ, 7, 28th January 1651 [1652], p78 - copy in D3287/1040/4
21 D258/31/10jb
22 DNB
23 HCJ, 7, 13th April 1652, p119 - copy in D3287/1040/4
24 D258/56/28b
25 D258/56/12b
26 D258/56/3
27 D258/44/1d
28 Craven, 1987
29 D258/42/14e
30D258/56/28i
31 D258/31/33o
32 D258/67/7c
33 D258/30/1
34 D3287/1043/4 - transcript
35 Waldo, 1912
36 D258/58/5y
37 D258/59/2m
38 Turner, 1967
39 D3287/1043/4
40 D258/56/28h
41 D3287/1043/4
42 D258/60/80
43 D258/52/16
44 PRO, S P, Charles II, CLXVI, 35 - in Reliquary, 6, new series, 1892, 11
45 D3287/1043/4
46 D258/59/2f
47 D258/61/50c
48 D258/29/44b
49 D258/56/51v
50 D258/41/31aa
51 D258/31/91f

52 D258/67/7c
53 D258/60/37
54 D258/56/47
55 Innes-Smith, 1980
56 DNB
57 D258/S/16a

INDEX